William J. Gedney's Concise Saek-English, English-Saek Lexicon

Oceanic Linguistics Special Publications
Numbers 1 through 25 and 28 are no longer available

1. English in Hawaii: An Annotated Bibliography. Stanley M. Tsuzaki and John E. Reinecke. 1966.
2. An Ivatan Syntax. Lawrence Andrew Reid. 1966.
3. Manobo-English Dictionary. Richard E. Elkins. 1968.
4. Nguna Texts. Albert J. Schütz. 1969.
5. Nguna Grammar. Albert J. Schütz. 1969.
6. A Grammar of Kaliai-Kove. David R. Counts. 1969.
7. Chrau Grammar. David D. Thomas. 1971.
8. Philippine Minor Languages: Word Lists and Phonologies. Edited by Lawrence A. Reid. 1971.
9. Japanese Pidgin English in Hawaii: A Bilingual Description. Susumu Nagara. 1972.
10. Kapampangan Syntax. Leatrice T. Mirikitani. 1972.
11. Isneg-English Vocabulary. Morice Vanoverbergh. 1972.
12. Outline of Sre Structure. Timothy M. Manley. 1972.
13. Austroasiatic Studies, Parts I and II. Edited by Philip N. Jenner, Laurence C. Thompson, and Stanley Starosta. 1976.
14. A Bibliography of Pidgin and Creole Languages. Compiled by John E. Reinecke, Stanley M. Tsuzaki, David DeCamp, Ian F. Hancock, and Richard E. Wood. 1975.
15. A Handbook of Comparative Tai. Fang Kuei Li. 1977.
16. Syntactic Derivation of Tagalog Verbs. Videa P. De Guzman. 1978.
17. The Genetic Relationship of the Ainu Language. James Patrie. 1982.
18. A Grammar of Manam. Frantisek Lichtenberk. 1983.
19. The History of the Fijian Languages. Paul A. Geraghty. 1983.
20. For Gordon H. Fairbanks. Edited by Veneeta Z. Acson and Richard L. Leed. 1985.
21. The Causatives of Malagasy. Charles Randriamasimanana. 1986.
22. Echo of a Culture: A Grammar of Rennell and Bellona. Samuel H. Elbert. 1988.
23. A guide to Austroasiatic Speakers and Their Languages. Robert Parkin. 1991.
24. Tonality in Austronesian Languages. Edited by Jerold A. Edmondson and Kenneth J. Gregerson. 1993.
25. Tinrin Grammar. Midori Osumi. 1995.
26. Toward a Reference Grammar of Tok Pisin: An Experiment in Corpus Linguistics. John W. M. Verhaar. 1995.
27. An Erromangan (Sye) Grammar. Terry Crowley. 1998.
28. From Ancient Cham to Modern Dialects: Two Thousand Years of Language Contact and Change. Graham Thurgood. 1999.
29. Grammatical Analysis: Morphology, Syntax, and Semantics: Studies in Honor of Stanley Starosta. Edited by Videa P. De Guzman and Byron W. Bender. 2000.
30. Nhanda: An Aboriginal Language of Western Australia. Juliette Blevins. 2001.
31. Bislama Reference Grammar. Terry Crowley. 2004.
32. Otto Dempwolff's *Grammar of the Jabêm language in New Guinea.* Translated and edited by Joel Bradshaw and Francisc Czobor. 2005.
33. A Grammar of South Efate: An Oceanic Language of Vanuatu. Nicholas Thieberger. 2006.
34. William J. Gedney's Comparative Tai Source Book. Thomas John Hudak. 2008
35. Kokota Grammar. Bill Palmer. 2009.
36. A Dictionary of Mah Meri as Spoken at Bukit Bangkong. Nicole Kruspe. 2010
37. William Gedney's Concise Saek-English, English-Saek Lexicon. Thomas John Hudak. 2010

Publications may be ordered electronically from www.uhpress.hawaii.edu or by mail from University of Hawai`i Press, 2840 Kolowalu Street, Honolulu, Hawai`I 96822, USA.

Oceanic Linguistics Special Publication No. 37

William J. Gedney's Concise Saek-English, English-Saek Lexicon

Thomas John Hudak

University of Hawai`i Press

Honolulu

Printed in the United States of America

15 14 13 12 11 10 6 5 4 3 2 1

Library of Congress Cataloguing-in-Publication Data

William J. Gedney's concise Saek-English, English-Saek lexicon / edited by Thomas John Hudak.
p. cm. -- (Oceanic linguistics special publication ; no. 37)
"The glossary reproduced here is from 1976 when Gedney first began to compile all of the material he had accumulated. It is an extensive lexical list arranged by rhyme. To this has been added an English-Saek section"--Introduction.
Includes bibliographical references.
ISBN 978-0-8248-3538-5 (softcover : alk. paper)
1. Saek language--Glossaries, vocabularies, etc. I. Hudak, Thomas J. II. Gedney, William J. III. Series: Oceanic linguistics special publication ; no. 37.
PL4251.S23W55 2010
495'.919--dc22

2010019922

Camera-ready copy for this book was prepared under the supervision of the series editor.

University of Hawai'i Press books are printed on acid-free paper and meet the guidelines for permanence and durability of the Council on Library Resources.

Printed by Integrated Book Technology, Inc.

Contents

Acknowledgments

This volume is the result of the encouragement of a group of people interested in and fascinated by Southeast Asian linguistics. Prominent among this group have been Karen L. Adams, Robert J. Bickner, Carol Compton, Anthony V. N. Diller, Jerold A. Edmondson, Thomas Gething, and Yongxian Luo. Once a project such as this one has begun, technical difficulties and decisions inevitably arise. Help with these issues came from Thanh-Lieu Duong, Christopher A. Miller, Judy Newland, Catherine Nichols, and Helene Ossipov. Early on Marin Julia Lewis provided considerable assistance in organizing the data into manageable groups. Toward the end of the project, Mitchell Darnell took on the task of proofreading with me. For assistance in producing the map, I once again turned to my friend and colleague, Barbara Stark, who is always generous with her time and ready for an adventure with new software. Finally, superb editorial assistance was offered by Keith Leber at the University of Hawai`i Press. All of these people have played significant parts in the production of this volume. To each of them, I extend my gratitude and thanks.

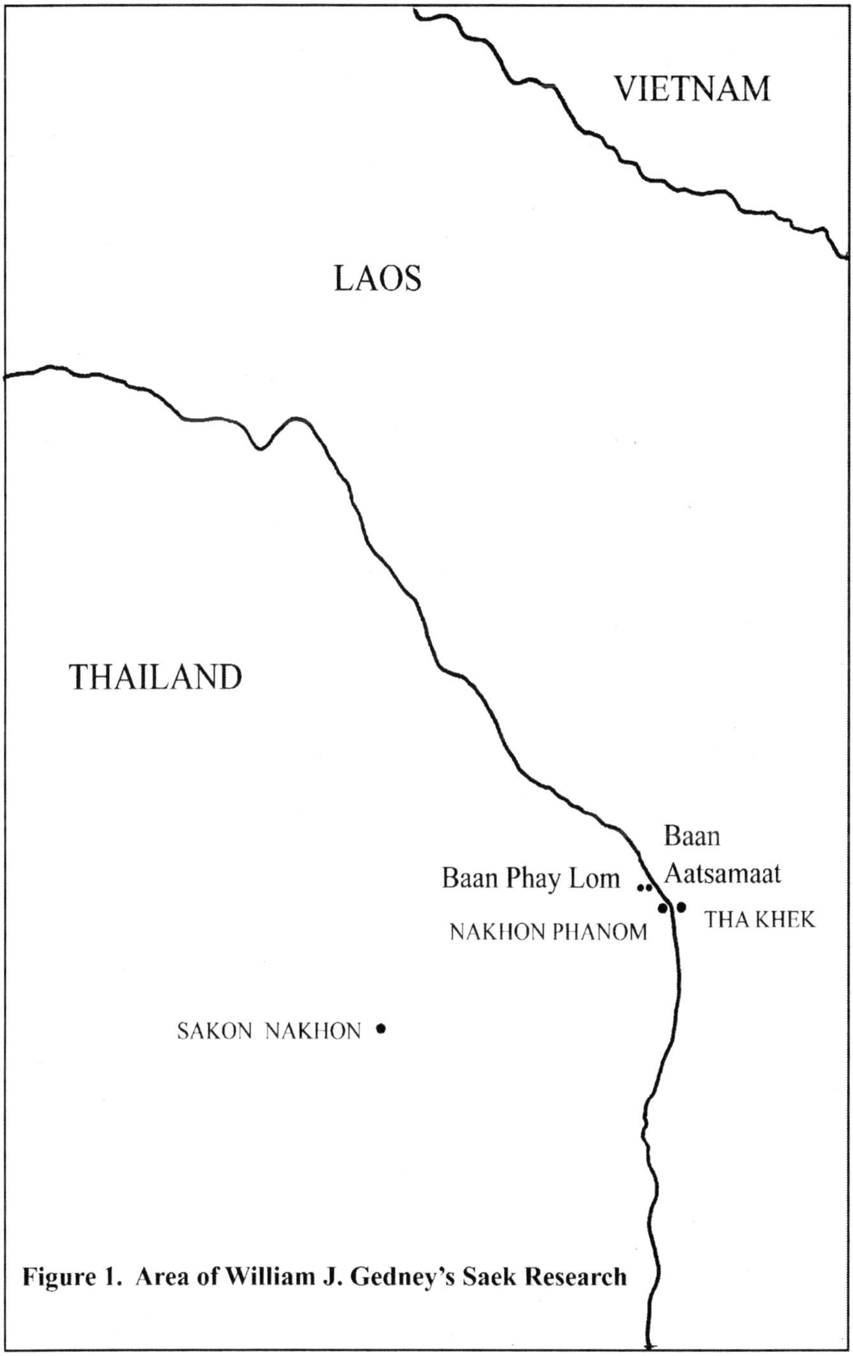

Figure 1. Area of William J. Gedney's Saek Research

Introduction

The Tai language family spreads across the whole of Southeast Asia, from Assam, the furthest point in the west where these languages are spoken, to the island of Hainan in the east where a number of dialects apparently related to the Tai family occur. In the north in Yunnan, Guizhou, and Guangxi provinces of southern China, a variety of Tai dialects exist, some mutually intelligible, others not. Siamese and related local dialects dominate Thailand while Lao and its dialects cover Laos as well as extend down into Northeast Thailand. Farther to the east in northeastern Laos and northwestern Vietnam are White, Red, and Black Tai, along with Yay. Still other dialects merge into northeastern Vietnam. Following Fang-kuei Li, scholars generally divide these languages and dialects into three branches: the Northern, the Central, and the Southwestern.

William J. Gedney began his study of Tai languages and dialects with Siamese in the 1950s. Then in 1964, with his usual meticulous attention to tonal and phonological systems, he expanded his studies to other Tai dialects. One of the most intensively studied of these dialects was Saek, a Northern Tai dialect unique for its geographical location on the border of Northeast Thailand and Laos among Southwestern Tai languages. Saek was first noted by French travelers and missionaries in the late nineteenth and early twentieth centuries: Aymonier (1895), Rivière (1902), Macy (1905), Maspero (1912), and Bonifacy (1919). Based on these reports and their own research, Seidenfaden (1930), Credner (1935), Blanchard (1957), and Lebar, Hickey, and Musgrave (1964) classified Saek as Mon-Khmer. In contrast, in a series of papers in the 1950s and 1960s, Haudricourt placed Saek in the Northern branch of the Tai family. Around this time, Fraisse (1950:338) also cited Saek as a 'Thai' language, although he did not speculate on its genetic classification. However, it was not until 1969 and 1970 that Gedney confirmed the Northern classification based upon his own extensive fieldwork. Saek continues to be of interest to linguists with more recent studies by Khanittanan (1975, 1976, 2008), Thongkųm (1976), Benedict (1979), Morev (1988), Boltz (1991), and Chamberlain (1998).

Gedney and Morev cite two different tales told by villagers about the history of the Saek. Gedney's informants place the origin of the Saek in northern Vietnam (Hudak 1993: 577, 585). There, because of a famine, they killed a white elephant of a local ruler and fled under threat of a heavy fine into Laos and then Thailand. Recounting a different origin, Morev's informant claims that in the nineteenth century the Thai forced the Saek to the Bangkok area to construct a canal around the city. Once the canal was completed, the Saek were then free to settle in the area (Morev 1988: 10).

Gedney conducted his research on Saek in a series of field trips in 1964, 1966, 1968, and 1976. Most of the data were provided by informants from baan^{3} ʔaat^{6} saa^{1} maat^{5} (Baan Atsamaat) with additional material from baan^{3} phay^{6} lɔɔm^{3} (Baan Phay Lom), both in Nakhon Phanom province in Northeast Thailand (see Figure 1). In the course of his research, Gedney noted that there were other Saek villages in Thailand, Laos, and Vietnam (see Appendix III), but had no opportunity to work there. Besides individual lexical items, Gedney also acquired important cultural information such as the names for the twelve cyclical years (see Appendix I) and the names for days of the New Year's festival known as Songkan (see Appendix II). The most complete record of Gedney's research can be found in the now out-of-print volume *William J. Gedney's The Saek Language: Glossary, Texts, and Translations* (Hudak 1993). The glossary reproduced here is from 1976 when Gedney first began to compile all of the material he had accumulated. It is an extensive lexical list arranged by rhyme. To this has been added an English-Saek section.

Phonology

Like other Tai languages, the phonological pattern of Saek is based on the syllable. Each syllable has distinctions in tone, initial (consonant or consonant cluster), nucleus (vowel or diphthong), and optional final consonant.

Tones. On open syllables (those ending with final vowel, semivowel, or nasal) Saek has six tones. In his 1970 publication on Saek, Gedney describes these tones. Here, pitch levels and contours based on the Chao 5-level pitch scale (Chao 1930) have been added to the descriptions:

1 – mid level, with rise on end, 34: pii^{1} year
2 – low level, 11: maa^{2} dog
3 – mid, falling to low, glottal constriction, 31: nii^{3} here
4 – high rising-falling, 454: naa^{4} ricefield
5 – high falling, 52: phii^{5} older sibling
6 – mid level, with slight fall, glottal constriction, nii^{6} this

Checked syllables in Saek (those ending in [p t k ʔ]) have tones phonetically similar to tones 4 5 6 on open syllables. Tones 4 and 6 are the most common on short checked syllables: kap^{4} 'frog' and suk^{6} 'cooked, ripe'. Tones 5 and 6 occur on long checked syllables: thaak^{5} 'land leech' and haat^{6} 'hungry'. Tone 2 rarely occurs on short syllables, phat^{2} 'and then', and tone 4 rarely on long syllables, ʔiit^{4} ʔɔɔy^{5} 'a little'. Tone 2 may also be found on long syllables: muak^{2} 'hat'.

The six tones of Saek had their origin in an earlier system that had three tones on open syllables, conventionally designated as A B C, and no contrast on checked syllables, designated as D. Conditioned by the phonetic nature of the initial consonant in each syllable, the tones in each proto-Tai category underwent phonemic splits. The proto-voiceless initials included aspirates, unaspirated or plain stops, and glottals. Further splits conditioned by vowel length occurred with tone D. In Saek, these splits can be represented as follows:

Initial\Tone	A	B	C	D-short	D-long
aspirate	2,1	6	3	4	6
plain	1	6	3	4	6
glottal	1	6	3	4	6
voiced	4	5	6	6	5

Saek exhibits a simple two-way split between proto-voiceless (aspirate, plain, and glottal) and proto-voiced initials; however, it shows two tones in the top box of column A. Most Tai dialects have a single tone in this category, for example, maa^{5} 'dog' and khaa^{5} 'leg' in Siamese. In Saek, tone 2 seems to be the normal development as in maa^{2} 'dog'. Saek kwaa^{1} 'leg', however, has tone 1. Gedney hypothesizes that this word and others lost their aspiration before the tone splits so that they fell together with other words having plain or unaspirated initials.

Initial Consonants. Initial consonants found in Saek include the following:

Voiceless unaspirated stops. p t c k ʔ: pii^{1} year, traa^{3} rice seedling, cɔɔ^{6} to put, kin^{1} to eat, ʔɔn^{1} thorn.

Voiceless aspirated stops. ph th ch (rare) kh: phuaŋ^{4} cluster, thiaŋ^{2} to argue, chom^{4} phuu^{4} thiip^{5} a mythical continent, khot^{6} crooked.

Voiced stops. b d: blian^{1} month, moon, din^{1} earth. Younger speakers almost always have a voiced velar stop [g] rather than the voiced spirant [ɣ]: gaw^{6} rice.

Voiceless spirants. f s h: sii^{2} faa^{3} blue, sin^{3} skirt, haa^{6} galangal. The spirant [f] does not appear in native Saek words, only in borrowings from Siamese or Lao which may have an initial [ph]: sii^{2} phaa^{3} blue.

Voiced spirants. ɣ: ɣɔɔn^{6} hammer, club.

Nasals. m n ɲ ŋ: mɔɔ^{2} shaman, nua^{3} crossbow, ɲam^{3} to chew, ŋaw^{2} to smell bad.

Sonorants. v r l y w: vɯn^{2} rain, rɔɔŋ^{4} bird nest, lɯm^{4} bundle, yap^{6} to chop up, wan^{6} that. Initial [r] is pronounced, apparently by speakers at all localities, with a preceding alveolar stop release: [^{d}r]. Initial [w] appears only as a result of assimilation with the preceding final consonant. Because of the low friction in the pronunciation of [v], Gedney grouped it with the sonorants.

Initial Clusters. Saek has a wide range of initial clusters some of which occur in no other Tai language. There are no final clusters.

Clusters with [w]. kw khw thw ʔw lw ŋw sw hw: kwii^6 to remove (a thorn), khwaak^6 sharpened stake, thwaay^2 to predict, guess, ʔwaay^6 to turn a car around, lwaat^5 overly full, ŋwɛɛk^5 to turn the head to look, swaa^5 famous, hwaaŋ^3 worried.

Clusters with [l]. pl phl tl thl bl ml: plaa^1 fish, phlam^4 bracelet, tlɤɤy^1 embarrassed, thlaa^2 tray, blɔɔ^3 to stick out the tongue, mlaay^4 saliva.

Clusters with [r]. pr phr tr thr: praa^1 eye, phrɔɔ^6 to squirt (water) from the mouth, traa^1 cockspur, thraw^3 head.

Final Consonants. As in other Tai languages, Saek has final nasals and final voiceless stops. It differs in also having final [l] among the older generation of speakers

Nasals. m n ŋ: rim^2 full, kian^1 oxcart, ɣeeŋ^5 foot, leg.

Voiceless stops. p t k ʔ: saap^6 cockroach, khɯt^6 to think, lɯk^6 child, tiʔ^4 to criticize.

Final [l]: mool^4 base of a plant.

Vowels. Saek has nine vowels, each occurring long and short. Final short vowels are reduced.

	Front	Back Unrounded	Back Rounded
High	i, ii	ɯ, ɯɯ	u, uu
Mid	e, ee	ɤ, ɤɤ	o, oo
Low	ɛ, ɛɛ	a, aa	ɔ, ɔɔ

i/ii	rip^4 raw	liin^6 tongue
ɯ/ɯɯ	ɣɯn^4 night	hɯɯt^6 tobacco
u/uu	luŋ^5 banana	kuuk^5 tiger
e/ee	leŋ^5 to hurry	peet^6 eight
ɤ/ɤɤ	ŋɤʔ^4 to think	trɤɤŋ^3 egg
o/oo	nom^4 milk	ʔoom^3 to have a fever
ɛ/ɛɛ	trɛk^4 fish scales	ʔɛɛŋ^1 older brother
a/aa	daŋ^1 nose	daaŋ^3 mushroom
ɔ/ɔɔ	kɔl^6 stump	rɔɔy^1 mountain

Diphthongs. There are three centering diphthongs, ia ɯa ua: plian^{3} smooth, hɯat^{6} dry, nuaŋ^{6} younger sibling. The [ua] diphthong is characteristic of the pronunciation of the younger generation.

Other diphthongs analyzed as consisting of a vocalic nucleus plus a final [w] or [y] also occur.

Diphthongs with final [w]. iw iaw iiw uaw eew ɛɛw aw aaw: siw^{1} pimple, yiaw^{3} granary, ŋiiw^{3} kapok, ruaw^{2} to laugh, theew^{4} to flee, ʔɛɛw^{1} waist, ʔaw^{1} to take, baaw^{6} young man.

Diphthongs with final [y]. ɯay uy uuy uay ɤɤy ooy ay aay ɔɔy: pɯay^{1} naked, khuy^{3} to scratch (of chickens), khuuy^{6} flute, suay^{6} tribute money, mɤɤy^{2} bear, phooy^{3} lungs, ʔay^{1} to cough, praay^{1} to die, ʔɔɔy^{3} sugarcane.

Final Rhymes. The following chart shows all possible rhymes in native Saek words. Final short vowels are reduced.

0	w	y	m	n	ŋ	l	p	t	k	ʔ
ii	iiw		iim	iin	iiŋ	iil	iip	iit	iik	
ɯɯ			ɯɯm	ɯɯn	ɯɯŋ	ɯɯl	ɯɯp	ɯɯt	ɯɯk	
uu		uuy	uum	uun		uul	uup	uut	uuk	
ee	eew		eem	een	eeŋ	eel	eep	eet	eek	
ɤɤ		ɤɤy	ɤɤm	ɤɤn	ɤɤŋ		ɤɤp	ɤɤt	ɤɤk	
oo		ooy	oom	oon	ooŋ	ool	oop	oot	ook	
ɛɛ	ɛɛw		ɛɛm	ɛɛn	ɛɛŋ	ɛɛl	ɛɛp	ɛɛt	ɛɛk	
aa	aaw	aay	aam	aan	aaŋ	aal	aap	aat	aak	
ɔɔ		ɔɔy	ɔɔm	ɔɔn	ɔɔŋ	ɔɔl	ɔɔp	ɔɔt	ɔɔk	
ia	iaw		iam	ian	iaŋ	ial	iap	iat	iak	
ɯa		ɯay	ɯam	ɯan	ɯaŋ		ɯap	ɯat	ɯak	
ua	uaw	uay	uam	uan	uaŋ	ual	uap	uat	uak	
i	iw		im	in	iŋ	il	ip	it	ik	iʔ
ɯ			ɯm	ɯn	ɯŋ	ɯl	ɯp	ɯt	ɯk	ɯʔ
u		uy	um	un	uŋ	ul	up	ut	uk	uʔ
e			em	en	eŋ		ep	et	ek	eʔ
ɤ					ɤŋ		ɤp			ɤʔ
o			om	on	oŋ		op	ot	ok	oʔ
ɛ			ɛm	ɛn	ɛŋ	ɛl	ɛp	ɛt	ɛk	ɛʔ
a	aw	ay	am	an	aŋ	al	ap	at	ak	aʔ
ɔ			ɔm	ɔn	ɔŋ	ɔl		ɔt	ɔk	ɔʔ

Other Phonetic Features. In his elicitations, Gedney noticed other phonetic features produced by both generations, particularly in fast speech, conversation, and storytelling.

1) The glottal stop ending short checked syllables is frequently deleted with a corresponding reduction in vowel and occasional tone change: paʔ^{4} maan^{4} and pa^{6} maan^{4} 'approximately'. The tone reduces to tone 6, and the vowel is slightly shorter than a short vowel in a closed syllable. At other times, the glottal stop may be deleted with no change in tone: ʔuʔ^{4} dɔɔn^{1} and ʔu^{4} dɔɔn^{1} 'Udorn'.

2) A final glottal stop sometimes appears with long vowels in hesitation particles: ʔaaʔ^{6} and ʔaa^{6}.

3) Sentence intonation may cause tone variation, with the tone almost always changed to tone 1: thaam^{2} and thaam^{1} 'to ask'.

4) Emphasis involves the repetition of two syllables with the first receiving a higher than normal tone. At other times, a short vowel may be lengthened.

5) The initial sound, generally with nan^{6} 'that', assimilates with the preceding final consonant: tɤɤ^{3} sum^{6} man^{6} 'under that chicken coop'. At other times, the final consonant assimilates with the following initial consonant: thua^{4} ŋua^{4} nal^{6} law^{6} 'that snake, you know'. In still other cases, both the initial and the final sounds assimilate: nɛɛn^{2} phiaŋ^{4} ŋal^{6} law^{6} 'in that city, you know'.

6) Glottal stops as in ʔun^{3} 'yonder, over there' frequently delete before following vowels and semivowels: lɯk^{6} yuu^{6} un^{3} 'child over there'.

7) Long vowels may reduce to short vowels with no change in tone: hɔɔy^{2} and hɔy^{2} 'to comb'.

Sociolinguistic Features. In the course of his elicitations, Gedney noted a variety of speech differences between older generation speakers (aged fifty and more) and younger ones. In the glossary, those features representative of the older generation are marked OG and those of the younger generation YG. These differences include the following:

1) OG speakers maintain a clear distinction between final [l] and final [n] whereas YG speakers merge the two. Thus, OG speakers distinguish between bɯl^{1} 'to fly' and bɯn^{1} 'sky'. YG speakers, on the other hand, have a single form bɯn^{1} for both meanings.

2) OG speakers maintain a clear distinction between clusters such as [pl] and [pr]: plaa^{1} 'fish' and praa^{1} 'eye, cockspur'. YG speakers use the single form praa^{1} for both meanings. Other clusters affected include [phl] and [phr], [tl] and [tr], [thl] and [thr].

3) OG speakers maintain clusters with an initial consonant plus the long vowel [aa] as in kwaay^{1} 'to sell'. YG speakers, through Lao influence, replace [aa] with the diphthong [ua] as in kuay^{1} 'to sell'.

4) OG speakers have a voiced velar spirant [ɣ] as an initial: ɣaw^6 'rice'. For this initial, YG speakers have substituted the voiced velar stop /g/: gaw^6 'rice'. In a recent diachronic study (2008; p. 389), Khanittanan notes that [g] is now stable in Saek. Because Gedney worked primarily with OG speakers, the glossary lists only the forms with initial [ɣ].

5) OG speakers have no contrast between short [iw] and long [iiw], using only the phonetic long form: ŋiiw^3 'kapok'. A similar case occurs with short [uy] and long [uuy]: muuy^6 'to sneeze'. For YG speakers, however, there is a clear distinction between the short and long forms. This situation suggests that Saek originally had no such contrasts and that the distinction has come about through the influence of Lao and Siamese loans.

Language Change and Saek

In his very early publication on Saek, Gedney, noting significant differences in the speech between older and younger generation speakers, voiced the fear that in one or two generations the language might very well disappear because of the increasing hegemony of Lao and Siamese in daily life (1970: 68). This same concern was echoed in several other publications through the years (Khanittanan 1975, 1976; Hudak 1993). Smalley (1994: 199) summed up the situation in the following multilingual terms for the Saek speakers in Thailand: "But for the present, at least, many Saek people move freely between three languages, Saek in the villages, Lao as the regional language, and Standard Thai [Siamese] as the national language and language of official affairs and education."

In one of the most recent publications on Saek, Khanittanan (2008) addresses this issue of Saek as an endangered language. In 2006, she returned to the Saek village of Ban Bawa to update her 1976 study, which had shown the same basic generational features as Gedney had elicited (see above **Sociolinguistic Features**). Using consonants as markers of language change in the same list of 1300 words as in the 1976 study and selecting a 23-year-old university student as a representative speaker, she notes the following changes:

Initial Consonants. The voiced velar stop [g] has become stable. In her 1976 study, her 45-year-old female informant also used initial [g]. While Gedney concentrated on the speech of the older generation, he recorded the widespread use of [g] by younger speakers. In many cases, he also noted older speakers varying their characteristic initial [ɣ] with /g/: gaw^6 for ɣaw^6 'rice'.

The voiceless spirant [f] has also become a stable sound in the initial consonant inventory, largely through Siamese borrowings. In Gedney's study, loan words from Lao and Thai with [f] were often borrowed as [ph]: Siamese fɯɯt^{2} Saek phɯɯt^{2} to move with difficulty; Siamese sii^{5} faa^{4} Saek sii^{2} phaa^{3} blue.

While initial [r] and [l] continue to remain distinct, there was an occasional substitution of [l] for [r].

Initial Clusters. Both initial [kw-] and [khw-] have disappeared and replaced with [k-] and [kh-]. Gedney notes this change as indicative of the speech of the younger generation: kuay^{1} for kwaay^{1} 'sell' and thuay^{4} for thwaay^{4} 'to guess'.

Initials with [ml-] have been simplified to [m-]: mɔɔn^{4} for mlɔɔn^{4} 'to open the eyes'.

Clusters with [-r-] and [-l-] are often interchanged, although this variation also appeared in Gedney's original data: thlaa^{4} and thraa^{4} 'late in the morning'.

Final Consonants. The final consonants have remained stable with the exception of the disappearance of final [-l].

Without specifically mentioning the older generation, Khanittanan suggests that the above changes also appear in the current older generation, the younger generation of her earlier study. She does claim, however, that "...it is natural for the younger generation of Saek speakers to be more open to the new vocabulary coming into the language" (2008: 392). This situation would suggest that further language change is probably inevitable. Nevertheless, a successful campaign to keep Saek alive and flourishing has been started by the father of her informant. With the rapid disappearance of many endangered languages, it is hoped that this interest and revival will continue.

The above linguistic background on Saek was originally published in different form in Thomas John Hudak, ed. 1993. *William J. Gedney's The Saek Language: Glossary, Texts, and Translations*. Michigan Papers on South and Southeast Asia No. 41. Ann Arbor: Center for South and Southeast Asian Studies, The University of Michigan. Reprinted courtesy of the publisher.

Introduction to the Lexicon

1. Saek-English Order:

1. Rhymes follow the Thai order: [i], [ia], [ɯ], [ɯa], [u], [ua], [e], [ɤ], [o], [ɛ], [a], [ɔ], final vowels first.

2. Vowels+glides follow final vowels: [vowel + w], [vowel + y].

3. Vowels+nasals follow vowels+glides: [vowel + m], [vowel + n], [vowel + ŋ].

4. Vowels+liquids follow vowels+nasals: [vowel + l].

5. Vowels+stops follow vowels+liquids: [vowel + p], [vowel + t], [vowel + k], [vowel + ʔ].

6. Reduced short vowels in open syllables follow vowels+stops. Reduced short vowels in open syllables are slightly shorter than short vowels in closed syllables.

7. Consonants appear in the following order: velars [ʔ], [k], [kh], [ɣ], [ŋ]; palatals [c], [ch]; alveolars [d], [t], [th], [n]; labials [b], [p], [ph], [m]; palatal glide, palatal nasal, and liquids [y], [ɲ], [r], [l]; spirants [v], [s], [f], [h].

8. Polysyllabic words are listed under each syllable: din^{1} cii^{6} 'brick' appears under din^{1} as well as cii^{6}.

9. For each entry, similar meanings are separated by commas; weakly related meanings are separated by semicolons. Unrelated meanings are listed as separate entries.

2. English-Saek Order:

All English meanings for each Saek word are listed. Thus the two meanings for blian^{1} 'moon, month' are listed under 'moon' as well as 'month'. Related meanings are then listed in regular alphabetical order.

3. Additional Information:

Because Saek has variations between the speech of the older and younger generations, both forms are listed, with OG identifying the older and YG the younger generation:

tray^{1} far (YG, = OG tlay^{1})
tlay^{1} far (OG, = YG tray^{1})

Other variations, such as reduced short vowels, are also listed: kii^{4} until (= maʔ^{6} kii^{4}, ma^{6} kii^{4}).

Saek-English

-ii

ʔii^{3} *in* taŋ^{6} ʔii^{3} chair (= taŋ^{6} ʔii^{6})
ʔii^{6} *in* taŋ^{6} ʔii^{6} chair (= taŋ^{6} ʔii^{3})
ʔii^{6} *in* luŋ^{5} ʔii^{6} tɔʔ^{4} kind of banana (clf. maak^{6})
kii^{1} to have or cause an itching feeling
kii^{3} how many
kii^{4} until (= maʔ^{6} kii^{4}, ma^{6} kii^{4})
kwii^{6} to remove (a thorn)
khii^{2} characterized by (= Siamese khii^{3})
  khii^{2} thii^{5} stingy
  khii^{2} sii^{4} resin
khii^{4} dorsal fin of a fish
ɣii^{4} algae
ɣii^{4} *in* ɣay^{6} ɣii^{4} dried sweat and dirt on the skin
ŋii^{5} to consider, weigh (a matter)
cii^{5} older sister
cii^{6} *in* din^{1} cii^{6} brick
cii^{6} *in* mit^{6} cii^{6} lii^{6} very quiet
dii^{1} good
dii^{1} *in* pha^{6} kha^{6} va^{6} dii^{1} name of a hall
dii^{1} *in* see^{1} naa^{4} bɔɔ^{1} dii^{1} minister, general
tii^{5} *in* pii^{1} tii^{5} sixth year in the Saek twelve-year cycle
tii^{6} *in* pii^{1} tii^{6} first year in the Saek twelve-year cycle
tii^{6} to unroll, unwrap
thii^{2} *in* seet^{6} thii^{2} rich man
thii^{4} thuu^{4} thii^{4} thaat^{5} descriptive of dragging
thii^{4} *in* ʔin^{1} thii^{4} eagle
thii^{4} *in* naa^{4} thii^{4} minute
thii^{5} closely spaced, finely woven; miserly
  khii^{2} thii^{5} stingy
thii^{6} which, that; morph used in ordinals
nii^{3} here
nii^{4} mit^{6} to cause, create
nii^{4} *in* kiʔ^{4} liʔ^{6} nii^{4} name of soŋ^{1} kaan^{1} day when it falls on Thursday
  (= ki^{4} li^{6} nii^{4})

nii^{4} *in* tha^{6} nii^{4} gibbon (clf. thua^{4})

nii^{4} *in* luŋ^{5} tha^{6} nii^{4} kind of banana

nii^{4} *in* praʔ^{6} phee^{4} nii^{4} customs

nii^{6} this, these

bii^{1} gallbladder (YG, = OG blii^{1})

bii^{6} twisted (mouth)

blii^{1} gallbladder (OG, = YG bii^{1})

blii^{1} calf of the leg

pii^{1} year *See Appendix I for a complete list of the twelve-year cycle.*

  pii^{1} ʔun^{3} the year after pii^{1} rɯɯ^{1}, three years from the current year

  pii^{1} ʔɛn^{3} the year after pii^{1} ʔun^{3}, four years from the current year

  pii^{1} naa^{3} next year

  pii^{1} rɯɯ^{1} the year after next

pii^{1} *in* cam^{1} pii^{1} kind of flowering tree (= cam^{6} pii^{1})

pii^{1} *in* cam^{6} pii^{1} kind of flowering tree (= cam^{1} pii^{1})

pii^{6} flute, pipe

pii^{6} to spread (a mat)

prii^{1} banana blossom (YG, = OG plii^{1})

plii^{1} banana blossom (OG, = YG prii^{1})

plii^{6} to lay aside; to leave; to divorce

phii^{1} pɯay^{1} naked (= pɯay^{1})

phii^{4} to fan, a fan

phii^{5} older sibling

mii^{2} a bear (< Siamese; = Saek mɤɤy^{2}, mɯay^{2}; clf. thua^{4})

mii^{2} thread

mii^{3} *in* plɔɔ^{6} mii^{3} dead coals, ashes of a dead fire

mii^{4} to have, there is, there are

mii^{4} khun^{4} mii^{4} noo^{4} to do a favor for

mii^{6} *in* mɛɛŋ^{4} mii^{6} small flies

ɲii^{6} to point (= nɛɛ^{4})

ɲii^{6} two

  blian^{1} ɲii^{6} second lunar month

rii^{3} mountain stream

rii^{4} chicken louse (clf. thua^{4})

rii^{4} track, footprint

rii^{5} dry field

rii^{6} *in* ʔa^{6} rii^{6} this one

lii^{1} *in* khan^{4} tha^{6} thu^{6} lii^{1} name of a cave

lii^{4} *in* buʔ^{6} lii^{4} cigar, cigarette (= bu^{6} lii^{4})

lii^{4} *in* sa^{6} lii^{4} Indian corn, maize

lii^{6} still, yet (= haa^{2} lii^{6}, haʔ^{6} lii^{6}, ha^{6} lii^{6}, hay^{2}; cf. khaa^{4})

lii^{6} *in* mit^{6} cii^{6} lii^{6} very quiet

vii^4 fire
vii^4 saay^2 flashlight
vii^4 *in* thee^4 vii^4 lady; queen
vii^5 crooked, not straight
vii^6 to winnow
sii^1 morph used in personal names
  sii^1 vay^4 personal name
sii^1 phɔɔŋ^4 face powder
sii^1 *in* saŋ^1 ka^6 sii^1 tin (= sɯɯn^4)
sii^2 color
  sii^2 phaa^3 blue (< Lao, = sii^2 faa^3 < Lao; = Saek muuy^4)
sii^2 paint
sii^2 to roll, make (candles)
sii^2 naa^3 gable
sii^2 *in* phaa^4 sii^2 tax
sii^2 *in* laa^4 sii^2 radiance, radiant glory (= raa^4 sii^2)
sii^2 *in* laat^5 sa^6 sii^2 lion
sii^2 *in* lɯɯ^4 sii^2 hermit, ascetic
sii^4 daa^1 Sita, wife of Rama
sii^4 *in* khii^2 sii^4 resin
sii^5 a boil
sii^5 *in* thɛk^4 sii^5 taxi
sii^6 four

-ia

kia^1 bat (the animal) (clf. thua^4, = cia^1)
khia^6 to scratch (of chickens)
cia^1 a moment ago
cia^1 bat (the animal) (clf. thua^4, = kia^1)
cia^5 paper
tia^3 low, short
bia^1 beer
pia^1 to braid
pia^3 weak, tired; crippled
phia^2 to harrow (= phɯa^2)
phia^3 side, part
phia^3 the edible, partially digested contents of a buffalo's intestines
phia^5 shirt, upper garment
mia^4 *in* pii^1 ma^6 mia^4 Year of the Horse, seventh year in the twelve-year cycle
ɲia^2 to hear; to listen
  saŋ^5 ɲia^2 to cock the ears to try to listen hard

lia^{4} to lick
via^{1} comb-like part of a loom, the beater (= via^{4})
via^{1} to poison (= bɯa^{1})
via^{3} cloud
via^{3} *in* plaa^{1} via^{3} water tortoise (= plaa^{1} pha^{6} ʔɔɔŋ^{1})
via^{4} comb-like part of a loom, the beater (= via^{1})
via^{6} to be poisoned, poisonous
hia^{3} monitor lizard (clf. thua^{4})

-ɯɯ

kɯɯ^{3} to put away, put aside, keep
cɯɯ^{1} heart
cɯɯ^{1} *in* thɯt^{4} cɯɯ^{1} to breathe (more frequent, = less frequent thit^{4} cɯɯ^{1})
cɯɯ^{1} *in* sɯɯn^{5} cɯɯ^{1} happy (= sɯɯn^{6} cɯɯ^{1})
  sɯɯn^{5} mɔk^{4} sɯɯn^{5} cɯɯ^{1} happy, cheerful
dɯɯ^{3} stubborn
thɯɯ^{4} to carry, hold
  nap^{4} thɯɯ^{4} to revere
thɯɯ^{5} *in* may^{6} thɯɯ^{5} naaŋ^{5} chopsticks (= thuu^{5}, may^{6} ta^{6} khiap^{2})
bɯɯ^{1} navel (= dua^{1})
plɯɯ^{6} to plow (a field) a second time
phɯɯ^{4} *in* ta^{6} phɯt^{6} ta^{6} phɯɯ^{4} scattered about
phɯɯ^{6} to raise, take up (a sheet, tablecloth)
mɯɯ^{4} hand
mɯɯ^{6} day
  mɯɯ^{6} thɔɔk^{5} nii^{6} tomorrow
rɯɯ^{1} day after tomorrow
  pii^{1} rɯɯ^{1} year after next
rɯɯ^{6} to gather in (clothes after they are dry)
lɯɯ^{4} sii^{2} hermit, ascetic
sɯɯ^{2} *in* naŋ^{4} sɯɯ^{2} writing, book
sɯɯ^{4} time (= sɯ^{6} sɯɯ^{4}, sɤɤ^{4})
sɯɯ^{5} to guard, watch
sɯɯ^{6} to buy
hɯɯ^{2} spoiled, damaged
hɯɯ^{4} to rush, hurry
hɯɯ^{6} dry

-ɯa

ʔɯa^{1} to do alone, do stubbornly
khɯa^{1} khɯa^{4} tomato (clf. maak^{6})
cɯa^{1} *in* cop^{4} cɯa^{1} good, proper
trɯa^{4} to be afraid; cured by a bad experience
thɯa^{5} a time
nɯa^{3} animal; meat (< Lao; = Saek mlɔɔ^{5})
bɯa^{1} to poison (= via^{1})
bɯa^{1} flour
phɯa^{2} to harrow (= phia^{2})
phɯa^{6} to save for someone; by the time
mɯa^{4} to return (< Lao)
ɲɯa^{2} bait (< Siamese; = Saek ɲɯa^{6})
ɲɯa^{4} a long time
ɲɯa^{6} bait (= ɲɯa^{2} < Siamese)
rɯa^{6} formerly
sɯa^{5} to believe
sɯa^{6} mattress

-uu

ʔuu^{6} cradle
kuu^{1} I
kuu^{3} nine
kuu^{3} term used in answer to a call
khuu^{1} to force, compel
khuu^{4} teacher
khuu^{4} *in* kuŋ^{6} khuu^{4} dung beetle
khuu^{4} *in* ɲaa^{4} khuu^{4} monk, senior monk (= caw^{3} hua^{2})
khuu^{6} to threaten
cuu^{3} breast
duu^{1} *in* la^{6} duu^{1} season
tuu^{1} *in* pak^{4} tuu^{1} door
  pak^{4} tuu^{1} bɔɔŋ^{6} window
tuu^{3} cupboard
tuu^{3} *in* ʔan^{3} tuu^{3} baffled
tuu^{3} *in* vaay^{4} tuu^{3} male buffalo with short horns
tuu^{6} thua^{4} the body (= tua^{6} thua^{4}, thua^{6} thua^{4}, tuŋ^{6} thua^{4}; cf. too^{1})
thuu^{1} *in* thiʔ^{4} thuu^{1} thiʔ^{4} thay^{1} descriptive of effort of dragging or carrying
thuu^{2} to rub

thuu^{3} fierce; to scold
  man^{3} thuu^{3} angry (cf. lɤɤ^{1}, bɯn^{3}, yak^{6})
thuu^{4} thaw^{3} an old person (= thua^{4} thaw^{3})
thuu^{4} *in* thii^{4} thuu^{4} thii^{4} thaat^{5} descriptive of dragging
thuu^{5} chopsticks (= may^{6} ta^{6} khiap^{2}, may^{6} thɯɯ^{5} naaŋ^{5})
thruu^{3} name of former Saek village in Vietnam
thruu^{4} like, alike, similar
  thruu^{4} ʔan^{6} like that (= thruu^{4} nan^{6}, thruu^{4} rɛn^{6}, thruun^{4})
  thruu^{4} ɣaa^{5} for example
nuu^{2} mouse, rat (clf. thua^{4})
nuu^{4} *in* tha^{6} nuu^{4} bow, arrow
buu^{1} saa^{4} to do reverence, offer, worship
buu^{1} *in* sa^{6} buu^{1} soap (< Siamese; = sa^{6} buu^{6})
buu^{6} *in* sa^{6} buu^{6} soap (< Siamese; = sa^{6} buu^{1})
puu^{1} *in* ta^{6} puu^{1} nail
pruu^{1} we (two or more) (= pruu^{1} hɔɔy^{6})
pruu^{6} empty (YG, = OG pluu^{6})
pluu^{6} empty (OG, = YG pruu^{6})
phuu^{4} *in* chom^{4} phuu^{4} thiip^{5} name of a mythical continent
phuu^{6} person
phuu^{6} male
phuu^{6} carpenter bee (clf. thua^{4})
phruu^{4} betel (YG, = OG phluu^{4})
phluu^{4} betel (OG, = YG phruu^{4})
muu^{2} pig (clf. thua^{4})
muu^{2} *in* sum^{2} muu^{2} a spear (= sam^{3} muu^{2}; clf. maak^{6})
muu^{3} *in* ɣaw^{6} muu^{3} roasted young rice pounded flat, used in making desserts
muu^{5} *in* ʔoŋ^{1} muu^{5} name of a spirit
muu^{6} friend; group
yuu^{4} to swim
yuu^{6} lover
yuu^{6} to live in a place
  ha^{6} lii^{6} yuu^{6} still alive (= hay^{2} lii^{2} yuu^{6})
  yuu^{6} maa^{2} time passed
ɲuu^{4} thaaŋ^{6} happy
ɲuu^{4} *in* khan^{4} ɲuu^{4} paper umbrella (< Lao)
ɲuu^{5} to urinate
luu^{1} *in* pii^{1} sa^{6} luu^{1} Year of the Ox, second year of the twelve-year cycle
luu^{5} to run
vuu^{1} to float
suu^{2} you (plural)
suu^{2} to push (someone)

suu^{3} own, self
suu^{4} *in* kaay^{1} suu^{4} a Vietnamese rank equivalent to Siamese ʔam^{1} maat^{2} thoo^{1}
suu^{6} for, toward
huu^{1} *in* tum^{3} huu^{1} earring (< Siamese; = Saek taaŋ^{3}, taaŋ^{6}, voŋ^{4} vɛɛn^{2})

-ua

ʔua^{1} *in* ʔon^{1} ʔua^{1} disorderly (of children)
kua^{1} leg (YG, = OG kwaa^{1})
kua^{1} to feed (animals)
kua^{3} crazy, mad (YG, = OG kwaa^{3})
kua^{6} more than, comparative (YG, = OG kwaa^{6})
khua^{4} to cut up (a slaughtered chicken or animal)
khua^{4} right (hand) (YG, = OG khwaa^{4})
khua^{4} small jar (for lime) (YG, = OG khwaa^{4})
khua^{4} to reach for (YG, = OG khwaa^{4})
khua^{4} to scratch, claw (YG, = OG khwaa^{4}; also OG khwaak^{6}, khwaaw^{4})
khua^{6} to struggle, writhe, move
ŋua^{4} snake (clf. thua^{4})
cua^{1} a novice
dua^{1} navel (= bɯɯ^{1})
tua^{6} thua^{4} the body (tuu^{6} thua^{4}, thua^{6} thua^{4}, tuŋ^{6} thaa^{4}, cf. too^{1})
trua^{1} salt (YG, = OG tlua^{1})
tlua^{1} salt (OG, = YG trua^{1})
thua^{1} white-headed wild bird kept as a pet
thua^{2} *in* praa^{1} thua^{2} poor vision
thua^{4} classifier for animals; body
thua^{4} thaw^{3} an old person (= thuu^{4} thaw^{3})
thua^{4} *in* tuu^{6} thua^{4} the body (= tua^{6} thua^{4}, thua^{6} thua^{4}, tuŋ^{6} thaa^{4}, cf. too^{1})
thua^{5} bean
thua^{5} everywhere
thua^{6} thua^{4} the body (= tua^{6} thua^{4}, tuu^{6} thua^{4}, tuŋ^{6} thaa^{4}, cf. too^{1})
thrua^{4} family
thrua^{6} wild fig
nua^{3} cross bow
nua^{4} delicious (= bua^{1})
bua^{1} lotus
bua^{1} delicious (= nua^{4})
pua^{1} to treat (the ill), care for (= pin^{6} pua^{1})
phua^{3} cluster (of fruit)
ɲua^{3} grass
ɲua^{6} to invite (only in a bad way)

rua^{1} boat
rua^{2} pig trough
rua^{4} ear
lua^{2} light firewood (such as bamboo)
lua^{2} spinning wheel (YG, = OG lwaa^{2})
lua^{2} to be left over
lua^{4} mule (clf. thua^{4})
vua^{6} he, you (respectful)
sua^{2} to be defeated
sua^{3} dead
sua^{4} to invite
sua^{5} period of time
sua^{6} bad
hua^{2} *in* caw^{3} hua^{2} monk, senior monk (= ɲaa^{4} khuu^{4})

-ee

ʔee^{5} ornament, to adorn
ʔee^{5} kaʔ^{6} reel^{4} ʔee^{5} sound of rooster crowing (OG, = OG ʔek^{4} kaʔ^{6} reel^{4} ʔeek^{4}, YG ʔee^{5} kaʔ^{6} reen^{4} ʔee^{5}, YG ʔek^{4} kaʔ^{6} reen^{4} ʔeek^{4})
kee^{3} to undo, remove, unbutton, untie
kee^{3} eggplant (clf. maak^{6})
kee^{3} *in* buat^{6} kee^{3} baʔ^{4} to become a monk to fulfill a promise
kee^{6} old (of living things), ripe, dark (color)
khee^{4} crippled, lame
ŋee^{4} to raise the head
cee^{1} to dislike, hate, be bored with
dee^{1} final particle
dee^{4} particle
dee^{5} particle
tlee^{1} *in* tloon^{1} tlee^{1} anus
thee^{4} to pour
thee^{4} vii^{4} lady; queen
  khoo^{4} laa^{4} khaʔ^{6} thee^{4} vii^{4} Lady khoo^{4} laa^{4} khaʔ^{6}, name of soŋ^{1} kaan^{1} day when it falls on Monday
  thuŋ^{4} saʔ^{4} thee^{4} vii^{4} Lady thuŋ^{4} saʔ^{4}, name of soŋ^{1} kaan^{1} day when it falls on Sunday
  mon^{4} thaa^{4} thee^{4} vii^{4} Lady mon^{4} thaa^{4}, name of soŋ^{1} kaan^{1} day when it falls on Wednesday
thee^{4} va^{6} daa^{1} divinity, god
thee^{4} va^{6} but^{4} angel, divine child
thee^{4} *in* thaŋ^{6} thee^{4} great numbers

pee^{1} flat
phee^{4} raft
phee^{4} *in* praʔ^{6} phee^{4} nii^{4} customs
mee^{3} mother (= mee^{5})
mee^{4} *in* ʔaʔ^{6} mee^{4} liʔ^{6} kaa^{1} America (= ʔa^{6} mee^{4} li^{4} kaa^{1})
mee^{4} *in* lot^{6} mee^{4} bus
mee^{5} mother (= mee^{3})
mee^{5} *in* phɔɔ^{3} mee^{5} an exclamation
ree^{2} sein
ree^{6} kind of bamboo
lee^{4} then, and then, so, and so, therefore (= leʔ^{4}, le^{4}, lɤɤy^{4})
lee^{5} to choose
lee^{6} *in* khoo^{6} lee^{6} shoulder
lee^{6} *in* thɔɔk^{6} lee^{6} to pour out
vee^{4} laa^{4} time
see^{1} naa^{4} bɔɔ^{1} dii^{1} minister, general
see^{4} to slant, lean over
see^{5} to soak
hee^{5} if

-ɤɤ

ʔɤɤ^{1} oh!
ʔɤɤ^{3} yes, o.k. (= ʔɤɤ^{5})
ʔɤɤ^{4} yes
ʔɤɤ^{5} yes, o.k. (= ʔɤɤ^{3})
khwɤɤ^{6} daughter-in-law (= phɤɤ^{6}, fɤɤ^{6})
dɤɤ^{1} who, everybody, anybody
tɤɤ^{1} gizzard
tɤɤ^{3} below, under, south
tɤɤ^{3} *in* bɯk^{4} naa^{4} tɤɤ^{3} name of former Saek village in Vietnam
tɤɤ^{5} *in* mat^{6} tɤɤ^{5} say^{4} motorcycle
tlɤɤ^{2} to talk in one's sleep (= thrɤɤ^{2})
trɤɤ^{3} near (YG, = OG tlɤɤ^{3})
tlɤɤ^{3} near (OG, = YG trɤɤ^{3})
thrɤɤ^{2} to talk in one's sleep (= tlɤɤ^{2})
thrɤɤ^{4} what, anything; why (= thaa^{4})
thrɤɤ^{4} *in* ca^{6} thrɤɤ^{4} lemongrass (= ca^{6} phrɤɤ^{4})
nɤɤ^{1} where; why (= nɤɤ^{2}) *Tone variation* (nɤɤ^{1}) *due to sentence intonation.*
nɤɤ^{2} where; why (= nɤɤ^{1})

nɤɤ^4 which, what, any
nɤɤ^4 *in* nap^4 nɤɤ^4 fontanelle
bɤɤ^1 leaf
bɤɤ^1 number
prɤɤ^6 to return (YG, = OG plɤɤ^6)
plɤɤ^6 to return (OG, = YG prɤɤ^6)
phɤɤ^5 *in* phak^6 phɤɤ^5 difficult
phɤɤ^6 daughter-in-law (= khwɤɤ^6, fɤɤ^6)
phrɤɤ^4 *in* ca^6 phrɤɤ^4 lemongrass (= ca^6 thrɤɤ^4)
yɤɤ^4 *in* day^3 yɤɤ^4 thank you
yɤɤ^5 to revile
ɲɤɤ^3 to remember
ɲɤɤ^6 big
rɤɤ^1 in, inside
rɤɤ^3 raaŋ^1 irritated, excited
rɤɤ^4 *in* tɛɛ^6 rɤɤ^4 formerly, in old times
rɤɤ^5 rɤɤ^5 bright, gleaming (red and yellow colors)
lɤɤ^1 angry (cf. bɯn^3, man^3 thuu^3, yak^6)
sɤɤ^4 time (= sɯɯ^4, sɯ^6 sɯɯ^4)
fɤɤ^6 daughter-in-law (= khwɤɤ^4, phɤɤ^6)
hɤɤ^3 to give; for; to cause

-oo

ʔoo^1 metal water bowl
ʔoo^1 oh!
ʔoo^3 oh!
ʔoo^4 oh!
ʔoo^5 oh!
ʔoo^6 thaŋ^4 to recollect
koo^1 mut^6 kind of flower
khoo^1 *in* leʔ^4 caŋ^1 leʔ^4 khoo^1 paralyzed
khoo^2 dry, dried, dried out,
khoo^4 laa^4 khaʔ^6 name of soŋ^1 kaan^1 day when it falls on Monday
  khoo^4 laa^4 khaʔ^6 thee^4 vii^4 Lady khoo^4 laa^4 khaʔ^6, name of soŋ^1 kaan^1 day when it falls on Monday
khoo^6 tree, plant
  khoo^6 taan^1 sugar palm tree
  khoo^6 hay^4 banyan tree

khoo^{6} base, first part
ŋoo^{4} to raise (the head)
doo^{5} ɣaa^{5} approximately
too^{1} the body (cf. tuu^{6} thua^{4}, tua^{6} thua^{4}, thua^{6} thua^{4}, tuŋ^{6} thua^{4})
too^{3} to challenge
thoo^{4} an exclamation (= paa^{4} thoo^{4}, paat^{4} thoo^{4})
thoo^{4} *in* thap^{6} thoo^{4} to beat, strike, batter
throo^{4} *in* thrɯaŋ^{5} throo^{4} things, possessions
noo^{4} swollen, as from a bruise
noo^{4} *in* mii^{4} khun^{4} mii^{4} noo^{4} to do a favor for
noo^{4} *in* saʔ^{4} ʔaʔ^{6} noo^{4} daat^{6} name of a pool
boo^{6} not
  boo^{6} day^{3} could not, do not (= bay^{3})
poo^{3} *in* ŋiaŋ^{5} poo^{3} thumb; big toe
phoo^{4} Bo tree
  phoo^{4} kham^{3} name of a Saek village in Laos
moo^{3} a skin disease
moo^{4} farmer's conical hat
moo^{4} *in* priaŋ^{1} moo^{4} watermelon (clf. maak^{6})
yoo^{5} shaky, in bad condition (of a house)
yoo^{5} interjection used to intensify
roo^{3} *in* sa^{6} roo^{3} the So people (= soo^{3})
roo^{4} we (inclusive)
loo^{5} to tell, narrate; to lie
loo^{5} again; also
soo^{2} to push
soo^{3} the So people (= sa^{6} roo^{3})
soo^{3} chain (< Siamese; = Saek soo^{6})
soo^{3} *in* ka^{6} soo^{3} a basket for scooping up water
soo^{4} very thin
soo^{4} *in* puay^{6} soo^{4} to be in pain
soo^{6} a heap (of dung)
soo^{6} chain (= soo^{3} < Siamese)
hoo^{1} *in* ma^{6} hoo^{1} thɔɔn^{4} name of soŋ^{1} kaan^{1} day when it falls on Saturday
hoo^{6} to hunt, go hunting
hoo^{6} to smoke (meat)

-ɛɛ

kɛɛ^{1} ɣay^{6} nonsense!
kɛɛ^{5} to poke in the ribs
kɛɛ^{5} *in* kap^{4} kɛɛ^{5} gecko (= kak^{4} kɛɛ^{5})

kɛɛ^{6} to, for

khɛɛ^{4} *in* thaa^{5} khɛɛ^{4} name of Saek village in Laos

khɛɛ^{5} line of joining of two floorboards

khɛɛ^{5} kwaa^{1} the groin

khɛɛ^{5} haa^{2} armpit (= khɛŋ^{5} haa^{2})

khɛɛ^{6} crocodile (clf. thua^{4})

ŋɛɛ^{4} *in* nɛɛŋ^{1} ŋɛɛ^{4} tusk of a boar

cɛɛ^{1} corner

cɛɛ^{1} kan^{1} vase

dɛɛ^{6} some

tɛɛ^{6} from, since

  tɛɛ^{6} moʔ^{6} at first

  taŋ^{3} tɛɛ^{6} from, since

tɛɛ^{6} but

  tɛɛ^{6} ɣaa^{3} but

trɛɛ^{1} small squirrel or chipmunk (clf. thua^{4})

thɛɛ^{2} to shave

thɛɛ^{3} real; really

thɛɛ^{4} *in* khan^{4} thɛɛ^{4} a dam

thrɛɛ^{3} small frog (clf. thua^{4})

thrɛɛ^{5} slowly, gradually

thrɛɛ^{5} kind of fish (YG, = OG thlɛɛ^{5}; = Siamese plaa^{1} chɔɔn^{3})

thlɛɛ^{5} kind of fish (OG, = YG thrɛɛ^{5}; = Siamese plaa^{1} chɔɔn^{3})

nɛɛ^{1} duckweed

nɛɛ^{4} to point (= ɲii^{6})

nɛɛ^{5} sure, certain

bɛɛ^{1} to lie flat on the back; to open the hand

bɛɛ^{3} goat (clf. thua^{4})

pɛɛ^{1} flat, flattened (cf. pɛɛ^{3})

pɛɛ^{1} a beam

pɛɛ^{3} flattened, pressed flat (cf. pɛɛ^{1})

phɛɛ^{5} to win, be victorious, defeat

mɛɛ^{4} final particle (= la^{6} mɛɛ^{4}; = Siamese si^{2})

mɛɛ^{4} *in* pii^{1} ma^{6} mɛɛ^{4} Year of the Goat, eighth year in the twelve-year cycle

ɲɛɛ^{3} kind of lizard (clf. thua^{4})

rɛɛ^{3} nonglutinous rice

rɛɛ^{6} to carry in a procession, have a procession

vɛɛ^{3} *in* vaŋ^{3} vɛɛ^{3} completely silent, as when a friend disappears

vɛɛ^{5} to stop in, visit

hɛɛ^{4} or

-aa

ʔaa^{1} kaat^{6} sky, air, atmosphere
  sat^{4} ta^{4} ʔaa^{1} kaat^{6} air, atmosphere
ʔaa^{1} caan^{1} teacher, scholar
ʔaa^{1} thit^{6} week
  van^{4} ʔaa^{1} thit^{6} Sunday (= van^{4} ʔa^{6} thit^{6}, van^{4} thit^{6})
ʔaa^{1} ɲuʔ^{6} age (= ʔa^{6} ɲuʔ^{6})
ʔaa^{1} saa^{1} *see* ʔaat^{6} saa^{1} maat^{5}
ʔaa^{1} saa^{1} maat^{5} *see* ʔaat^{6} saa^{1} maat^{5}
ʔaa^{1} say^{2} to live (in a place)
ʔaa^{1} siip^{5} occupation
ʔaa^{1} *in* ʔeek^{6} ʔaa^{1} saa^{1} *see* ʔaat^{6} saa^{1} maat^{5}
ʔaa^{3} to open (the mouth)
ʔaa^{6} hesitation particle (= ʔaaʔ^{6})
ʔaat^{6} sa^{6} maat^{5} *see* ʔaat^{6} saa^{1} maat^{5}
kaa^{1} crow (clf. thua^{4})
kaa^{1} teakettle, teapot
kaa^{1} *in* ʔaʔ^{6} mee^{4} liʔ^{6} kaa^{1} America (= ʔa^{6} mee^{4} li^{4} kaa^{1})
kaa^{1} *in* naa^{4} li^{4} kaa^{1} watch, clock
kaa^{1} *in* paak^{6} kaa^{1} pen
kaa^{1} *in* pii^{1} la^{6} kaa^{1} Year of the Cock, tenth year in the twelve-year cycle
kaa^{1} *in* saŋ^{1} kaa^{1} kind of gambling game
kaa^{3} to kill
kaa^{3} brave, bold (cf. tlaa^{3})
kwaa^{1} leg (OG, = YG kua^{1})
kwaa^{3} mad, crazy (OG, = YG kua^{3})
kwaa^{6} more than, comparative (OG, = YG kua^{6})
khaa^{4} still, yet (cf. lii^{6})
khaa^{4} to be stuck
khaa^{4} *in* laa^{4} khaa^{4} price (< Siamese)
khaa^{5} value, price; tax
khaa^{6} to engage in trade
khwaa^{4} right (hand) (OG, = YG khua^{4})
khwaa^{4} to scratch, claw (OG, = YG khua^{4}; also OG khwaak^{6}, khwaaw^{4})
khwaa^{4} to reach for (OG, = YG khua^{4})
khwaa^{4} small jar (for lime) (OG, = YG khua^{4})
ɣaa^{3} *in* tɛɛ^{6} ɣaa^{3} but
ɣaa^{4} thatchgrass
ɣaa^{5} to say; that (= Siamese waa^{3})
ŋaa^{4} elephant's tusk, ivory

ŋaa^{5} branch
caa^{1} *in* phiʔ^{4} caa^{1} la^{6} naa^{4} to reflect, consider (= phiʔ^{6} caa^{1} la^{6} naa^{4}, phit^{4} caa^{1} la^{6} naa^{4}, phit^{6} caa^{1} la^{6} naa^{4})
daa^{1} will, would; about to
daa^{1} *in* tham^{4} ma^{6} daa^{1} usual, ordinary
daa^{1} *in* thee^{4} va^{6} daa^{1} divinity, god
daa^{1} *in* sii^{4} daa^{1} Sita, wife of Rama
taa^{1} maternal grandfather; old man
  caw^{3} khoot^{5} voŋ^{4} taa^{1} the elder who is an arranger at a wedding
taa^{1} able, worthy of being (= Siamese naa^{3})
  taa^{1} kin^{1} edible
  taa^{1} sɯɯ^{6} good at shopping
  taa^{1} saat^{5} of low quality
taa^{6} *in* ka^{6} taa^{6} basket
traa^{1} cockspur
traa^{3} rice seedling (YG, = OG tlaa^{3})
traa^{3} bamboo (YG, = OG tlaa^{3})
traa^{3} brave, bold (YG, = OG tlaa^{3})
tlaa^{3} rice seedling (OG, = YG traa^{3})
tlaa^{3} bamboo (OG, = YG traa^{3})
tlaa^{3} brave, bold (OG, = YG traa^{3}; cf. kaa^{3})
thaa^{3} if (= khan^{4})
thaa^{3} to wait
thaa^{4} to smear on, paint
thaa^{4} partridge (clf. thua^{4})
thaa^{4} what, anything; why (= thuʔ^{4} thaa^{4}, thrɤɤ^{4})
thaa^{4} vine
thaa^{4} *in* kiʔ^{4} miʔ^{6} thaa^{4} name of soŋ^{1} kaan^{1} day when it falls on Friday (= ki^{4} mi^{6} thaa^{4})
thaa^{4} *in* tuŋ^{6} thaa^{4} what, something, everything
thaa^{4} *in* mon^{4} thaa^{4} name of soŋ^{1} kaan^{1} day when it falls on Wednesday
thaa^{4} *in* saa^{1} thaa^{4} laʔ^{6} naʔ^{6} public
thaa^{5} landing
  thaa^{5} khɛɛ^{4} name of Saek village in Laos
  thaa^{5} khɛɛk^{6} place name
  thaa^{5} vaay^{4} name of abandoned Saek village in Thailand
thaa^{5} way, means
thaa^{6} big knife, machete (clf. maak^{6})
  thaa^{6} koʔ^{4} cleaver-like knife with big blade curved at top (clf. maak^{6})
  thaa^{6} khat^{4} vuat^{6} knife put in waist at back
thraa^{2} tray (YG, = OG thlaa^{2})
thraa^{4} late in the morning (YG, = OG thlaa^{4})
thraa^{6} orphan (= Saek lɯk^{6} thraa^{6}; = kam^{1} phaa^{3} < Lao)

thraa^{6} shelf
thlaa^{2} tray (OG, = YG thraa^{2})
thlaa^{4} late in the morning (OG, = YG thraa^{4})
naa^{2} thick
naa^{2} *in* saat^{6} sa^{6} naa^{2} religion
naa^{3} face
  pii^{1} naa^{3} next year
naa^{4} ricefield
  naa^{4} laʔ^{6} vaay^{4} name of abandoned Saek village in Thailand
  bɯk^{4} naa^{4} tɤɤ^{3} name of abandoned Saek village in Vietnam
naa^{4} final particle
naa^{4} thii^{4} minute
naa^{4} naa^{4} various
naa^{4} li^{4} kaa^{1} watch, clock
naa^{4} *in* phiʔ^{4} caa^{1} la^{6} naa^{4} to reflect, consider (= phiʔ^{6} caa^{1} la^{6} naa^{4}, phit^{4} caa^{1} la^{6} naa^{4}, phit^{6} caa^{1} la^{6} naa^{4})
naa^{4} *in* vɔɔ^{4} la^{6} naa^{4} old term for the end of Buddhist Lent (= paʔ^{6} vɔɔ^{4} la^{6} naa^{4})
naa^{4} *in* see^{1} naa^{4} bɔɔ^{1} dii^{1} minister, general
naa^{4} *in* sin^{4} naa^{4} mɤɤy^{4} name of abandoned Saek village in Vietnam
naa^{5} final particle
naa^{6} mother's younger sibling
naa^{6} arrow of a crossbow
baa^{1} to skip, omit
baa^{1} vaa^{3} *see* baa^{6} vaa^{3}
baa^{3} *in* buŋ^{6} baa^{3} butterfly (clf. thua^{4})
baa^{4} oh!
baa^{6} vaa^{3} name of Saek village in Thailand (also recorded as baa^{1} vaa^{3})
paa^{1} *in* cam^{1} paa^{1} kind of flowering tree (= cam^{6} paa^{1})
paa^{3} aunt, older sister of either parent
paa^{4} thoo^{4} an exclamation (= thoo^{4}, paat^{4} thoo^{4})
paa^{6} group
paa^{6} palm, sole (= vaa^{1})
paa^{6} forest, thicket
paa^{6} reew^{5} maaŋ^{4} cemetery
praa^{1} fish (YG, = OG plaa^{1})
praa^{1} cockspur
praa^{1} eye
plaa^{1} fish (OG, = YG praa^{1})
  plaa^{1} dɛɛk^{6} fermented fish paste
phaa^{1} saat^{2} palace, mansion (= phaa^{1} saat^{6})
phaa^{2} to force one's way through (= phaa^{6})
phaa^{3} *in* kam^{1} phaa^{3} orphan (< Lao; = Saek thraa^{6}, lɯk^{6} thraa^{6})

phaa^{3} *in* caw^{3} phaa^{3} prince
phaa^{3} *in* sii^{2} phaa^{3} blue (< Lao, = sii^{2} faa^{3} < Lao; = Saek muuy^{4})
phaa^{4} wife, woman
phaa^{4} sii^{2} tax
phaa^{4} *in* saa^{1} laʔ^{6} phat^{6} saa^{1} laʔ^{6} phaa^{4} every sort of thing
phaa^{5} (not) yet
phaa^{6} to split
phaa^{6} to carry slung over the shoulder
phaa^{6} to force one's way through (= phaa^{2})
phraa^{2} rocky cliff
phraa^{3} thunder
maa^{2} dog (clf. thua^{4})
  maa^{2} nay^{4} jackal (clf. thua^{4})
maa^{2} to come, return
  yuu^{6} maa^{2} time passed
maa^{3} *in* kha^{6} maa^{3} bathing cloth
maa^{4} iron (the metal)
maa^{6} horse (clf. thua^{4})
maa^{6} to soak (e.g., rice)
  maa^{6} ɣaw^{6} to soak rice
yaa^{1} to mend (a boat)
yaa^{1} naaŋ^{4} kind of leaf boiled with bamboo shoots to make bamboo curry
yaa^{1} thaay^{6} laxative (< Siamese)
yaa^{1} raan^{4} house lizard (clf. thua^{4})
yaa^{4} to roast
yaa^{5} paternal grandmother; old woman
yaa^{6} don't; to stop, refrain from
yaa^{6} to divorce
ɲaa^{4} khuu^{4} monk, senior monk (= caw^{3} hua^{2})
ɲaa^{4} *in* ʔan^{6} ɲaa^{4} an official
ɲaa^{4} *in* pan^{1} ɲaa^{4} intelligence, wits
ɲaa^{4} *in* pha^{6} ɲaa^{4} king, prince, chief, lord
ɲaa^{4} *in* sɛn^{3} ɲaa^{4} to promise; a contract
raa^{2} to seek
raa^{4} sii^{2} radiance, radiant glory (= laa^{4} sii^{2})
  raa^{4} sii^{2} som^{1} phaan^{4} radiant glory (of a king)
raa^{5} flattened, crushed, smashed
raa^{5} way, road; side
  raa^{5} ʔan^{6} that way (= raan^{5})
raa^{6} shower
raa^{6} *in* kɔɔŋ^{1} raa^{6} large pile of firewood
laa^{1} final particle

laa^{2} final particle
laa^{3} final particle
laa^{4} donkey (clf. thua^{4})
laa^{4} to take one's leave
laa^{4} khaa^{4} price (< Siamese)
laa^{4} sii^{2} radiance, radiant glory (= raa^{4} sii^{2})
laa^{4} *in* khoo^{4} laa^{4} khaʔ^{6} thee^{4} vii^{4} name of soŋ^{1} kaan^{1} day when it falls on Monday
laa^{4} *in* saa^{1} laa^{4} pavilion
laa^{4} *in* vee^{4} laa^{4} time
lwaa^{2} spinning wheel (OG, = YG lua^{2})
vaa^{1} palm, sole (= paa^{6})
vaa^{1} lid; wall, partition
  vaa^{1} ka^{6} tɛʔ^{4} wall of woven bamboo
vaa^{1} leew^{2} bamboo star to ward off spirits
vaa^{2} kind of fruit called luuk^{3} waa^{1} in Siamese (clf. maak^{6})
vaa^{2} theen^{5} broom (YG, = OG vaay^{2} theel^{5})
vaa^{3} *in* baa^{1} vaa^{3} *see* baa^{6} vaa^{3}
vaa^{3} *in* baa^{6} vaa^{3} *see* baa^{6} vaa^{3}
vaa^{4} armspread, fathom; to measure with armspreads
vaa^{4} *in* vat^{6} vaa^{4} monasteries
vaa^{6} shoulder
saa^{1} thaa^{4} laʔ^{6} naʔ^{6} public
saa^{1} laa^{4} pavilion
saa^{1} laʔ^{6} phat^{6} saa^{1} laʔ^{6} phaa^{4} every sort of thing
saa^{1} *in* ʔa^{6} saa^{1} *see* ʔaat^{6} saa^{1} maat^{5}
saa^{1} *in* ʔaa^{1} saa^{1} *see* ʔaat^{6} saa^{1} maat^{5}
saa^{1} *in* ʔaa^{1} saa^{1} maat^{5} *see* ʔaat^{6} saa^{1} maat^{5}
saa^{1} *in* ʔaat^{6} saa^{1} maat^{5} *see* ʔaat^{6} saa^{1} maat^{5}
saa^{1} *in* ʔit^{4} saa^{1} to envy
saa^{1} *in* ʔeek^{6} ʔaa^{1} saa^{1} *see* ʔaat^{6} saa^{1} maat^{5}
saa^{2} *in* phan^{4} saa^{2} Buddhist Lent
saa^{2} *in* rak^{6} saa^{2} to take care of
saa^{3} a dish made of chopped raw fish or meat
  saa^{3} plaa^{1} dish made of chopped fish
  saa^{3} mlɔɔ^{5} dish made of chopped meat
saa^{4} tea
saa^{4} Indian hemp, marijuana
saa^{4} *in* kam^{1} laŋ^{4} vaŋ^{4} saa^{4} troops
saa^{4} *in* buu^{1} saa^{4} to do reverence, offer, worship
saa^{5} *in* kaay^{1} saa^{5} a Vietnamese rank equivalent to Siamese ʔam^{1} maat^{2} ʔeek^{2}
saa^{6} sediment, as in water, liquor, soup

saa^{6} far apart, widely spaced; coarse, coarsely woven
swaa^{5} famous
faa^{3} *in* sii^{2} faa^{3} blue (< Lao, = sii^{2} phaa^{3} < Lao; = Saek muuy^{4})
haa^{1} *in* ma^{6} haa^{1} great (used in various expressions)
  ma^{6} haa^{1} phom^{4} great Brahma
haa^{2} lii^{6} still, yet (= lii^{6}, haʔ^{6} lii^{6}, ha^{6} lii^{6}, hay^{2}; cf. khaa^{4})
haa^{2} *in* khɛŋ^{5} haa^{2} armpit (= khɛɛ^{5} haa^{2})
haa^{2} *in* ban^{3} haa^{2} riddle
haa^{3} five
haa^{3} final question particle (= haa^{5})
haa^{5} final question particle (= haa^{3})
haa^{6} epidemic
  praay^{1} haa^{6} a curse meaning ‘a disgrace upon you’
haa^{6} galangal, root similar to ginger

-ɔɔ

ʔɔɔ^{5} father’s younger sister
ʔɔɔ^{5} oh!
kɔɔ^{1} clump (of bamboo)
kɔɔ^{3} spool, reel
kɔɔ^{6} knee
kɔɔ^{6} to build, construct, erect
ɣɔɔ^{4} neck
  ɣɔɔ^{4} ʔɤɤm^{1} goiter
  ɣɔɔ^{4} cɔɔ^{6} lɔɔ^{6} up to the neck
  ɣɔɔ^{4} hɔɔy^{1} Adam’s apple
ɣɔɔ^{5} joint
ɣɔɔ^{5} item
ŋɔɔ^{5} *in* pii^{1} ŋɔɔ^{5} seventh year in the Saek twelve-year cycle
ŋɔɔ^{5} *in* ŋɯt^{6} ŋɔɔ^{5} strange
cɔɔ^{1} *in* pii^{1} cɔɔ^{1} Year of the Dog, eleventh in the twelve-year cycle
cɔɔ^{6} to put
dɔɔ^{1} each, every
dɔɔ^{1} early ripening (of rice, beans)
dɔɔ^{3} *in* ka^{6} det^{4} ka^{6} dɔɔ^{3} really, very
tɔɔ^{3} to fight (of cocks)
tɔɔ^{6} wasp (clf. thua^{4})
tɔɔ^{6} to join; continue
tɔɔ^{6} *in* ka^{6} tɔɔ^{6} small basket used for marketing

trɔɔ^{1} *in* ŋua^{4} trɔɔ^{1} python (YG, = OG ŋua^{4} tlɔɔ^{1}, OG ŋua^{4} tlɛn^{1}, YG ŋua^{4} trɛn^{1})

tlɔɔ^{1} *in* ŋua^{4} tlɔɔ^{1} python (OG, = YG ŋua^{4} trɔɔ^{1}, OG ŋua^{4} tlɛn^{1}, YG ŋua^{4} trɛn^{1})

thɔɔ^{4} *in* ka^{6} thɔɔ^{4} basket

thɔɔ^{5} pipe

thrɔɔ^{2} to beg

thrɔɔ^{5} to project, stick out, stick up (YG, = OG thlɔɔ^{5})

thrɔɔ^{6} only (YG, = OG thlɔɔ^{6})

taŋ^{3} thrɔɔ^{6} only

thlɔɔ^{5} to project, stick out, stick up (OG, = YG thrɔɔ^{5})

thlɔɔ^{6} only (OG, = YG thrɔɔ^{6})

nɔɔ^{1} khay^{4} to look (= nɔɔm^{1} khay^{4})

nɔɔ^{4} horn of a rhinoceros

nɔɔ^{4} final particle

bɔɔ^{1} li^{6} veen^{4} area

bɔɔ^{1} *in* see^{1} naa^{4} bɔɔ^{1} dii^{1} minister, general

bɔɔ^{4} ox (clf. thua^{4})

bɔɔ^{4} final particle

bɔɔ^{5} final particle

bɔɔ^{6} a mine

bɔɔ^{6} ɣam^{4} gold mine

bɔɔ^{6} ɲɛn^{4} silver mine

blɔɔ^{3} to stick out (the tongue)

pɔɔ^{1} a fiber plant

pɔɔ^{1} to wash (the hair)

pɔɔ^{1} *in* mɛɛŋ^{4} pɔɔ^{1} larva of the dragonfly

pɔɔ^{3} a bundle; to tie in a bundle

prɔɔ^{6} a stick (of firewood) (YG, = OG plɔɔ^{6})

plɔɔ^{6} a stick (of firewood) (OG, = YG prɔɔ^{6})

plɔɔ^{6} mii^{3} dead coals, ashes of a dead fire

phɔɔ^{3} mee^{5} an interjection

phɔɔ^{4} enough

phɔɔ^{4} when

phɔɔ^{5} father; man

phɔɔ^{5} ʔɔɔŋ^{1} old man, old fellow

phɔɔ^{5} saay^{2} man

phɔɔ^{6} to play, blow (a wind instrument)

phrɔɔ^{6} to squirt (water) from the mouth (= phiw^{2} < Lao)

mɔɔ^{2} doctor; shaman

mɔɔ^{2} mon^{4} magician

mɔɔ^{3} pot

mɔɔ^{3} thɛɛŋ^{2} frying pan

mɔɔ^{3} *in* mɛɛw^{4} mɔɔ^{3} soot
mɔɔ^{4} *in* doŋ^{1} su^{6} mɔɔ^{4} *see* dɔŋ^{1} sa^{6} mɔɔ^{4}
mɔɔ^{4} *in* doŋ^{1} sa^{6} mɔɔ^{4} *see* dɔŋ^{1} sa^{6} mɔɔ^{4}
mɔɔ^{4} *in* dɔɔn^{1} suʔ^{6} mɔɔ^{4} *see* dɔŋ^{1} sa^{6} mɔɔ^{4}
mɔɔ^{4} *in* dɔŋ^{1} sa^{6} mɔɔ^{4} *see* dɔŋ^{1} sa^{6} mɔɔ^{4}
mɔɔ^{6} new; again; another
mlɔɔ^{5} meat, flesh
  saa^{3} mlɔɔ^{5} dish made of chopped meat
yɔɔ^{1} to put away, keep
yɔɔ^{3} *in* naŋ^{5} yɔɔŋ^{3} yɔɔ^{3} to squat down (= naŋ^{5} yɔɔŋ^{3} yɔɔ^{6})
yɔɔ^{5} straight; honest
yɔɔ^{6} *in* naŋ^{5} yɔɔŋ^{3} yɔɔ^{6} to squat down (= naŋ^{5} yɔɔŋ^{3} yɔɔ^{3})
rɔɔ^{2} an itching foot disease caused by foul water
rɔɔ^{4} turtle (clf. thua^{4})
rɔɔ^{5} to leak
rɔɔ^{6} to know
  thɛn^{4} rɔɔ^{6} knowledge
lɔɔ^{3} wheel; cart
lɔɔ^{4} blind
lɔɔ^{6} *in* ɣɔɔ^{4} cɔɔ^{6} lɔɔ^{6} up to the neck
vɔɔ^{3} mad (of a dog)
vɔɔ^{4} la^{6} naa^{4} old term for the end of Buddhist Lent (= paʔ^{6} vɔɔ^{4} la^{6} naa^{4})
vɔɔ^{6} *in* phrak^{4} vɔɔ^{6} onion
sɔɔ^{2} pencil, pen
sɔɔ^{5} name
  sɔɔ^{5} ɣa^{3} named
sɔɔ^{5} to seek, go to see someone
sɔɔ^{6} to repair
hɔɔ^{2} tower
hɔɔ^{2} hook
hɔɔ^{2} *in* phrak^{4} hɔɔm^{1} hɔɔ^{2} the aromatic plant called yii^{3} raa^{2} in Siamese

-iw

khiw^{2} unpleasantly pungent (YG, = OG khiiw^{2})
khiw^{3} eyebrow (YG, = OG khiiw^{3})
ŋiw^{3} kapok (YG, = OG ŋiiw^{3}; = nun^{6} < Lao)
ciw^{3} to ache (YG, = OG ciiw^{3})
diw^{3} kidneystones (YG, = OG diiw^{3}; = niw^{3} probably < Siamese)
diw^{3} a whittled stick (YG, = OG diiw^{3})
tiw^{3} *in* yaaŋ^{1} ka^{6} tiw^{3} rubber band

tiw^6 clitoris (YG, = OG tiiw^6)
thiw^2 to whistle (= phriw^2, hiw^2, hiiw^2)
thriw^3 in pii^1 thriw^3 second year in the Saek twelve-year cycle
niw^3 kidneystones (YG, = OG niiw^3 probably < Siamese; = Saek diw^3)
priw^1 to blow away (YG, = OG pliw^1)
pliw^1 to blow away (OG, = YG priw^1)
phiw^2 to spurt (water) from the mouth (< Lao; = Saek phrɔɔ^6)
phriw^2 to whistle (= thiw^2, hiw^2, hiiw^2)
riw^3 to carry hanging from the hand (YG, = OG riiw^3; = hiiw^5)
riw^4 swift (of current) (YG, = OG riiw^4)
liw^4 *in* naŋ^2 liw^4 buffalo hide cut into strips (< Lao; = Saek niiw^4)
siw^1 pimple (YG, = OG siiw^1)
siw^2 spoiled (of food) (YG, = OG siiw^2)
siw^3 light green (YG, = OG siiw^3)
siw^4 kind of fish (YG, = OG siiw^4)
siw^6 chisel (YG, = OG siiw^6)
hiw^2 very tired (YG, = OG hiiw^2)
hiw^2 to whistle (YG, = OG hiiw^2; thiw^2, phriw^2)

-iiw

khiiw^2 unpleasantly pungent (OG, = YG khiw^2)
khiiw^3 eyebrow (OG, = YG khiw^3)
ŋiiw^3 kapok (OG, = YG ŋiw^3; = nun^6 < Lao)
ciiw^3 to ache (OG, = YG ciw^3)
diiw^3 kidneystones (OG, = YG diw^3; = niiw^3 probably < Siamese)
diiw^3 a whittled stick (OG, = YG diw^3)
tiiw^3 kind of tree
tiiw^3 kind of vegetable
tiiw^6 clitoris (OG, = YG tiw^6)
niiw^3 kidneystones (OG, = YG niw^3 probably < Siamese; = Saek diiw^3)
niiw^4 *in* naŋ^2 niiw^4 buffalo hide cut into strips (= liw^4)
riiw^3 to carry hanging from the hand (OG, = YG riw^3; = hiiw^5)
riiw^4 swift (of current) (OG, = YG riw^4)
liiw^6 to close one eye
siiw^1 pimple (OG, = YG siw^1)
siiw^2 spoiled (of food) (OG, = YG siw^2)
siiw^3 light green (OG, = YG siw^3)
siiw^4 kind of fish (OG, = YG siw^4)
siiw^6 chisel (OG, = YG siw^6)
hiiw^2 very tired (OG, = YG hiw^2)

hiiw^{2} to whistle (OG, = YG hiw^{2}; thiw^{2}, phriw^{2}
hiiw^{5} to carry hanging from the hand (= YG riw^{3}, OG riiw^{3})

-iaw

kiaw^{1} screwthreads (= tlɛɛw^{1}, trɛɛw^{1}, triaw^{1})
khiaw^{1} green (< Lao; cf. heew^{2})
khiaw^{4} affected, flirtatious, putting on airs (of a young woman)
diaw^{1} only one
tiaw^{6} loincloth
triaw^{1} screwthreads (= kiaw^{1}, tlɛɛw^{1}, trɛɛw^{1})
thiaw^{4} to walk, pass
thiaw^{4} *in* thɔŋ^{2} ka^{6} thiaw^{4} kind of bag
thiaw^{6} to travel around
thriaw^{2} to hurry (YG, = OG thliaw^{2})
thliaw^{2} to hurry (OG, = YG thriaw^{2})
niaw^{2} tough, sticky; glutinous (rice)
biaw^{3} crooked, twisted
yiaw^{3} granary
riaw^{4} charcoal
siaw^{2} friend (< Lao; = Saek siaw^{6})
siaw^{6} friend (= siaw^{2} < Lao)

-uaw

khuaw^{4} to scratch (YG, = OG khwaaw^{4})
ruaw^{2} to laugh
luaw^{4} wife of father's younger brother

-eew

ʔeew^{6} to wheedle, entreat
keew^{1} Vietnamese
kheew^{2} to push aside
theew^{4} to flee; away
preew^{1} flame (YG, = OG pleew^{1})
pleew^{1} flame (OG, = YG preew^{1})
reew^{5} *in* paa^{6} reew^{5} maaŋ^{4} cemetery
reew^{6} a snare
leew^{2} *in* vaa^{1} leew^{2} bamboo star to ward off spirits

leew^{4} to fight
seew^{2} to fight (of buffaloes); to collide
heew^{2} green (cf. khiaw^{1})
heew^{6} ring around handle of a knife

-ɛɛw

ʔɛɛw^{1} waist (= vuat^{6})
  trɔɔy^{3} ʔɛɛw^{1} belt (= taay^{3} ʔɛɛw^{1}, tɔɔy^{3} ʔɛɛw^{1}, saay^{2} ʔɛɛw^{1}; khem^{1} khat^{6} < Lao)
kɛɛw^{1} to tease
kɛɛw^{3} jewel
  ɲɛn^{4} ɣam^{4} kam^{1} kɛɛw^{3} silver and gold and jewels
kɛɛw^{3} glass; drinking glass; bottle
  kɔɔŋ^{3} kɛɛw^{3} bottle
kɛɛw^{3} scissors (clf. maak^{6})
kɛɛw^{3} *in* ɣay^{6} kɛɛw^{3} lead ore
kɛɛw^{6} favorite place to which people or animals like to return
khɛɛw^{3} khoŋ^{4} invulnerable
ŋɛɛw^{3} to turn (the face) away
ŋɛɛw^{4} a fruit similar to the lychee (clf. maak^{6})
cɛɛw^{6} kind of salad made from raw papaya called som^{3} tam^{1} in Siamese
trɛɛw^{1} strand (of rope), screwthreads (YG, = OG tlɛɛw^{1}; kiaw^{1}, triaw^{1})
trɛɛw^{2} tamarind (YG, = OG tlɛɛw^{2}; YG thrɛɛw^{2}, OG thlɛɛw^{2}; clf. maak^{6})
trɛɛw^{6} thick, sticky (of liquids)
tlɛɛw^{1} strand (of rope), screwthreads (OG, = YG trɛɛw^{1}; kiaw^{1}, triaw^{1})
tlɛɛw^{2} tamarind (OG, = YG trɛɛw^{2}; YG thrɛɛw^{2}, OG thlɛɛw^{2}; clf. maak^{6})
tlɛɛw^{3} to wind (a rope) around
thɛɛw^{2} a row, column
thɛɛw^{4} to walk
thrɛɛw^{2} tamarind (YG, = OG thlɛɛw^{2}; YG trɛɛw^{2}, OG tlɛɛw^{2}; clf. maak^{6})
thlɛɛw^{2} tamarind (OG, = YG thrɛɛw^{2}; YG trɛɛw^{2}, OG tlɛɛw^{2}; clf. maak^{6})
nɛɛw^{4} kind (< Lao)
mɛɛw^{3} the Hmong people
mɛɛw^{3} *in* pii^{1} mɛɛw^{3} fourth year in the Saek twelve-year cycle
mɛɛw^{4} cat (clf. thua^{4})
mɛɛw^{4} mɔɔ^{3} soot
lɛɛw^{1} liquid, soft
lɛɛw^{1} to go near the edge

lɛɛw^{1} finished; already; then (= lɛɛw^{6}) *Tone variation* (lɛɛw^{1}) *due to sentence intonation.*
lɛɛw^{3} tɛɛ^{6} depending upon
lɛɛw^{6} finished; already; then (= lɛɛw^{1})
  lɛɛw^{6} kuŋ^{2} and then
sɛɛw^{4} sɛɛw^{4} loud (of talking, crying out)
sɛɛw^{6} to swoop down (of a bird)
hɛɛw^{3} wrinkled, withered

-aw

ʔaw^{1} to take
ʔaw^{3} very hot
kaw^{1} horn (of an animal)
kaw^{1} to scratch
kaw^{1} owl
kaw^{6} old (of things)
khaw^{3} *in* khiim^{4} khaw^{3} tongs, pincers, pliers (= khiim^{4})
khaw^{4} bridge
ɣaw^{6} rice
  ɣaw^{6} khiap^{2} crisp rice
  ɣaw^{6} ŋaw^{4} kind of rice that ripens late
  ɣaw^{6} tum^{2} preek^{6} popped rice
  ɣaw^{6} thɔɔk^{6} unhusked rice, paddy
  ɣaw^{6} nom^{1} cake, dessert
  ɣaw^{6} muu^{3} roasted young rice pounded flat, used in making desserts
  ɣaw^{6} maa^{2} ɲɛɛŋ^{6} kind of wild rice with very short grains
  ɣaw^{6} saal^{2} white rice (OG, = YG ɣaw^{6} saan^{2})
  ɣaw^{6} viaŋ^{3} millet (clf. maak^{6})
ŋaw^{2} to smell bad
ŋaw^{4} shadow, reflection
ŋaw^{4} *in* mɛɛŋ^{4} ŋaw^{4} scorpion (= mɛɛŋ^{4} ŋɔɔt^{6})
ŋaw^{4} *in* ɣaw^{6} ŋaw^{4} kind of rice that ripens late
caw^{3} you (very polite)
caw^{3} prince, lord, chief
  caw^{3} khoot^{5} voŋ^{4} taa^{1} the elder who is an arranger at a wedding
caw^{3} hu̥a^{2} monk, senior monk (= ɲaa^{4} khuu^{4})
taw^{1} to light (a fire, lamp)
taw^{1} liit^{5} an iron
taw^{3} gourd

taw^{3} *in* nam^{6} taw^{3} water bottle used as a vessel
taw^{3} *in* lɯk^{6} taw^{3} one's children
traw^{1} rich (= ruay^{4})
thaw^{3} old; old person
  thuu^{4} thaw^{3} an old person (= thua^{4} thaw^{3})
thaw^{3} *in* thuŋ^{1} thaw^{3} socks
thaw^{4} rope in the nose of a buffalo
thaw^{5} ashes
thraw^{3} head
  ta^{6} poʔ^{4} bak^{2} thraw^{3} skull
naw^{5} rotten
naw^{5} *in* phrak^{4} naw^{5} the plant called cha^{4} ʔoom^{1} in Siamese
naw^{6} pubic mound (< Siamese)
baw^{1} *in* ka^{6} baw^{1} kind of tree called ka^{2} baw^{1} in Siamese
baw^{3} crucible
paw^{1} crab (clf. thua^{4})
paw^{1} *in* ka^{6} paw^{1} bag, suitcase
paw^{3} target
phaw^{3} to guard; go to see royalty
phraw^{2} to burn (something)
maw^{2} to make a contract
maw^{3} idle, indolent
maw^{4} drunk
raw^{2} they, other people
raw^{2} headlouse (clf. thua^{4})
raw^{3} warm (of a body from the fire or sun)
raw^{3} *in* pii^{1} raw^{3} tenth year in the Saek twelve-year cycle
raw^{3} nuun^{4} sleepy
law^{1} to whittle
law^{3} liquor
  hun^{4} kin^{1} law^{3} drunkard
law^{3} *in* saw^{1} law^{3} *see* phay^{6} lɔɔm^{3}
law^{4} kind of reed cut into sections then tied to top of a seine
law^{4} gunbarrel, classifier for guns
law^{6} final particle meaning 'you see'
vaw^{1} light (in weight)
saw^{1} law^{3} *see* phay^{6} lɔɔm^{3}
saw^{1} *in* van^{4} saw^{1} Saturday
saw^{6} to rent
haw^{2} dove
haw^{3} to enter
haw^{3} sharp
haw^{6} to bark

-aaw

ʔaaw^{5} father's younger brother
kaaw^{6} to speak, tell
khaaw^{6} news (= khaaw^{6} raaw^{4})
khwaaw^{4} to scratch (OG, = YG khuaw^{4})
ɣaaw^{4} fishy smell
ŋaaw^{6} *in* luŋ^{5} ŋaaw^{6} kind of banana
caaw^{1} bud, sprout, as in a coconut
traaw^{1} star
  traaw^{1} phek^{6} morning star
traaw^{1} small knife
traaw^{3} to speak
thaaw^{3} to dismantle, demolish
thaaw^{4} to seek out
thaaw^{6} title for a hero
thraaw^{2} *in* thruŋ^{6} thraaw^{2} spider
naaw^{4} lime fruit (clf. maak^{6})
baaw^{6} young man
paaw^{6} to announce
phraaw^{5} to spill (YG, = OG phlaaw^{5})
phraaw^{6} coconut (YG, = OG phlaaw^{6}; clf. maak^{6})
phlaaw^{5} to spill (OG, = YG phraaw^{5})
phlaaw^{6} coconut (OG, = YG phraaw^{6}; clf. maak^{6})
maaw^{3} man's name
mlaaw^{6} old woman
yaaw^{6} clothesline, pole for drying clothes; pole for picking fruit
ɲaaw^{2} *in* ɲuŋ^{6} ɲaaw^{2} mussed, disheveled, tangled
ɲaaw^{4} *in* ɲuŋ^{6} ɲaaw^{4} mosquito larva
raaw^{2} to yawn (= haaw^{2} < Siamese)
raaw^{2} sword (= daap^{6} < Lao)
raaw^{4} *in* khaaw^{6} raaw^{4} news (= khaaw^{6})
laaw^{2} to fear, be afraid
laaw^{4} Lao
  thɛn^{4} laaw^{4} Lao language
saaw^{2} young woman
saaw^{2} to pull in (a rope) hand over hand
saaw^{4} twenty
saaw^{4} people, inhabitants
haaw^{2} white
haaw^{2} to yawn (< Siamese; = Saek raaw^{2})
haaw^{3} *in* hɯŋ^{1} haaw^{3} vigorous

-ɯay

thɯay^{4} *in* khan^{4} thɯay^{4} an effeminate man
pɯay^{1} naked (= phii^{1} pɯay^{1})
pɯay^{6} soft and rotten; tender (of meat)
mɯay^{2} bear (clf. thua^{4}) (= mii^{2} < Siamese; = Saek mɤɤy^{2})
lɯay^{3} steadily, continually (= lɯay^{5})
lɯay^{5} steadily, continually (= lɯay^{3})
lɯay^{6} to saw, a saw

-uy

khuy^{3} to scratch (of chickens)
khuy^{3} to dip ball of rice in food and take it up
khuy^{4} to converse, chat (YG, = OG khuuy^{4})
khuy^{6} flute (YG, = OG khuuy^{6})
tuy^{5} fat (= phuuy^{4})
tuy^{5} *in* mlɛk^{6} tuy^{5} hail
muy^{4} *in* pii^{1} muy^{4} eighth year in the Saek twelve-year cycle
muy^{6} to sneeze (YG, = OG muuy^{6})

-uuy

khuuy^{4} to converse, chat (OG, = YG khuy^{4})
khuuy^{6} flute (OG, = YG khuy^{6})
buuy^{4} an interjection
phuuy^{4} fat (= tuy^{5})
muuy^{4} blue (= sii^{2} faa^{3} and sii^{2} phaa^{3} < Lao)
muuy^{6} to sneeze (OG, = YG muy^{6})

-uay

ʔuay^{6} almost ripe (of fruit) (= hɤɤm^{6})
ʔuay^{6} to turn (a car) around (YG, = OG ʔwaay^{6})
kuay^{1} to sell (YG, = OG kwaay^{1})
duay^{3} with, together
tuay^{3} year
thuay^{1} to offer, present (= thuay^{2}) *Tone variation* (thuay^{1}) *due to sentence intonation.*
thuay^{2} to offer, present (YG, = OG thwaay^{2}; = thuay^{1})

thuay^{4} to guess, predict (YG, = OG thwaay^{4})
buay^{3} when
puay^{6} to be in pain (< Siamese)
muay^{4} to box
yuay^{3} soft, decayed (= ɲuay^{3})
ɲuay^{3} to drool (< Lao; = Saek hɤɤy^{1})
ɲuay^{3} soft, decayed (= yuay^{3})
ruay^{4} rich (= traw^{1})
suay^{4} funnel made of bamboo leaves
suay^{4} kind of fish (YG, = OG swaay^{4})
suay^{6} tribute money

-ɤɤy

ʔɤɤy^{1} vocative particle
ʔɤɤy^{3} oh!
ʔɤɤy^{4} vocative particle
ʔɤɤy^{5} vocative particle
khɤɤy^{4} used to, to have ever
ŋɤɤy^{4} naa^{3} to tilt the head back
cɤɤy^{3} at an angle (= pɤɤy^{3})
dɤɤy^{1} free; idle
tɤɤy^{1} the *Pandanus* tree (= caan^{3}, caal^{3})
trɤɤy^{1} embarrassed, ashamed (YG, = OG tlɤɤy^{1})
tlɤɤy^{1} embarrassed, ashamed (OG, = YG trɤɤy^{1})
nɤɤy^{4} cheese, butter
pɤɤy^{3} at an angle (= cɤɤy^{3})
phɤɤy^{1} to spread in the sun to dry
mɤɤy^{2} bear (clf. thua^{4}) (= mii^{2} < Siamese; = Saek mɯay^{2})
mɤɤy^{4} to revile
mɤɤy^{4} *in* sin^{4} naa^{4} mɤɤy^{4} name of abandoned Saek village in Vietnam
rɤɤy^{1} to disappear
lɤɤy^{4} then, and then, so, and so, therefore (= lee^{4}, leʔ^{4}, le^{4})
vɤɤy^{1} *in* sa^{6} vɤɤy^{1} to rule over (a kingdom)
sɤɤy^{1} simply (= Siamese chɤɤy^{5})
sɤɤy^{4} a go-between; a spy
hɤɤy^{1} to flow, drool (of saliva) (= ɲuay^{3})
hɤɤy^{1} to evaporate
hɤɤy^{1} final particle

hɤɤy^{3} an interjection
hɤɤy^{4} an interjection
hɤɤy^{5} an interjection
hɤɤy^{5} *in* pii^{1} hɤɤy^{5} twelfth year in the Saek twelve-year cycle

-ooy

ʔooy^{1} oh!
ʔooy^{3} guava (clf. maak^{6})
ʔooy^{4} an interjection
ʔooy^{5} an interjection
kooy^{1} *in* ca^{6} kooy^{1} kind of red-headed lizard (clf. thua^{4})
kooy^{5} kaay^{5} to move in a lazy, indolent manner
khooy^{4} male in-law
  lɯk^{6} khooy^{4} son-in-law
khooy^{5} to ride
dooy^{1} with, by
dooy^{3} to put on (a hat)
tooy^{1} a pair, couple
trooy^{1} the seeds called Job's tears
trooy^{1} to flow (YG, = OG tlooy^{1})
tlooy^{1} to flow (OG, = YG trooy^{1})
thooy^{2} *in* ciʔ^{6} thooy^{2} never mind, let it be, no matter
thooy^{6} dish, cup, bowl
phooy^{3} lungs
phooy^{4} phay^{4} danger
phrooy^{2} pile of dust outside an animal's hole
mooy^{1} *in* ta^{6} mooy^{1} big spoon, ladle (= ta^{6} mooy^{4})
mooy^{4} *in* kha^{6} mooy^{4} thief
mooy^{4} *in* ta^{6} mooy^{4} big spoon, ladle (= ta^{6} mooy^{1})
yooy^{4} sand
rooy^{2} bee
rooy^{2} to give birth to
rooy^{4} to sprinkle
looy^{1} to pull, drag
looy^{5} to release, set free
sooy^{2} steam, vapor; odor
sooy^{5} to help
sooy^{6} to wash
hooy^{4} time, when

-ay

ʔay^{1} to cough
ʔay^{5} you
kay^{1} laat^{5} name of a mythical mountain
kay^{2} don't (OG, = YG kay^{3})
kay^{3} don't (YG, = OG kay^{2})
kay^{6} chicken (clf. thua^{4})
kway^{1} to stir; to swing, rock
khay^{1} tallow
khay^{2} basket or container (for betel)
khay^{4} final imperative particle (= hay^{4})
khay^{4} *in* lak^{6} khit^{6} lak^{6} khay^{4} to ask indirectly
khay^{6} egg
khway^{6} to cross
ɣay^{6} excrement
  ɣay^{6} suʔ^{6} diarrhea
ŋay^{6} to pry up, pry open
day^{1} emphatic final particle
day^{3} (past tense marker)
day^{3} to get, obtain; to be able
  boo^{6} day^{3} could not, do not (= bay^{3})
day^{5} pocket, bag
tay^{1} kidney
tay^{3} to weep, cry
tay^{6} to crawl, creep
tray^{1} far (YG, = OG tlay^{1})
tlay^{1} far (OG, = YG tray^{1})
thay^{1} *in* thiʔ^{4} thuu^{1} thiʔ^{4} thay^{1} descriptive of effort of dragging or carrying
thay^{2} to plow, a plow
thay^{4} people; Thai, Tai (= thay^{5})
thay^{5} people; Thai, Tai (= thay^{4})
thay^{6} to redeem, ransom
thray^{4} to spin (cotton)
nay^{4} spindle; a skein
nay^{4} *in* maa^{2} nay^{4} jackal (clf. thua^{4})
nay^{4} lɔn^{5} nylon
nay^{5} nay^{5} very small (= nɔɔy^{5} nɔɔy^{5})
phay^{4} thuun^{4} kind of gem
bay^{1} *in* ta^{6} bay^{1} a file (the tool)
bay^{3} could not, do not (= boo^{6} day^{3})
pay^{1} to go

phay^{3} playing cards
phay^{4} impetigo
phay^{4} to tie in bundles
phay^{4} *in* phooy^{4} phay^{4} danger
phay^{6} lɔɔm^{3} name of Saek village in Thailand (= saw^{1} law^{3})
phray^{6} *in* may^{6} phray^{6} thual^{5} kind of bamboo
may^{1} to fine (= may^{2})
may^{2} to fine (= may^{1})
may^{6} wood, tree, plant
  may^{6} thɯɯ^{5} naaŋ^{5} chopsticks (= thuu^{5}, may^{6} ta^{6} khiap^{2})
yay^{1} *in* mɛɛŋ^{4} yay^{1} kind of insect that makes mud nests on walls
yay^{4} fishtrap
ɲay^{6} big (< Lao)
ray^{1} stairs, ladder (= ŋan^{5} ray^{1})
ray^{4} long
ray^{5} to be without, have none
  boo^{6} day^{3} ray^{5} there is some, we are not without
lay^{4} stinger of an insect
lay^{4} wooden bar for a door
lay^{4} to rinse soap off after washing
lay^{4} green algae
lay^{4} *in* plaa^{1} pha^{6} lay^{4} kind of fish (= plaa^{1} pha^{6} lay^{5})
lay^{5} to chase
lay^{5} *in* plaa^{1} pha^{6} lay^{5} kind of fish (= plaa^{1} pha^{6} lay^{4})
lay^{6} to make obeisance
vay^{4} naaŋ^{4} bamboo shoot before it is cut
vay^{4} *in* sii^{1} vay^{4} personal name
vay^{6} vɔɔn^{4} to ask, pray (< Siamese, Lao)
say^{1} *in* nit^{4} say^{1} character, personality, disposition
say^{1} *in* soŋ^{1} say^{1} to doubt, wonder
say^{2} *in* ʔaa^{1} say^{2} to live in (a place)
say^{3} intestines
say^{3} one length of warp in weaving
say^{3} to use (< Lao)
say^{4} *in* mat^{6} tɤɤ^{5} say^{4} motorcycle
say^{6} debt
hay^{1} beautiful
  hay^{+} very, very beautiful *The superscript plus indicates a tone much higher than the normal, tone 1 in this case.*
hay^{2} to open
hay^{2} jug, jar
hay^{2} still, yet (= lii^{6}, haa^{2} lii^{6}, haʔ^{6} lii^{6}, ha^{6} lii^{6}, cf. khaa^{4})
  hay^{2} lii^{6} yuu^{6} still alive (= ha^{6} lii^{6} yuu^{6})

hay^{3} since
hay^{4} final imperative particle (= khay^{4})
hay^{4} banyan tree
  khoo^{6} hay^{4} banyan tree

-aay

ʔaay^{4} maternal grandmother
ʔwaay^{6} to turn (a car) around (OG, = YG ʔuay^{6})
kaay^{1} suu^{4} Vietnamese rank equivalent to Siamese ʔam^{1} maat^{2} thoo^{1}
kaay^{1} saa^{5} Vietnamese rank equivalent to Siamese ʔam^{1} maat^{2} ʔeek^{2}
kaay^{5} *in* kooy^{5} kaay^{5} to move in a lazy, indolent manner
kaay^{6} to lay (e.g., a leg) across
kwaay^{1} to sell (OG, = YG kuay^{1})
khaay^{4} *in* nɔɔŋ^{1} khaay^{4} Nong Khai, city in Northeast Thailand
ɣaay^{4} to put out of the mouth
ɣaay^{4} irritating to the skin
ŋaay^{2} (to lie) face up
ŋaay^{2} full (moon)
  blian^{1} ŋaay^{2} full moon
ŋaay^{4} midday meal, lunch
ŋaay^{5} easy, simple
ŋaay^{5} not yet
caay^{1} *in* ka^{6} cat^{4} ka^{6} caay^{1} scattered about
caay^{6} to pay
daay^{3} thread sold in shops (< Siamese, Lao)
taay^{3} ʔɛɛw^{1} belt (= tɔɔy^{3} ʔɛɛw^{1}, trɔɔy^{3} ʔɛɛw^{1}, saay^{2} ʔɛɛw^{1};
    khem^{1} khat^{6} < Lao)
taay^{3} vat^{6} wall or fence of a monastery
taay^{6} *in* ka^{6} taay^{6} rabbit (clf. thua^{4})
traay^{1} to pass; last (year) (YG, = OG tlaay^{1})
tlaay^{1} to pass; last (year) (OG, = YG traay^{1})
thaay^{6} to take a picture
thaay^{6} *in* yaa^{1} thaay^{6} a laxative
thraay^{2} to use, employ; to send (someone)
thraay^{3} really (= tha^{6} raay^{3})
thwaay^{2} to give, offer (OG, = YG thuay^{2}; thuay^{1})
thwaay^{4} to guess, predict (OG, = YG thuay^{4})
naay^{4} master, boss
naay^{6} tired (of)
baay^{1} to take hold of

baay^{6} to spread, smear
baay^{6} afternoon, nightfall
paay^{1} cotton, cotton cloth
paay^{6} to strike (e.g., fruit) with a pole
praay^{1} to die
  praay^{1} phɛɛp^{6} a cursing expression
  praay^{1} haa^{6} a curse meaning ‘a disgrace upon you’
praay^{1} end, tip (YG, = OG plaay^{1})
plaay^{1} end, tip (OG, = YG praay^{1})
phaay^{1} a dam (< Siamese)
phaay^{4} to row (a boat)
  may^{6} phaay^{4} oar
phaay^{6} to try, make an effort
maay^{2} to make a mark, to mark; to intend, aim
maay^{2} *in* cot^{4} maay^{2} a letter
maay^{5} always, continually
maay^{6} widowed
mlaay^{4} saliva
yaay^{1} to distribute, pass out
yaay^{4} eaves
yaay^{6} mute, unable to speak; stupid
raay^{3} ramie
raay^{3} *in* tha^{6} raay^{3} really (= thraay^{3})
raay^{5} to move one’s dwelling
raay^{6} to pour
raay^{6} bad
  thrɔʔ^{6} raay^{6} bad luck
raay^{6} naa^{4} a single ricefield
laay^{1} much, many, very (= laay^{2}) *Tone variation* (laay^{1}) *due to sentence intonation.*
laay^{1} to unroll, come unrolled
laay^{2} much, many, very (= laay^{1})
laay^{4} stripe, design, mark, spots
  naa^{3} laay^{4} pock-marked face
  laay^{4} lɔɔŋ^{6} striped
  sak^{4} laay^{4} to tattoo, tattoo designs
laay^{4} *in* priaŋ^{1} laay^{4} kind of squash
laay^{6} idiomatic word meaning something like ‘to hold one’s own, defeat’
  boo^{6} laay^{6} man^{4} couldn’t defeat him
vaay^{1} to scoop up water in the palms to drink
vaay^{2} rattan
vaay^{2} *in* tha^{6} vaay^{2} to offer, present
vaay^{4} bufflao (clf. thua^{4})

thaa^{5} vaay^{4} name of abandoned Saek village in Thailand
naa^{4} laʔ^{6} vaay^{4} name of abandoned Saek village in Thailand
vaay^{4} *in* la^{6} vaay^{4} really, truly
saay^{1} chain, necklace (< Siamese, Lao)
saay^{2} cord, string
saay^{2} ʔɛɛw^{1} belt (= taay^{3} ʔɛɛw^{1}, tɔɔy^{3} ʔɛɛw^{1}, trɔɔy^{3} ʔɛɛw^{1}; khem^{1} khat^{6} < Lao)
saay^{2} *in* vii^{4} saay^{2} flashlight
saay^{2} *in* phɔɔ^{5} saay^{2} man
saay^{2} to dance
swaay^{4} kind of fish (OG, = YG suay^{4})
haay^{6} to pity, take pity (on)

-ɔɔy

ʔɔɔy^{3} sugarcane
ʔɔɔy^{4} an interjection
ʔɔɔy^{5} *in* ʔiit^{4} ʔɔɔy^{5} a little
sip^{4} ʔiit^{4} sip^{4} ʔɔɔy^{5} a little
kɔɔy^{1} kind of edible wild tuber eaten as substitute for rice
kɔɔy^{3} *in* ŋiaŋ^{5} kɔɔy^{3} little finger, little toe
khɔɔy^{4} to wait
khɔɔy^{6} from
ŋɔɔy^{4} to perch
tɔɔy^{3} to touch lightly
tɔɔy^{3} ʔɛɛw^{1} belt (= saay^{2} ʔɛɛw^{1}, taay^{3} ʔɛɛw^{1}, trɔɔy^{3} ʔɛɛw^{1}; khem^{1} khat^{6} < Lao)
tɔɔy^{3} *in* ka^{6} tɔɔy^{3} old-fashioned lower garment
tɔɔy^{6} to knock, strike
trɔɔy^{3} to touch lightly (YG, = OG tlɔɔy^{3})
trɔɔy^{3} ʔɛɛw^{1} belt (= saay^{2} ʔɛɛw^{1}, taay^{3} ʔɛɛw^{1}, tɔɔy^{3} ʔɛɛw^{1}; khem^{1} khat^{6} < Lao)
tlɔɔy^{3} to touch lightly (OG, = YG trɔɔy^{3})
thɔɔy^{1} to back up
thɔɔy^{4} to tell
thɔɔy^{6} low, evil
nɔɔy^{1} *in* mɛk^{6} nɔɔy^{1} kind of ant called mot^{4} ta^{2} nɔɔy^{1} in Siamese
nɔɔy^{3} to talk, say, speak, tell
nɔɔy^{3} ŋɔɔŋ^{6} to be unable to speak
nɔɔy^{5} small

nɔɔy^{6} person
nɔɔy^{6} small (used in certain expressions < Lao)
pɔɔy^{1} *in* phal^{4} pɔɔy^{1} raveled out
phrɔɔy^{2} silk
yɔɔy^{5} with, together
rɔɔy^{1} mountain
rɔɔy^{1} switch
rɔɔy^{4} *in* sa^{6} rɔɔy^{4} mortar
rɔɔy^{6} hundred
  saam^{3} rɔɔy^{6} three hundred
rɔɔy^{6} to string
lɔɔy^{5} *in* liap^{5} lɔɔy^{5} proper
sɔɔy^{2} *in* kiiŋ^{6} sɔɔy^{2} shuttle of a loom
sɔɔy^{3} necklace (< Siamese)
hɔɔy^{1} *in* ɣɔɔ^{4} hɔɔy^{1} Adam's apple
hɔɔy^{2} a comb, to comb
hɔɔy^{6} I
hɔɔy^{6} slave, servant

-im

kim^{1} needle
cim^{3} to pick (the teeth) (= ciim^{6})
nim^{5} pangolin (= lin^{5}, lil^{5}, lin^{6}, lil^{6}; clf. thua^{4})
rim^{2} full
rim^{4} edge
  rim^{4} muam^{4} lips (= muam^{4})
lim^{3} couplet paired with saaŋ^{1} 'granaries' (also recorded as lim^{5})
lim^{5} couplet paired with saaŋ^{1} 'granaries' (also recorded as lim^{3})
him^{1} ma^{6} phaan^{4} name of a mythical forest

-iim

ʔiim^{6} full (after eating)
  ʔiim^{6} nam^{1} sam^{1} raan^{4} full, satiated
khiim^{4} tongs, pincers, pliers (= khiim^{4} khaw^{3})
ŋiim^{4} section (of garlic, orange)
ciim^{6} to pick (the teeth) (= cim^{3})
ɲiim^{5} to whisper (= ɲiim^{5} ɲia^{2})
ɲiim^{5} ɲia^{2} to be careful; to whisper (= ɲiim^{5})

liim^{3} wedge
siim^{4} ugly
  soŋ^{4} siim^{4} ugly
siim^{4} dirty, soiled (= pɯan^{3} < Lao)

-iam

ciam^{1} modest, humble
thiam^{4} garlic
thriam^{2} to prepare (< Lao)
liam^{4} sickle (clf. maak^{6})
liam^{5} angle, corner, edge

-ɯm

dɯm^{5} overripe
trɯm^{5} slow
lɯm^{4} bundle, faggot
sɯm^{6} to dip up fish with a sieve

-ɯɯm

tɯɯm^{6} to add

-ɯam

ʔɯam^{3} to belch
kɯam^{3} kaaŋ^{1} a waste of effort
khɯam^{4} khɯam^{4} (oil) floating on the surface of water
lɯam^{3} smooth and shiny
lɯam^{4} to vanish, disappear (by magic power)
sɯam^{4} kind of fish

-um

kum^{1} to capture, arrest; to abduct
kum^{1} *in* kɔɔt^{6} kum^{1} to embrace

kum^{1} phan^{4} name of a giant
khum^{1} a pit (< Siamese, Lao; = Saek khum^{4}; cf. lum^{1})
khum^{4} a pit (= khum^{1} < Siamese, Lao; cf. lum^{1})
khum^{4} to stoke (a fire)
ɣum^{4} to itch
ŋum^{4} to grope (for fish) under water
ŋum^{5} to cover (e.g., a small animal) with the hand
tum^{1} sound of something falling
tum^{2} *in* ɣaw^{6} tum^{2} preek^{6} popped rice
tum^{3} cage; trap for frogs
tum^{3} huu^{1} earring (< Siamese; = Saek taaŋ^{3}, taaŋ^{6}, voŋ^{4} vɛɛn^{2})
tum^{3} *in* mlɛk^{6} tum^{3} beads
tum^{6} pɔŋ^{3} a toy balloon
tum^{6} *in* nam^{6} tum^{6} sweat
trum^{3} worth it (YG, = OG tlum^{3})
tlum^{3} worth it (OG, = YG trum^{3})
thum^{6} to flood
num^{6} young
bum^{3} dented
bum^{6} to put fruit away to ripen
pum^{1} a knot (= OG plum^{1}, YG prum^{1})
pum^{5} to roll into a ball
prum^{1} round (YG, = OG plum^{1})
prum^{1} a knot (YG, = OG plum^{1}; pum^{1})
plum^{1} round (OG, = YG prum^{1})
plum^{1} a knot (OG, = YG prum^{1}; pum^{1})
plum^{6} to drop into water
mum^{4} *in* mɛɛŋ^{4} mum^{4} spider
yum^{1} shade
ɲum^{1} to pick up with all five fingers, or claws
ɲum^{3} to constrict, pucker up
ɲum^{6} to dye
rum^{2} mortar
rum^{2} in disorder
rum^{3} the lap
lum^{1} pit, hole (cf. khum^{1}, khum^{4})
lum^{4} wind
sum^{2} muu^{2} a spear (= sam^{3} muu^{2}; clf. maak^{6})
sum^{3} twilight, dusk
sum^{3} arch, archway (of gate)
sum^{4} to assemble
sum^{6} chicken cage; fish trap
hum^{2} to warm up, reheat

hum^{3} to wrap up, cover
hum^{6} to cover, as with a cloth

-uum

ʔuum^{3} to hold or carry in the arms
cuum^{1} knob
  cuum^{1} khɔɔŋ^{6} ankle bone
cuum^{1} to be in bud (of a flower)
thuum^{4} *in* ɣaaŋ^{4} thuum^{4} swollen jaws; mumps

-uam

kuam^{1} to cover, as with a big lid
nuam^{4} stuffing, padding (as of a quilt)
nuam^{5} overripe (of fruit)
phuam^{4} to be doing (cf. kam^{1} laŋ^{4})
muam^{4} lips (= rim^{4} muam^{4})
ruam^{5} to share in (something)

-em

khem^{1} khat^{6} belt (< Lao; = tɔɔy^{3} ʔɛɛw^{1}, trɔɔy^{3} ʔɛɛw^{1},
  taay^{3} ʔɛɛw^{1}, saay^{2} ʔɛɛw^{1})
khem^{3} dark (of color)
  sii^{2} khem^{3} dark color

-eem

ʔeem^{1} nearly healed (of a wound)
keem^{3} cheek
ɣeem^{4} edge, gunwale (of a boat)
deem^{3} to taste
teem^{6} to paint (a picture)
threem^{5} that fellow, that person
meem^{4} a game, one game (in sports)

-ɤɤm

ʔɤɤm^{1} *in* ɣɔɔ^{4} ʔɤɤm^{1} goiter
ɲɤɤm^{4} ɲɤɤm^{4} descriptive of dragging
lɤɤm^{4} kind of large, shark-like fish
hɤɤm^{6} almost ripe (of fruit) (= ʔuay^{6})

-om

ʔom^{3} *in* ɲɛn^{2} ʔom^{3} civet cat (clf. thua^{4})
khom^{6} to press down
chom^{4} phuu^{4} thiip^{5} name of a mythical continent
thom^{1} to fill in (a hole)
nom^{1} *in* ɣaw^{6} nom^{1} cake, dessert
nom^{4} milk
nom^{4} *in* na^{6} khɔɔn^{4} pha^{6} nom^{4} Nakhon Phanom, city in Northeast Thailand (= la^{6} khɔɔn^{4})
phom^{4} Brahma divinity, Brahma
ka^{6} bin^{1} la^{6} phom^{4} name of a Brahma divinity (= ka^{6} bin^{1} laʔ^{6} phom^{4})
ma^{6} haa^{1} phom^{4} great Brahma
ɲom^{4} gooseberry (clf. maak^{6})
som^{1} bat^{4} property
som^{1} phaan^{4} glory (of a king)
raa^{4} sii^{2} som^{1} phaan^{4} radiant glory (of a king)
hom^{4} to steam; to smoke

-oom

ʔoom^{1} to take up in both arms
ʔoom^{3} sick, ill; to have a fever
khoom^{4} to sit or lie on top of someone
khoom^{4} eyebrow ridge
khoom^{4} fay^{4} lantern
coom^{1} to lift, raise in two hands
moom^{4} *in* kha^{6} moom^{4} pubic mound
ɲoom^{2} to stand on a branch and bounce it up and down (= ɲoom^{3})
ɲoom^{3} to stand on a branch and bounce it up and down (= ɲoom^{2})
room^{4} together
loom^{4} to cover (e.g., a book)

-ɛm

khɛm^4 salty
lɛm^2 to sharpen to a point
lɛm^3 classifier for books, knives, boats, oxcarts, various sharp objects

-ɛɛm

kɛɛm^1 to mix, mixed
kɛɛm^3 food eaten with liquor
kɛɛw^3 *in* kam^1 kɛɛw^3 jewels
ŋɛɛm^3 to open (a door) a little
thrɛɛm^4 edge, side; beside
nɛɛm^4 to look, watch, see (= nɔɔm^1)
rɛɛm^3 to trim a tree after it has been cut down; cut into pieces
rɛɛm^4 waning (of the moon)
  blian^1 rɛɛm^4 waning moon
lɛɛm^2 sharp-pointed
sɛɛm^1 heavily laden (of a boat)
hɛɛm^3 dry and crisp (of roasted meat)

-am

ʔam^1 to hold in the mouth
ʔam^1 to conceal
ʔam^6 to carry an infant against the side in cloth
kam^1 food regarded as harmful
kam^1 to hold in the closed hand
kam^1 punishment, misfortune
kam^1 unit of weight equal to a gram
kam^1 kɛɛw^3 jewels
  ɲɛn^4 ɣam^4 kam^1 kɛɛw^3 silver and gold and jewels
kam^1 not^4 limit, period (= kam^1 not^6)
kam^1 not^6 limit, period (= kam^1 not^4)
kam^1 phaa^3 orphan (< Lao; = Saek thraa^6, lɯk^6 thraa^6)
kam^1 laŋ^4 to be doing (cf. phuam^4)
kam^1 laŋ^4 vaŋ^4 saa^4 troops
kam^1 *in* pha^6 veet^5 su^4 kam^1 name of the architect of the gods
kam^3 to bend over, bow
kam^6 pan^6 steamboat

kham^{3} because (= kham^{5})

kham^{3} *in* phoo^{4} kham^{3} name of Saek village in Laos

kham^{4} gold (used in a personal name)

kham^{5} because (= kham^{3})

kham^{6} to borrow

kham^{6} to prop up, support

ɣam^{4} gold

ɲɛn^{4} ɣam^{4} kam^{1} kɛɛw^{3} silver and gold and jewels

ɣam^{4} bitter

ɣam^{4} sharp, sharp edge

ɣam^{5} evening, nightfall, night

ŋam^{1} to grow slowly because shaded by a big tree

ŋam^{3} (to lie) face down; to overturn, place upside down

ŋam^{4} to cover with a lid

cam^{1} to sink (= cɔm^{1})

cam^{1} to stab deeply

cam^{1} to force, compel

cam^{1} pii^{1} kind of flowering tree (= cam^{6} pii^{1})

cam^{1} paa^{1} kind of flowering tree (= cam^{6} paa^{1})

cam^{1} *in* pra^{6} cam^{1} regular, usual

cam^{3} to dip (food) in sauce

cam^{3} to stick, plant (e.g., a stake in the ground)

cam^{6} pii^{1} kind of flowering tree (= cam^{1} pii^{1})

cam^{6} paa^{1} kind of flowering tree (= cam^{1} paa^{1})

dam^{1} to smell

dam^{1} *in* dɯk^{4} dam^{1} ban^{1} olden times

tam^{1} to stab, pierce; to pound; collide

tam^{1} ʔaaŋ^{1} the chest (= ta^{6} baaŋ^{1})

tam^{1} bon^{1} a commune (= Siamese tam^{1} bon^{1})

tam^{3} to weave

tam^{3} huuk^{6} to weave

tam^{6} short, low

tram^{1} to transplant young rice plants

tham^{2} to visit

tham^{3} cave

tham^{4} the Buddhist Dharma

tham^{4} maʔ^{6} baan^{1} personal name (= tham^{4} ma^{6} baan^{1})

tham^{4} ma^{6} daa^{1} ordinary, usual

tham^{4} ma^{6} baan^{1} personal name (= tham^{4} maʔ^{6} baan^{1})

tham^{4} *in* ɲut^{6} ti^{4} tham^{4} just (= ɲot^{6} ti^{4} tham^{4})

tham^{4} *in* laat^{5} sa^{6} tham^{4} royal precepts

thram^{2} to prepare (= thram^{3})

thram^{3} to prepare (= thram^{2})
thram^{3} nearly, almost
nam^{1} *in* ʔiim^{6} nam^{1} sam^{1} raan^{4} full, satiated
nam^{4} to accompany, follow; to go in search of; with; from; along
nam^{6} water
  nam^{6} khɛŋ^{1} ice
  nam^{6} cɛn^{3} a spring (of water)
  nam^{6} tum^{6} sweat
  nam^{6} bun^{3} whirlpool (= nam^{6} pun^{3})
  nam^{6} pun^{3} whirlpool (= nam^{6} bun^{3})
  nam^{6} maak^{5} high water (< Lao)
  nam^{6} saaŋ^{3} a well
pram^{3} to fell a tree (YG, = OG plam^{3})
pram^{3} to wrestle (YG, = OG plam^{3})
plam^{3} to fell a tree (OG, = YG pram^{3})
plam^{3} to wrestle (OG, = YG pram^{3})
pham^{1} an edible green algae (= pham^{2})
pham^{2} an edible green algae (= pham^{1})
pham^{2} tetanus, any infection from a wound (= pham^{3})
pham^{3} tetanus, any infection from a wound (= pham^{2})
pham^{3} to chop fine
phram^{2} hair of the head
phlam^{1} bracelet (= phlam^{4})
phlam^{4} bracelet (= phlam^{1})
yam^{1} *in* khet^{4} yam^{1} magically efficacious
yam^{6} also; to repeat
ɲam^{3} to chew
ɲam^{4} quick, fast, quickly
ram^{1} black
  ram^{1} pit^{4} completely black
ram^{2} testicle
ram^{4} bran
ram^{4} wet
lam^{1} hump on back of an ox or buffalo
lam^{1} to repeat, redo
lam^{4} trunk of a tree
lam^{4} voŋ^{4} circle dancing (= Siamese ram^{1} woŋ^{1})
lam^{4} *in* mɔɔ^{2} lam^{4} singer, singing
lam^{5} hawk
lam^{6} to fall, fall over
  lam^{6} tɯɯŋ^{4} to fall flat
  lam^{6} phuap^{5} to fall down, fall flat (= lam^{6} phuak^{5})
  lam^{6} phuak^{5} to fall down, fall flat (= lam^{6} phuap^{5})

sam^{1} raan^{4} happy
  ʔiim^{6} nam^{1} sam^{1} raan^{4} full, satiated
sam^{2} to have sexual intercourse (cf. ɲuut^{5}, suut^{5})
sam^{3} sour
sam^{3} muu^{2} a spear (= sum^{2} muu^{2}; clf. maak^{6})
sam^{3} haaŋ^{2} white rice roasted and then pounded
sam^{4} glad, happy
sam^{5} maʔ^{6} almost, about to, will
sam^{6} bruised
sam^{6} size; kind, like
ham^{2} to burn (intransitive)
ham^{4} to roll (a cigarette), roll up, coil up
ham^{6} to cover (with a blanket)

-aam

kaam^{1} orange (the fruit) (clf. maak^{6})
khaam^{4} indigo
ŋaam^{5} fork of a tree
ŋaam^{5} maak^{6} ka^{6} thun^{1} slingshot
ŋaam^{5} *in* mɛk^{6} ŋaam^{5} kind of ant
daam^{3} handle of knife, sword, etc. (= taam^{1})
taam^{1} handle of knife, sword, etc. (= daam^{3})
taam^{1} to light (a light or lamp)
taam^{1} to follow; to go in search of; along, according to
  kuŋ^{2} taam^{1} no matter
thaam^{1} to ask (= thaam^{2}) *Tone variation* (thaam^{1}) *due to sentence intonation.*
thaam^{2} to ask (= thaam^{1})
thraam^{4} to grumble, complain
naam^{4} kind of box-shaped fishnet
phaam^{4} to meet, encounter
maam^{3} spleen (= maam^{6}, paaŋ^{3})
maam^{6} spleen (= maam^{3}, paaŋ^{3})
ɲaam^{4} season; watchman, a watch
raam^{2} (two or more) carry
laam^{4} to spread (of fire)
laam^{5} to tie up (an animal)
laam^{5} to drag on the ground (of a long garment)
laam^{5} interpreter
saam^{2} three

saam^{2} rɔɔy^{6} three hundred
sip^{6} saam^{2} thirteen
saam^{4} dish, bowl, basin
haam^{3} to cross, go across
haam^{4} jaw (= ɣaaŋ^{4})
kaaŋ^{3} haam^{4} jaw; chin

-ɔm

cɔm^{1} to sink (= cam^{1})
thɔm^{5} *in* ka^{6} thɔm^{5} small hut (< Siamese)
pɔm^{3} fort, police box (fast speech form, = pɔɔm^{3})

-ɔɔm

ʔɔɔm^{1} to spend (money) cautiously, to be saving
ʔɔɔm^{3} to go around, make a detour
ʔɔɔm^{6} to stew, cook for a long time
kɔɔm^{1} to bend into a curve
cɔɔm^{1} peak, pinnacle
tɔɔm^{1} to swarm
tɔɔm^{3} to gather (rice, sand) into a heap
nɔɔm^{1} to look, watch, see (= nɛɛm^{4})
pɔɔm^{3} fort, police box (= fast speech form pɔm^{3})
pɔɔm^{3} to coil up (of a centipede)
phrɔɔm^{2} thin (not fat)
phrɔɔm^{6} together, altogether
yɔɔm^{1} to be frugal (in eating), eat sparingly
ɲɔɔm^{4} to yield, submit, consent, allow
rɔɔm^{6} to boil
lɔɔm^{3} *in* phay^{6} lɔɔm^{3} *see* phay^{6} lɔɔm^{3}
lɔɔm^{5} morning, early morning
hɔɔm^{1} fragrant
phrak^{4} hɔɔm^{1} hɔɔ^{2} the aromatic plant called yii^{3} raa^{2} in Siamese

-in

ʔin^{1} tendon
ʔin^{1} Indra

ʔin^{1} thii^{4} eagle
kin^{1} to eat
  kin^{1} trɔɔŋ^{1} to get married; to have a wedding feast
kin^{1} each other
din^{1} earth
  din^{1} cii^{6} brick
tin^{3} short
thin^{2} *in* thɔɔt^{5} ka^{6} thin^{2} Buddhist ceremony of giving robes to the monks
bin^{1} *in* ka^{6} bin^{1} la^{6} phom^{4} name of a Brahma divinity (= ka^{6} bin^{1} laʔ^{6} phom^{4})
pin^{6} to spin, whirl, turn, revolve
pin^{6} hairpin
pin^{6} pua^{1} to treat (the ill), care for (= pua^{1})
phin^{4} phaat^{5} music, orchestra
min^{6} placed near the edge
lin^{4} water pipe
lin^{5} pangolin (YG, = OG lil^{5}; also recorded as lil^{6}, lin^{6}, nim^{6}; clf. thua^{4})
lin^{6} pangolin (YG, = OG lil^{6}; also recorded as lil^{5}, lin^{5}, nim^{6}; clf. thua^{4})
vin^{6} having a piece torn off the corner or edge (fast speech form of OG viil^{6})
sin^{3} skirt
sin^{4} *in* pii^{1} sin^{4} fifth year in the Saek twelve-year cycle
sin^{4} naa^{4} mɤɤy^{4} name of abandoned Saek village in Vietnam
sin^{6} all, all gone

-iin

ʔiin^{3} to lose; to disappear; to spoil; to die
ʔiin^{3} to pay
ʔiin^{3} to pull up, cut grass
khiin^{2} to be irritating or offensive to (the ear, the eye)
khiin^{3} to knock aside with the hand, foot, or stick
ŋiin^{6} turmeric (YG, = OG ŋiil^{6})
tiin^{1} foot, base (of a tree)
thiin^{4} wasp (YG, = OG thiil^{4}; clf. thua^{4})
biin^{3} grass mat
piin^{1} to climb a tree
priin^{3} to turn upside down or inside out (YG, = OG pliin^{3})
pliin^{3} to turn upside down or inside out (OG, = YG priin^{3})
ɲiin^{6} to go without (food or water)
riin^{2} stone (YG, = OG riil^{2})
  ŋɤɤp^{5} riin^{2} blocks of stone on a mountain (YG, = OG ŋɤɤp^{5} riil^{2})

riin^{6} a gnat (clf. thua^{4})
liin^{6} tongue

-ian

kian^{1} oxcart (clf. lɛm^{3})
khian^{2} to write, draw
khian^{4} to wind (a cord) around
khian^{4} cockcomb (YG, = OG khial^{4})
cian^{5} language
cian^{5} matter, thing
tian^{3} *in* tuŋ^{6} tian^{3} cricket (YG, = OG tuŋ^{6} tial^{3}; clf. thua^{4})
thian^{4} candle
nian^{6} a dish made by boiling certain fruit and vegetables and then pounding them and adding spices
bian^{1} *in* thaʔ^{6} bian^{1} registry (= tha^{6} bian^{1})
bian^{1} *in* biat^{6} bian^{1} to crowd, oppress, annoy
blian^{1} moon
  blian^{1} pheŋ^{4} full moon
  blian^{1} rɛɛm^{4} waning moon
blian^{1} month
  blian^{1} ciaŋ^{1} first month
  blian^{1} ɲii^{6} second lunar month
blian^{3} to avoid (< Lao)
pian^{6} to change, exchange
plian^{1} ɣaa^{4} a flat of woven thatchgrass for roofing (YG, = OG plial^{1} ɣaa^{4})
plian^{3} smooth, clean
phian^{4} diligent, to persevere
mian^{6} to gather up, put away
rian^{4} to study
lian^{1} eel (clf. thua^{4})
lian^{1} coin, medal
lian^{4} a row, column
lian^{4} *in* thu^{6} lian^{4} durian (= thuʔ^{6} lian^{4}; clf. maak^{6})
lian^{4} *in* thua^{5} lian^{4} peas
vian^{4} very much
vian^{4} to go around, make a circuit
sian^{4} to reap, harvest
hian^{2} torn, chipped (< Lao)

-ɯn

khɯn^{4} on, above, upper, north
ɣɯn^{4} night
dɯn^{6} a pond or marsh in the forest with soft clay into which one sinks
(YG, = OG dɯl^{6})
thɯn^{4} capital, investment
lup^{4} thɯn^{4} to lose one's investments
thrɯn^{1} *in* pii^{1} thrɯn^{1} ninth year in the Saek twelve-year cycle
bɯn^{1} sky, weather
bɯn^{1} to fly (YG, = OG bɯl^{1})
bɯn^{3} angry (cf. man^{3} thuu^{3}, lɤɤ^{1}, yak^{6})
phɯn^{4} classifier for mats, cloth articles (fast speech form, = phɯɯn^{4})
mɯn^{1} a rash on the body (< Lao, = mɯɯn^{6})
mɯn^{4} the foot 'goes to sleep'
rɯn^{4} *in* pii^{1} rɯn^{4} third year in the Saek twelve-year cycle
vɯn^{1} firewood (YG, = OG vɯl^{1})
vɯn^{2} rain
hɯn^{3} to rise, ascend, go up, come up, up, grow
hɯn^{4} having the flavor of orange or lime rinds

-ɯɯn

ʔɯɯn^{6} other
trɯɯn^{1} to swallow (YG, = OG tlɯɯn^{1})
tlɯɯn^{1} to swallow (OG, = YG trɯɯn^{1})
thɯɯn^{3} to snatch things away from someone
bɯɯn^{1} obstinate, stubborn
phɯɯn^{4} classifier for mats, cloth articles (= fast speech form phɯn^{4})
phɯɯn^{6} floor, ground
phɯɯn^{6} story, level
phɯɯn^{6} matter
mɯɯn^{6} ten thousand
mɯɯn^{6} a rash on the body (= mɯn^{1} < Lao)
mlɯɯn^{5} slippery (YG, = OG mlɯɯl^{5})
ɲɯɯn^{4} long-lasting, enduring
lɯɯn^{5} to get ahead of another, surpass; more
sɯɯn^{4} tin (= saŋ^{1} ka^{6} sii^{1})
sɯɯn^{4} *in* sɯ^{6} sɯɯn^{4} now

sɯɯn^{5} cɯɯ^{1} happy, cheerful (= sɯɯn^{6} cɯɯ^{1})
  sɯɯn^{5} mɔk^{4} sɯɯn^{5} cɯɯ^{1} happy, cheerful
sɯɯn^{6} cɯɯ^{1} happy, cheerful (= sɯɯn^{5} cɯɯ^{1})

-ɯan

ʔɯan^{1} not pretty
ŋɯan^{5} leftover food
thɯan^{6} illegal
bɯan^{1} to turn (the face) away
pɯan^{3} dirty, soiled (< Lao; = Saek siim^{4})
phɯan^{4} to shake, quake, quiver
ɲɯan^{3} *in* ʔot^{4} ɲɯan^{3} to endure

-un

ʔun^{3} yonder, there
ʔun^{3} *in* pii^{1} ʔun^{3} the year after pii^{1} rɯɯ^{1}, three years after the current year
kun^{1} *in* pii^{1} kun^{1} Year of the Pig, twelfth year in the twelve-year cycle
khun^{2} to carry, transport
khun^{2} turbid
khun^{4} merit, favor, good deeds
  mii^{4} khun^{4} mii^{4} noo^{4} do a favor for
khun^{6} tame; familiar
thun^{1} *in* ŋaam^{5} maak^{6} ka^{6} thun^{1} slingshot
nun^{6} kapok (< Lao; = Saek ŋiw^{3}, ŋiiw^{3})
bun^{1} merit; merit-making ceremony
  bun^{1} phaʔ^{6} veet^{6} name of a merit-making ceremony
bun^{3} *in* nam^{6} bun^{3} whirlpool (= nam^{6} pun^{3})
pun^{1} body hair (YG, = OG pul^{1})
pun^{3} to rob
pun^{3} *in* nam^{6} pun^{3} whirlpool (= nam^{6} bun^{3})
phun^{3} yonder, over there (< Lao)
phun^{5} dust (< Lao; = Saek OG mul^{4}, YG mun^{4})
phun^{6} areca nut
mun^{2} to spin (a wheel), whirl, turn (fast speech form, = muun^{2})
mun^{4} dust; crushed or smashed to small pieces (YG, = OG mul^{4}; = phun^{5} < Lao)
mun^{5} mud
mun^{6} to force one's way into or through (YG, = OG mul^{6})

hun^{4} person, human being
pa?^{6} hun^{4} people (= pa^{6} hun^{4})
hun^{4} to come, return
hun^{6} figure, image

-uun

?uun^{6} soft; young; light (of color)
khuun^{2} clever, intelligent
khuun^{4} a blessing
cuun^{6} phuun^{6} a big heap or pile
tuun^{1} to pull up or out; to take off, remove
thuun^{4} to say to (royalty)
thuun^{4} *in* phay^{4} thuun^{4} kind of gem
thuun^{4} *in* phi?^{6} thuun^{4} kind of gem (= phi^{6} thuun^{4})
thruun^{4} like that (= thruu^{4} ?an^{6}, thruu^{4} nan^{6}, thruu^{4} rɛn^{6})
nuun^{3} a bump on the skin
nuun^{4} to lie down, sleep
buun^{1} heaped up (in a container)
puun^{1} to repay (a debt)
puun^{6} to feed (an infant or invalid)
phuun^{6} *in* cuun^{6} phuun^{6} a big heap or pile
muun^{2} to spin (a wheel), whirl, turn (= fast speech form mun^{2})
muun^{2} to support (as a pillow under the head)
muun^{4} legacy
muun^{6} lime eaten with betel or used for plaster, etc. (YG, = OG muul^{6})
ruun^{6} hot (YG, = OG ruul^{6})
luun^{2} skinned (= luun^{3})
luun^{3} skinned (= luun^{2})
suun^{4} to touch lightly
huun^{4} huun^{4} gleaming (red)

-uan

kuan^{1} *in* ku?^{4} kuan^{1} to disturb
kuan^{3} to coil up (a rope) (YG, = YG khuan^{3}, OG khwaan^{3})
khuan^{3} to coil up (a rope) (YG, = OG khwaan^{3}; YG kuan^{3})
khuan^{4} elephant rider (YG, = OG khwaan^{4})
khuan^{4} fitting, suitable
tuan^{1} top for spinning (YG, = OG tual^{1}; clf. maak^{6})
truan^{1} worm (YG, = OG trual^{1}; clf. thua^{4})

thuan^{6} forest (YG, = OG thual^{6})
nuan^{4} seed of jackfruit or durian (< Lao)
phuan^{4} restless
muan^{5} fun, amusing
muan^{6} to roll up, coil up
yuan^{5} to hand to someone (YG, = OG yual^{5})
ɲuan^{6} gnat, gadfly (YG, = OG ɲual^{6}; clf. thua^{4})
ruan^{5} leprosy (of humans; = ka^{6} thuut^{5})
ruan^{6} leprosy (of dogs, although some also use it for people)
luan^{4} to crawl
luan^{4} yesterday
suan^{2} garden
suan^{3} spade, shovel (YG, = OG swaan^{3}; clf. maak^{6})
suan^{4} to invite
suan^{6} part; while; as for (YG, = OG sual^{6})

-en

khen^{1} to oppress
pen^{1} to be
  yuu^{6} yen^{1} pen^{1} suk^{4} to live happily (< Lao)
men^{3} porcupine (clf. thua^{4})
yen^{1} *in* yuu^{6} yen^{1} pen^{1} suk^{4} to live happily (< Lao)
sen^{5} time, period

-een

ʔeen^{3} to pull in one's back when struck
ʔeen^{6} swallow (the bird) (= ʔɛɛn^{6})
keen^{1} arm
keen^{1} to conscript
keen^{6} hard, solid, firm (YG, = OG keel^{6})
kheen^{4} to present (to monks)
kheen^{6} splinter (YG, = OG kheel^{6})
kheen^{6} to stick in the throat
ŋeen^{4} curving (of the buttocks)
deen^{4} a spirit shrine
theen^{5} *in* vaa^{2} theen^{5} broom (YG, = OG vaay^{2} theel^{5})
neen^{3} crowded; stuffed
peen^{3} a board

peen^{6} sheet (of paper)
peen^{6} bal^{1} the world (OG, = YG peen^{6} ban^{1})
pheen^{4} noon meal of monks
meen^{4} *in* su^{4} meen^{4} Mt. Meru (= su^{6} meen^{4})
reen^{1} *in* ʔek^{4} kaʔ^{6} reen^{1} ʔeek^{4} sound of rooster crowing (YG, = YG ʔee^{5} kaʔ^{6} reen^{1} ʔee^{5}, OG ʔek^{4} kaʔ^{6} reel^{1} ʔeek^{4}, OG ʔee^{5} kaʔ^{6} reel^{1} ʔee^{5})
leen^{1} great-grandchild (< Siamese; = Saek leen^{2})
leen^{2} great-grandchild (= leen^{1} < Siamese)
leen^{5} *in* khook^{5} leen^{5} thaŋ^{6} anvil
veen^{2} to hang up
veen^{4} misfortune (YG, = OG veel^{4})
veen^{4} *in* bɔɔ^{1} li^{6} veen^{4} area
heen^{3} pillow (YG, = OG heel^{3})
heen^{3} thɤɤŋ^{3} triangular pillow

-ɤɤn

ʔɤɤn^{1} *in* ʔɛŋ^{3} ta^{6} ʔɤɤn^{1} kind of potato
kɤɤn^{1} to exceed; too
khɤɤn^{2} too short (of a skirt)
khɤɤ̇n^{3} overjoyed, very glad
thɤɤn^{6} imperative final particle
vɤɤn^{6} to swoop back and forth (of vultures, etc.)
sɤɤn^{4} to invite
sɤɤn^{6} to play; to court, woo
hɤɤn^{1} to fly through the air

-on

ʔon^{1} disorderly
khon^{3} to search
con^{1} until, so much that
ton^{3} tree (used in certain expressions)
thon^{4} to endure
bon^{1} *in* ʔuʔ^{4} bon^{1} Ubon, city in Northeast Thailand
bon^{1} *in* tam^{1} bon^{1} a commune
pon^{1} mixed

mon^{4} thaa^{4} name of soŋ^{1} kaan^{1} day when it falls on Wednesday
mon^{4} thaa^{4} thee^{4} vii^{4} Lady mon^{4} thaa^{4}
mon^{4} *in* niʔ^{6} mon^{4} to invite (monks)
mon^{4} *in* mɔɔ^{2} mon^{4} magician
ɲon^{4} machine, engine
lon^{3} to overflow
von^{4} to go in a circle
hon^{4} to hurry

-oon

khoon^{3} poor
ŋoon^{5} a big lump
coon^{1} bandit
toon^{1} to leap into water
toon^{3} a stone or other object used as a weight
troon^{1} buttocks (YG, = OG tloon^{1})
tloon^{1} buttocks (OG, = YG troon^{1})
thoon^{1} *in* ka^{6} thoon^{1} spittoon (= ŋiaŋ^{5}, khɔɔk^{5} ŋiaŋ^{5})
thoon^{4} kind of drum
moon^{4} base of a plant (YG, = OG mool^{4})
ɲoon^{4} to toss, throw
ɲoon^{6} *in* pa^{6} ɲoon^{6} small bits of rubbish (YG, = OG pa^{6} ɲool^{6})
yoon^{6} trellis, as for cucumbers (YG, = OG yool^{6})
soon^{3} soon^{3} big (of a heap)
hoon^{1} to swing

-ɛn

ʔɛn^{3} term used in expressions for certain years, days
pii^{1} ʔɛn^{3} the year after pii^{1} ʔun^{3}, four years from the current year
cɛn^{1} *in* ʔat^{4} sa^{6} cɛn^{1} amazing
cɛn^{1} *in* viaŋ^{4} cɛn^{1} Vientiane, capital of Laos
cɛn^{1} *in* van^{4} cɛn^{1} Monday
cɛn^{3} *in* nam^{6} cɛn^{3} a spring (of water)
tɛn^{1} plugged up
tɛn^{3} to put on, wear
trɛn^{1} *in* ŋua^{4} trɛn^{1} python (YG, = OG ŋua^{4} tlɛn^{1}; YG ŋua^{4} trɔɔ^{1}, OG ŋua^{4} tlɔɔ^{1}; clf. thua^{4})

trɛn^{6} *in* ca^{6} trɛn^{6} skink (YG, = OG ca^{6} tlɛn^{6}; YG caʔ^{6} trɛn^{6}, OG caʔ^{6} tlɛn^{6}; clf. thua^{4})
tlɛn^{1} *in* ŋua^{4} tlɛn^{1} python (OG, = YG ŋua^{4} trɛn^{1}; YG ŋua^{4} trɔɔ^{1}, OG ŋua^{4} tlɔɔ^{1}; clf. thua^{4})
tlɛn^{6} *in* ca^{6} tlɛn^{6} skink (OG, = YG ca^{6} trɛn^{6}; YG caʔ^{6} trɛn^{6}, OG caʔ^{6} tlɛn^{6}; clf. thua^{4})
thɛn^{4} to be in time, to catch up with
thɛn^{4} language in various expressions
  thɛn^{4} laaw^{4} Lao language
  thɛn^{4} rɔɔ^{6} knowledge
thɛn^{4} *in* ka^{6} thɛn^{4} Chinese date (clf. maak^{6})
thɛn^{6} to snore (YG, = OG thɛl^{6})
nɛn^{4} noisy
  nɔɔŋ^{4} nan^{4} noisy
blɛn^{3} to protrude, as a body part or something in the pocket (YG, = OG blɛl^{3})
mlɛn^{3} body louse (YG, = OG mlɛl^{3}; clf. thua^{4})
yɛn^{1} to push with the feet (YG, = OG yɛl^{1})
ɲɛn^{2} civet cat (YG, = OG ɲɛl^{2}; clf. thua^{4})
ɲɛn^{2} fly (YG, = OG ɲɛl^{2})
ɲɛn^{3} to press down
ɲɛn^{4} silver
  ɲɛn^{4} ɣam^{4} kam^{1} kɛɛw^{3} silver and gold and jewels
ɲɛn^{4} money
  ɲɛn^{4} haaŋ^{4} kind of ancient money
ɲɛn^{4} day, daytime; the sun
rɛn^{2} to see (YG, = OG rɛl^{2})
rɛn^{6} that (YG, = OG rɛl^{6})
  thruu^{4} rɛn^{6} like that (= thruu^{4} ʔan^{6}, thruu^{4} nan^{6}, thruun^{4})
lɛn^{1} to roll
sɛn^{2} back of a knife
sɛn^{2} ɲaa^{4} to promise; a contract
sɛn^{3} classifier for long, thin objects (YG, = OG sɛl^{3})
sɛn^{4} steep
sɛn^{6} level, story; layer

-ɛɛn

ʔɛɛn^{1} to bend backwards
ʔɛɛn^{6} swallow (the bird) (= ʔeen^{6})

kɛɛn^{1} hard core
kwɛɛn^{6} familiar, well acquainted
khɛɛn^{4} a Lao musical instrument made from reeds
ŋɛɛn^{3} to crave
dɛɛn^{1} boundary; territory
thɛɛn^{4} to substitute for
nɛɛn^{1} at, in, there (= nɛɛn^{2}) *Tone variation* (nɛɛn^{1}) *due to sentence intonation.*
nɛɛn^{2} at, in, there (= nɛɛn^{1})
nɛɛn^{4} *in* sa^{6} nɛɛn^{4} bamboo frame on which people sit in a boat
bɛɛn^{1} pressed flat
bɛɛn^{1} *in* laaŋ^{4} bɛɛn^{1} skin disease
mɛɛn^{5} it is
mɛɛn^{5} if
lɛɛn^{4} kind of big striped lizard (clf. thua^{4})
vɛɛn^{2} a ring
  voŋ^{4} vɛɛn^{2} earring (= Saek taaŋ^{3}, taaŋ^{6}; = tum^{3} huu^{1} < Siamese)
vɛɛn^{4} to get more than others
vɛɛn^{5} mirror
vɛɛn^{6} kind of vegetable
vɛɛn^{6} left (hand) (YG, = OG vɛɛl^{6})
sɛɛn^{2} hundred thousand
hɛɛn^{3} to gnaw

-an

ʔan^{1} classifier for things (YG, = OG ʔal^{1})
ʔan^{3} plugged up
ʔan^{3} to stammer
ʔan^{3} tuu^{3} baffled
ʔan^{6} there (= man^{6})
ʔan^{6} that (= nan^{6}, man^{6})
  thruu^{4} ʔan^{6} like that (= thruu^{4} nan^{6}, thruu^{4} rɛn^{6}, thruun^{4})
kan^{1} to prevent, protect from
kan^{1} *in* cɛɛ^{1} kan^{1} vase
kan^{1} kind of fruit (clf. maak^{5})
kan^{3} to hold (the breath)
kan^{3} to partition off (a room) (< Lao)
kan^{6} haft of a knife
kan^{6} to make an incision or mark around (e.g., a stick)

kan^{6} that (allomorph of nan^{6} following [k])
  lɯk^{6} kan^{6} that child
kwan^{1} *in* khɔɔk^{5} kwan^{1} rice cooked in a bamboo tube
khan^{1} *in* khɛɛŋ^{6} khan^{1} to compete
khan^{2} a footed stand
khan^{2} *in* mɛɛŋ^{6} khan^{2} handkerchief
khan^{4} umbrella (= khan^{4} ɲuu^{4} < Lao)
  khan^{4} kot^{4} cloth umbrella
khan^{4} a dam
khan^{4} if (= thaa^{3})
  khan^{4} ɣa^{3} if
khan^{4} classifier for spoons, pencils, saws (YG, = OG khal^{4})
khan^{4} thɯay^{4} an effeminate man
khan^{4} tha^{6} thu^{6} lii^{1} name of a cave
khan^{6} to squeeze juice out (YG, = OG khal^{6})
ɣan^{4} *in* ɣum^{4} ɣan^{4} to itch (YG, = OG ɣum^{4} ɣal^{4})
ŋan^{4} music, entertainment
ŋan^{4} late ripening (of rice, beans)
ŋan^{5} ray^{1} stairs, ladder (= ray^{1})
tan^{6} that (allomorph for nan^{6} following [t])
  phaa^{1} saat^{2} tan^{6} that mansion
nan^{6} that, there (= ʔan^{6}, kan^{6}, tan^{6}, man^{6}, yan^{6})
  thruu^{4} nan^{6} like that (= thruu^{4} ʔan^{6}, thruu^{4} rɛn^{6}, thruun^{4})
nan^{6} *in* nɔɔŋ^{4} nan^{6} noisy
ban^{1} dirt, earth, ground (YG, = OG bal^{1})
  ban^{1} buŋ^{6} mud (YG, = OG bal^{1} bluŋ^{6})
  peen^{6} ban^{1} the world (YG, = OG peen^{6} bal^{1})
ban^{1} thɛt^{6} ruler
ban^{1} *in* dɯk^{4} dam^{1} ban^{1} olden times
ban^{3} to cut into sections (= ban^{6})
ban^{3} haa^{2} riddle
ban^{6} to cut into sections (= ban^{3})
pan^{1} to divide, share
pan^{1} to spin cotton (YG, = OG pal^{1}; = pan^{6})
pan^{1} ɲaa^{4} wits, intelligence
pan^{3} to twist, wring; to form (rice) into a ball (YG, = OG val^{3})
pan^{6} to spin cotton (= YG pan^{1}, OG pal^{1})
pan^{6} *in* kam^{6} pan^{6} steamboat
phan^{4} to be, become; to have a disease (YG, = OG phal^{4})
phan^{4} thousand
phan^{4} saa^{2} Buddhist Lent
phan^{4} *in* kum^{1} phan^{4} name of a giant

man^{1} sterile
man^{2} to want, would like to (= man^{3})
man^{3} to want, would like to (= man^{2})
man^{3} to get engaged
man^{3} porcupine (clf. thua^{4})
man^{3} ɲɯɯn^{4} to have long life
man^{3} thuu^{3} angry (cf. lɤɤ^{1}, bɯn^{3}, yak^{6})
man^{4} oil
man^{4} it, he, she, they
man^{4} potato, tuber
man^{6} there (allomorph for nan^{6} following [m])
man^{6} that (allomorph for nan^{6} following [m])
yan^{6} that (allomorph for nan^{6} following [y])
  khoo^{6} hay^{4} yan^{6} that banyan tree
van^{1} to slash, cut (YG, = OG val^{1})
van^{2} seed; kind
van^{4} day (< Lao)
  van^{4} ʔaa^{1} thit^{6} Sunday (= van^{4} ʔa^{6} thit^{6}, van^{4} thit^{6})
  van^{4} ʔaŋ^{1} khaan^{4} Tuesday
  van^{4} cɛn^{1} Monday
  van^{4} phut^{6} Wednesday
  van^{4} phaʔ^{6} hat^{4} Thursday
  van^{4} suk^{4} Friday
  van^{4} saw^{1} Saturday
van^{4} to dream
san^{4} steep (< Lao)
han^{1} to spin (a top)
han^{2} to crow (YG, = OG hal^{2})
han^{3} there
han^{6} to slice

-aan

ʔaan^{1} saddle
ʔaan^{1} to read (= ʔaan^{2})
ʔaan^{2} to read (= ʔaan^{1})
kaan^{1} act, action, work
kaan^{1} *in* soŋ^{1} kaan^{1} New Year's
kaan^{3} stem of leaf, flower, fruit
kaan^{6} to mark; striped
khaan^{1} *in* pii^{1} khaan^{1} Year of the Tiger, third year in the twelve-year cycle

khaan^{2} to fasten (a button) (YG, = OG khaal^{2})
khaan^{4} *in* van^{4} ʔaŋ^{1} khaan^{4} Tuesday
khwaan^{3} to wind (a rope) into a coil (OG, = YG khuan^{3}, kuan^{3})
khwaan^{4} elephant rider (OG, = YG khuan^{4})
ɣaan^{4} carrying pole
ŋaan^{2} to answer, reply
ŋaan^{3} the medicinal plant called waan^{3} in Siamese (YG, = OG ŋaal^{3})
ŋaan^{4} stubborn, naughty
ŋaan^{4} work
caan^{1} dish
caan^{1} man who has been a monk
caan^{1} *in* ʔaa^{1} caan^{1} teacher, scholar
caan^{1} *in* peeŋ^{1} caan^{1} name of a city in a story
caan^{3} the *Pandanus* tree (YG, = OG caal^{3}; = tɤɤy^{1})
caan^{6} phaan^{6} to be scattered about
daan^{6} border; frontier post
taan^{1} sugar palm
  khoo^{6} taan^{1} sugar palm tree
thaan^{1} toilet
thaan^{4} alms
thaan^{4} *in* niʔ^{4} thaan^{4} story (=niʔ^{6} thaan^{4})
thaan^{6} charcoal
naan^{1} a bed in a garden
naan^{1} *in* sa^{6} nuk^{4} sa^{6} naan^{1} happily
baan^{1} to bloom (of a flower)
baan^{1} *in* tham^{4} maʔ^{6} baan^{1} personal name (= tham^{4} ma^{6} baan^{1})
baan^{3} village, home
baan^{4} to consult
baan^{6} nicked, chipped (YG, = OG baal^{6})
paan^{1} time, amount
paan^{1} like, similar
paan^{1} birthmark
paan^{3} to dam up water (YG, = OG paal^{3})
phaan^{4} bad, wicked
phaan^{4} hunter
phaan^{4} *in* som^{1} phaan^{4} glory (of a king)
phaan^{4} *in* him^{1} ma^{6} phaan^{4} name of a mythical forest
phaan^{6} I
phaan^{6} to pass
phaan^{6} *in* caan^{6} phaan^{6} to be scattered about
maan^{3} certain
maan^{4} pregnant
maan^{4} Mara; illusion

maan^{4} *in* ku^{6} maan^{4} boy (= kuʔ^{4} maan^{4})
maan^{4} *in* pa^{6} maan^{4} about, approximately
maan^{6} to borrow; ask for help
yaan^{4} slack (YG, = OG yaal^{4})
ɲaan^{5} area, district
raan^{4} house (clf. laŋ^{2})
raan^{4} *in* ʔiim^{6} nam^{1} sam^{1} raan^{4} full, satiated
raan^{5} that way (< raa^{5} ʔan^{6})
laan^{2} grandchild; nephew, niece
laan^{3} store, shop
laan^{3} million
laan^{3} bald
laan^{4} threshing ground
laan^{4} to skin (the penis)
laan^{4} kind of tree called ben^{1} ca^{2} phan^{1} in Siamese (YG, = OG laal^{4})
vaan^{1} to cry out
vaan^{2} sweet (YG, = OG vaal^{2})
vaan^{2} axe (clf. maak^{6})
vaan^{4} kind of deer (YG, = OG vaal^{4}; clf. thua^{4})
vaan^{6} to throw, cast, sow (YG, = OG vaal^{6})
saan^{1} official building
saan^{2} to weave baskets, nets
swaan^{3} spade, shovel (OG, = YG suan^{3}; clf. maak^{6})
haan^{1} kind of stinging caterpillar (YG, = OG haal^{1}; YG haan^{2}, OG haal^{2}; clf. thua^{4})
haan^{2} kind of stinging caterpillar (YG, = OG haal^{2}; YG haan^{1}, OG haal^{1}; clf. thua^{4})
haan^{2} *in* tha^{6} haan^{2} soldier
haan^{3} platform in a tree
haan^{6} goose (clf. thua^{4})

-ɔn

ʔɔn^{1} thorn
kɔn^{3} to tie
kɔn^{6} stump, stubble (YG, = OG kɔl^{6})
ɣɔn^{4} smoke
cɔn^{1} poor
cɔn^{1} phɔɔn^{4} mongoose (fast speech form, = cɔɔn^{1} phɔɔn^{4}; clf. thua^{4})
phɔn^{6} across, away
mɔn^{4} round

lɔn^{5} *in* nay^{4} lɔn^{5} nylon
lɔn^{6} to fall (of a leaf, etc.)
sɔn^{3} heel; butt, end
hɔn^{2} whorl in the hair
hɔn^{2} spirit
hɔn^{2} idiomatic term meaning something like 'ever' or 'indeed'
  raw^{2} hɔn^{2} hit^{6} Indeed, they're going to do it (for us).

-ɔɔn

kɔɔn^{6} before, first
khɔɔn^{4} to carry on one end of a pole over the shoulder (YG, = OG khɔɔl^{4})
khɔɔn^{4} *in* na^{6} khɔɔn^{4} city
khɔɔn^{4} *in* la^{6} khɔɔn^{4} Nakhon Phanom, city in Northeast Thailand
  (= na^{6} khɔɔn^{4} pha^{6} nom^{1})
khɔɔn^{5} to slip loose, fall off, fall out (YG, = OG khɔɔl^{5})
ɣɔɔn^{6} hammer, club (YG, = OG ɣɔɔl^{6})
ŋɔɔn^{2} delicious, to enjoy one's food
ŋɔɔn^{5} back of the head
cɔɔn^{1} tender, crisp, brittle
cɔɔn^{1} sideburns
cɔɔn^{1} phɔɔn^{4} mongoose (= fast speech form cɔn^{1} phɔɔn^{4}; clf. thua^{4})
cɔɔn^{3} to tuck up (a skirt)
dɔɔn^{1} island
dɔɔn^{1} suʔ^{6} mɔɔ^{4} *see* dɔŋ^{1} sa^{6} mɔɔ^{4}
dɔɔn^{1} *in* ʔuʔ^{4} dɔɔn^{1} Udorn, city in Northeast Thailand (= ʔu^{4} dɔɔn^{1})
dɔɔn^{1} *in* laat^{5} sa^{6} dɔɔn^{1} people
tɔɔn^{1} to castrate; part, section
tɔɔn^{3} to receive, welcome
tɔɔn^{6} to scrape off (fish scales) (YG, = OG tɔɔl^{6}; cf. tlɛk^{4}, trɛk^{4})
thɔɔn^{3} to put away (neatly); to save (money)
thɔɔn^{4} to make change (money)
thɔɔn^{4} *in* ma^{6} hoo^{1} thɔɔn^{4} name of soŋ^{1} kaan^{1} day when it falls on Saturday
thɔɔn^{5} a piece, a length
thɔɔn^{5} a lump
thɔɔn^{5} a classifier
thɔɔn^{6} kind of tree
nɔɔn^{1} worm (< Siamese, Lao; = Saek OG nɔɔl^{2}, YG nɔɔn^{2}; clf. thua^{4})
nɔɔn^{2} worm (YG, = OG nɔɔl^{2}; = nɔɔn^{1} < Siamese, Lao; clf. thua^{4})
bɔɔn^{1} yam

bɔɔn^{3} to jump out of water (of fish)
bɔɔn^{6} place
prɔɔn^{1} to put inside (YG, = OG plɔɔn^{1}; YG prɔɔn^{6}, OG plɔɔn^{6})
prɔɔn^{6} to put inside (YG, = OG plɔɔn^{6}; YG prɔɔn^{1}, OG plɔɔn^{1})
plɔɔn^{1} to put inside (OG, = YG prɔɔn^{1}; YG prɔɔn^{6}, OG plɔɔn^{6})
plɔɔn^{6} to put inside (OG, = YG prɔɔn^{6}; YG prɔɔn^{1}, OG plɔɔn^{1})
phɔɔn^{4} day before yesterday
phɔɔn^{4} blessing
phɔɔn^{4} *in* cɔɔn^{1} phɔɔn^{4} mongoose (= fast speech form cɔn^{1} phɔɔn^{4}; clf. thua^{4})
phɔɔn^{6} to pay in installments
mlɔɔn^{4} to open (the eyes)
mlɔɔn^{5} to turn freely (as a wheel)
yɔɔn^{3} to dance
yɔɔn^{3} yɔɔ^{3} to squat (= yɔɔn^{3} yɔɔ^{6})
yɔɔn^{5} to hide (YG, = OG yɔɔl^{5})
ɲɔɔn^{4} kind of fish
ɲɔɔn^{4} to dig out (the ear) (YG, = OG ɲɔɔl^{4})
rɔɔn^{4} to trim
rɔɔn^{6} to slice
lɔɔn^{2} (to eat) all
lɔɔn^{2} to lose the skin
lɔɔn^{4} waves, as in the hair
vɔɔn^{3} to turn (something) over
vɔɔn^{4} *in* vay^{6} vɔɔn^{4} to ask, pray
sɔɔn^{2} to teach (YG, = OG sɔɔl^{2})
sɔɔn^{3} kind of fish trap (YG, = OG sɔɔl^{3})
sɔɔn^{3} to scoop up (fish) (YG, = OG sɔɔl^{3})
sɔɔn^{3} to spend money wastefully, to waste
hɔɔn^{1} to howl (of a dog)
hɔɔn^{1} cockscomb

-iŋ

ʔiŋ^{1} to lean back, lean something against the wall, etc. (< Siamese, Lao; = Saek biŋ^{1})
kiŋ^{6} twig; one chopstick (fast speech form, = kiiŋ^{6})
khiŋ^{3} wheel (clf. maak^{6})
ciŋ^{1} true
diŋ^{1} *in* ka^{6} diŋ^{1} kind of wind
diŋ^{1} *in* ka^{6} diŋ^{1} name of a river
diŋ^{6} *in* lɯk^{6} diŋ^{6} plumb line with weight on the end

tiŋ^{6} *in* say^{3} tiŋ^{6} appendix
biŋ^{1} to lean back, lean something against the wall, etc. (= ʔiŋ^{1} < Siamese, Lao)
biŋ^{3} kind of bat (clf. thua^{4})
priŋ^{1} leech (YG, = OG pliŋ^{1}; clf. thua^{4})
pliŋ^{1} leech (OG, = YG priŋ^{1}; clf. thua^{4})
phriŋ^{4} *in* ŋaw^{2} phriŋ^{4} phriŋ^{4} to smell very bad (YG, = OG phliŋ^{4})
phliŋ^{4} *in* ŋaw^{2} phliŋ^{4} phliŋ^{4} to smell very bad (OG, = YG phriŋ^{4})
miŋ^{5} spirit, soul
ɲiŋ^{4} to shoot (fast speech form, = ɲiiŋ^{4})
riŋ^{6} to pour
liŋ^{1} to look
siŋ^{4} scales, balance

-iiŋ

kiiŋ^{6} twig; one chopstick (= fast speech form kiŋ^{6})
ciiŋ^{1} to lead by the hand
piiŋ^{4} sound of fruit falling
ɲiiŋ^{4} to shoot (= fast speech form ɲiŋ^{4})
riiŋ^{1} red
liiŋ^{4} monkey (clf. thua^{4})
siiŋ^{2} to struggle over, vie for
hiiŋ^{2} ginger
hiiŋ^{4} oneself, we

-iaŋ

ʔiaŋ^{1} not straight, tilted
ʔiaŋ^{3} mynah bird (= ʔiaŋ^{6})
ʔiaŋ^{6} mynah bird (= ʔiaŋ^{3})
kiaŋ^{1} *in* ta^{6} kiaŋ^{1} lamp
kiaŋ^{3} kind of orange (clf. maak^{6})
khiaŋ^{4} tripod
ŋiaŋ^{5} finger, toe
ŋiaŋ^{5} spittoon (= khɔɔk^{5} ŋiaŋ^{5}, ka^{6} thoon^{1})
ciaŋ^{1} *in* blian^{1} ciaŋ^{1} first month
tiaŋ^{1} bed
triaŋ^{1} a hard spot in fruit
triaŋ^{3} smooth (YG, = OG tliaŋ^{3})
tliaŋ^{3} smooth (OG, = YG triaŋ^{3})
thiaŋ^{2} to argue

thiaŋ^{4} a hut in the fields
thiaŋ^{5} noon (= theeŋ^{5})
thiaŋ^{5} honest (= theeŋ^{5})
thiaŋ^{5} straight (= theeŋ^{5})
thriaŋ^{2} hard, stiff
biaŋ^{6} diagonal (= viaŋ^{6})
piaŋ^{6} a round ball (of sugar)
priaŋ^{1} cucumber, melon, gourd (clf. maak^{6})
  priaŋ^{1} prɔɔŋ^{6} cucumber (YG, = OG priaŋ^{1} plɔɔŋ^{6})
phiaŋ^{4} city; country, kingdom
phiaŋ^{4} level, even
phiaŋ^{6} jackfruit when still small (clf. maak^{6})
phiaŋ^{6} *in* phiaʔ^{4} phiaŋ^{6} sound of an elephant trumpeting
miaŋ^{4} miaŋ^{4} shiny
miaŋ^{5} mango (clf. maak^{6})
miaŋ^{6} a substance that is chewed, consisting of betel, tamarind, pepper, figs, and fish paste
riaŋ^{4} to line up in a row
liaŋ^{6} to raise, feed, tend, keep; to feast
viaŋ^{1} rice straw
viaŋ^{1} starfruit (clf. maak^{6})
viaŋ^{3} side, direction
viaŋ^{3} bank of a river
viaŋ^{3} classifier for one of a pair
viaŋ^{3} *in* ɣaw^{6} viaŋ^{3} millet (clf. maak^{6})
viaŋ^{4} cɛn^{1} Vientiane, capital of Laos
viaŋ^{6} diagonal (= biaŋ^{6})
siaŋ^{2} sound, noise, voice
siaŋ^{2} diligent, industrious
siaŋ^{5} to take a chance, take a risk; make a wish (= siaŋ^{6})
siaŋ^{5} to shine (a light)
siaŋ^{5} to show off (something)
siaŋ^{6} to take a chance, take a risk; make a wish (= siaŋ^{5})
hiaŋ^{3} to reheat dried meat or fish

-ɯŋ

ʔɯŋ^{3} hard of hearing
kɯŋ^{3} praa^{1} to stare fixedly
khɯŋ^{1} to stretch taut, pull taut
khɯŋ^{4} to hold up, support
tɯŋ^{1} taut

thɯŋ^{4} all, both, together with
thɯŋ^{4} even though
thrɯŋ^{5} traaŋ^{1} middle, in the middle (YG, = OG thrɯŋ^{5} tlaaŋ^{1})
thrɯŋ^{5} tlaaŋ^{1} middle, in the middle (OG, = YG thrɯŋ^{5} traaŋ^{1})
thrɯŋ^{6} *in* cooŋ^{3} thrɯŋ^{6} walking stick
nɯŋ^{3} to steam
nɯŋ^{4} *in* la^{6} nɯŋ^{4} la^{6} naat^{5} in disorder
nɯŋ^{5} one
nɯŋ^{6} a little, only a little
bɯŋ^{1} marsh
bɯŋ^{3} a small, edible, spider-like animal that lives in the ground (clf. thua^{4})
pɯŋ^{1} kind of very large leech (clf. thua^{4})
phɯŋ^{6} to unroll (cloth) (fast speech form, = phɯɯŋ^{6})
mɯŋ^{4} you
rɯŋ^{4} *in* rɛt^{6} rɯŋ^{4} to tie tightly
vɯŋ^{1} sesame
sɯŋ^{4} kind of small bee (clf. thua^{4})
hɯŋ^{1} haaw^{3} vigorous

-ɯɯŋ

ʔɯɯŋ^{6} bullfrog (clf. thua^{4})
kɯɯŋ^{6} to pry up
khɯɯŋ^{6} *in* cɯɯŋ^{6} khɯɯŋ^{6} gleaming red and yellow
cɯɯŋ^{6} khɯɯŋ^{6} gleaming red and yellow
tɯɯŋ^{4} *in* lam^{6} tɯɯŋ^{4} to fall flat
pɯɯŋ^{6} a big hole (e.g., large nostrils)
phɯɯŋ^{6} to unroll (cloth) (= fast speech form phɯŋ^{6})

-ɯaŋ

ʔɯaŋ^{1} to plant, germinate (seeds)
ʔɯaŋ^{3} kind of orchid
khɯaŋ^{4} swollen (of the eye)
thɯaŋ^{4} kind of tree
thrɯaŋ^{3} to rejoice in or admire another's good fortune
thrɯaŋ^{5} things, possessions; food; clothing; utensil
bɯaŋ^{3} *in* ka^{6} bɯaŋ^{3} tile
pɯaŋ^{1} to waste

mɯaŋ^{1} a ditch
lɯaŋ^{4} bamboo basket with handles called ka^{2} buŋ^{1} in Siamese
lɯaŋ^{6} story
sɯaŋ^{2} to love
hɯaŋ^{4} *in* huŋ^{6} hɯaŋ^{4} to prosper

-uŋ

kuŋ^{1} theep^{5} Bangkok, capital of Thailand
kuŋ^{2} then, so (= kuŋ^{3})
  kuŋ^{2} taam^{1} no matter
  lɛɛw^{6} kuŋ^{2} and then
kuŋ^{3} then, so (= kuŋ^{2})
kuŋ^{6} shrimp (clf. thua^{4})
kuŋ^{6} khuu^{4} dung beetle (clf. thua^{4})
khuŋ^{4} thrust in all the way, pushed to the limit
duŋ^{3} *in* sa^{6} duŋ^{3} kind of square fishnet
tuŋ^{6} to throw, throw away
tuŋ^{6} tian^{3} cricket (YG, = OG tuŋ^{6} tial^{3}; clf. thua^{4})
tuŋ^{6} tial^{3} cricket (OG, = YG tuŋ^{6} tian^{3}; clf. thua^{4})
tuŋ^{6} thua^{4} the body (= tuu^{6} thua^{4}, tua^{6} thua^{4}, thua^{6} thua^{4}; cf. too^{1})
tuŋ^{6} thaa^{4} what, something, everything
thuŋ^{1} thaw^{3} socks
thuŋ^{3} raŋ^{2} a sieve
thuŋ^{3} vii^{6} winnowing basket
thuŋ^{4} flag
thuŋ^{4} saʔ^{4} name of soŋ^{1} kaan^{1} day when it falls on Sunday
  thuŋ^{4} saʔ^{4} thee^{4} vii^{4} Lady thuŋ^{4} saʔ^{4}, name of soŋ^{1} kaan^{1} day when it falls on Sunday
thuŋ^{6} stomach, belly (= phuŋ^{4})
thruŋ^{3} gun
thruŋ^{6} thraaw^{2} spider
buŋ^{3} baa^{3} butterfly
buŋ^{6} *in* ban^{1} buŋ^{6} mud (YG, = OG bal^{1} bluŋ^{6})
bluŋ^{6} *in* bal^{1} bluŋ^{6} mud (OG, = YG ban^{1} buŋ^{6})
phuŋ^{4} belly (= thuŋ^{6})
muŋ^{3} mosquito net
yuŋ^{3} granary
ɲuŋ^{4} mosquito (clf. thua^{4})
ɲuŋ^{6} confused
ɲuŋ^{6} ɲaaw^{2} confused, disheveled, entangled

ɲuŋ^{6} ɲaaw^{4} mosquito larva (clf. thua^{4})
ruŋ^{1} to temble, shiver
ruŋ^{2} to cook (rice); to boil; to distil
ruŋ^{2} in disorder
ruŋ^{2} the lap (= ruŋ^{3})
ruŋ^{3} the lap (= ruŋ^{2})
luŋ^{2} kind of mousetrap
luŋ^{4} uncle, older brother of either parent
luŋ^{5} banana (clf. maak^{6})
 nɔk^{6} luŋ^{5} a bunch of bananas
 luŋ^{5} ʔii^{6} tɔʔ^{4} kind of banana
 luŋ^{5} ŋaaw^{6} kind of banana
 luŋ^{5} tha^{6} nii^{4} kind of banana
 luŋ^{5} tha^{6} nii^{4} ʔɔɔŋ^{1} kind of banana
huŋ^{2} papaya (clf. maak^{6})
huŋ^{3} kind of giant in stories
huŋ^{6} hɯaŋ^{4} to prosper

-uaŋ

kuaŋ^{6} calf of the leg
khuaŋ^{2} not good, bad (of a person)
ŋuaŋ^{4} elephant's trunk, spout of a teapot
cuaŋ^{1} kind of tree
duaŋ^{3} coconut grub (clf. thua^{4})
tuaŋ^{1} to guess, assume, presume; to estimate (weight, length)
thuaŋ^{4} to ask for repayment
nuaŋ^{6} younger sibling
buaŋ^{6} spoon
buaŋ^{6} loop in a snare
buaŋ^{6} water-hyacinth
puaŋ^{6} mentally deficient
phuaŋ^{4} cluster (of fruit)
yuaŋ^{3} to roast or smoke over fire
yuaŋ^{6} a step, to pace; to step
ruaŋ^{2} tail
ruaŋ^{4} ear or head of rice
ruaŋ^{4} beehive
luaŋ^{1} kind of potato (YG, = OG lwaaŋ^{1})
luaŋ^{2} royal; the government
luaŋ^{3} kind of mousetrap
luaŋ^{4} copper, brass, bronze

luaŋ^5 space underneath an elevated house
luaŋ^5 (year) before last
vuaŋ^4 deer (clf. thua^4)
suaŋ^4 loom
suaŋ^5 to race
suaŋ^6 to recover from illness or drunkenness
huaŋ^3 worried (YG, = OG hwaaŋ^3)
huaŋ^6 a loop (of a rope)

-eŋ

keŋ^1 *in* lot^6 keŋ^1 sedan automobile
keŋ^6 skilled, clever (fast speech form, = keeŋ^6)
kheŋ^1 kind of fish
neŋ^5 to pull (a rope) taut (= nɛŋ^5)
beŋ^6 to strain, as in defecating or in childbirth (= bɛŋ^6)
pheŋ^4 full (moon)
  blian^1 pheŋ^4 full moon
leŋ^5 to hurry
seŋ^1 *in* pii^1 ma^6 seŋ^1 Year of the Snake, sixth year in the twelve-year cycle
heŋ^4 cancer (= ma^6 heŋ^4)

-eeŋ

ʔeeŋ^1 self, oneself
keeŋ^1 curry
keeŋ^6 skilled, clever (= fast speech form keŋ^6)
ɣeeŋ^5 foot, leg
treeŋ^1 to make (the hair) into a knot (YG, = OG tleeŋ^1)
tleeŋ^1 to make (the hair) into a knot (OG, = YG treeŋ^1)
theeŋ^5 noon (= thiaŋ^5)
  theeŋ^5 ɣɯn^4 midnight
  theeŋ^5 ɲɛn^4 noon
theeŋ^5 honest (= thiaŋ^5)
theeŋ^5 straight (= thiaŋ^5)
beeŋ^6 to divide, share
peeŋ^1 caan^1 name of a city in a story
reeŋ^1 to moan
reeŋ^4 strength, strong
reeŋ^6 bamboo bell on buffalo's neck
leeŋ^4 equal; degree, quantity

veeŋ^{3} small brinjals (clf. maak^{6})
seeŋ^{2} cold

-ɤŋ

khɤŋ^{4} kind of fish
khɤŋ^{5} half
tɤŋ^{3} term used to call a small child, similar to ʔay^{3} nuu^{5} in Siamese
ɲɤŋ^{4} to lift up

-ɤɤŋ

ʔɤɤŋ^{1} *in* caʔ^{6} ʔɤɤŋ^{1} big cup or glass; old-fashioned Chinese earthen bowl
khɤɤŋ^{6} to try
ŋɤɤŋ^{4} to raise oneself from a sitting position
cɤɤŋ^{1} to protrude (of teeth)
trɤɤŋ^{1} name of abandoned Saek village in Vietnam
trɤɤŋ^{3} egg; to lay an egg (YG, = OG tlɤɤŋ^{3})
tlɤɤŋ^{3} egg; to lay an egg (OG, = YG trɤɤŋ^{3})
thɤɤŋ^{3} to sit leaning against a triangular pillow
  heen^{3} thɤɤŋ^{3} triangular pillow
thrɤɤŋ^{6} ceiling
pɤɤŋ^{1} to raise, lift
sɤɤŋ^{4} to mate (of animals)

-oŋ

ʔoŋ^{1} classifier for royal persons
  ʔoŋ^{1} muu^{5} name of a spirit
ʔoŋ^{1} term used before Vietnamese titles
ʔoŋ^{6} arrogant
koŋ^{1} wheel
koŋ^{1} balustrade
khoŋ^{1} arched gateway as at a monastery
khoŋ^{4} invulnerable
coŋ^{1} dorsal fin
coŋ^{6} to save (food) for someone

doŋ^{1} su^{6} mɔɔ^{4} *see* dɔŋ^{1} sa^{6} mɔɔ^{4}
doŋ^{1} sa^{6} mɔɔ^{4} *see* dɔŋ^{1} sa^{6} mɔɔ^{4}
boŋ^{1} kind of plant formerly used in mortar between bricks
phoŋ^{3} to splash (of water); to swirl up (of dust)
voŋ^{4} vɛɛn^{2} earring (= Saek taaŋ^{3}, taaŋ^{6}; = tum^{3} huu^{1} < Siamese)
voŋ^{4} *in* caw^{3} khoot^{5} voŋ^{4} taa^{1} the elder who is an arranger at a wedding
voŋ^{4} *in* lam^{4} voŋ^{4} circle dancing
soŋ^{1} kaan^{1} New Year's *See Appendix II for the names of the days.*
soŋ^{1} say^{1} to doubt, wonder
soŋ^{4} (in combination with a verb) worthy of, likely to
  soŋ^{4} siim^{4} ugly
  soŋ^{4} saŋ^{4} hateful, detestable
soŋ^{6} sa^{6} kaan^{1} to have a funeral (< Lao)

-ooŋ

ʔooŋ^{1} *in* phaʔ^{6} ʔooŋ^{1} simple ladder made of a bamboo pole
ʔooŋ^{4} paternal grandfather
kooŋ^{1} effort
khooŋ^{3} curved, bent
khooŋ^{3} a coil
khooŋ^{3} to bow respectfully
cooŋ^{3} thrɯŋ^{6} walking stick
tooŋ^{1} to touch
tooŋ^{6} kind of fishnet
tooŋ^{6} *in* viaŋ^{6} tooŋ^{6} diagonal, as of a stole over the shoulder
tlooŋ^{1} to coil up (a rope)
pooŋ^{1} *in* ka^{6} pooŋ^{1} skirt
prooŋ^{5} to slip off, slip down (of a lower garment)
phooŋ^{4} blistered (= phɔɔŋ^{4})
phooŋ^{6} hollow, a hole (in a tree, in bamboo)
mooŋ^{1} to wipe oneself after defecating
mooŋ^{3} knitted cap worn in cold weather
mooŋ^{4} time, hour
mooŋ^{6} ʔɛɛk^{1} the moon (in talking to children)
yooŋ^{1} very tall (of a person)
yooŋ^{1} *in* may^{6} yooŋ^{1} yeek^{6} teeter-totter
rooŋ^{3} *in* sa^{6} rooŋ^{3} sarong (= sa^{6} looŋ^{2})
rooŋ^{4} building, hall
rooŋ^{6} wide, broad
looŋ^{2} *in* sa^{6} looŋ^{2} sarong (= sa^{6} rooŋ^{3})

looŋ^{4} coffin
  ka^{6} looŋ^{4} wooden box that is nailed shut
looŋ^{4} *in* pii^{1} ma^{6} looŋ^{4} Year of the Dragon, fifth year in the twelve-year cycle
sooŋ^{3} pants, trousers
sooŋ^{5} pillar
hooŋ^{2} the sides (of the body), ribs

-ɛŋ

ʔɛŋ^{3} potato, tuber
  ʔɛŋ^{3} ta^{6} ʔɤɤn^{1} kind of potato
khɛŋ^{1} *in* nam^{6} khɛŋ^{1} ice
khɛŋ^{5} taut
khɛŋ^{5} haa^{2} armpit (= khɛɛ^{5} haa^{2})
ŋɛŋ^{5} section of garlic
ŋɛŋ^{5} chevrons on a uniform
nɛŋ^{2} to weigh down with something heavy
nɛŋ^{5} to pull (a rope) taut (= neŋ^{5})
bɛŋ^{4} howdah (= yɛɛŋ^{6} < Lao)
bɛŋ^{6} to strain, as in defecating or in childbirth (= beŋ^{6})
ɲɛŋ^{3} *in* kha^{6} ɲɛŋ^{3} afterbirth
lɛŋ^{6} *in* ka^{6} lɛŋ^{6} small metal bell (clf. maak^{6})
vɛŋ^{6} having a piece out (of the mouth) (fast speech form, = vɛɛŋ^{6})
sɛŋ^{6} metal clappers (fast speech form, = sɛɛŋ^{6})

-ɛɛŋ

ʔɛɛŋ^{1} older brother
ʔɛɛŋ^{5} fellow, person (used only with males)
ʔɛɛŋ^{6} small jug for water
kɛɛŋ^{6} to throw (= kwɛɛŋ^{6})
kwɛɛŋ^{6} to throw (= kɛɛŋ^{6})
khɛɛŋ^{4} *in* ta^{6} khɛɛŋ^{4} (to lie) on the side
khɛɛŋ^{6} a lath, a small, thin board
khɛɛŋ^{6} to compete (< Lao)
ŋɛɛŋ^{4} *in* sa^{6} ŋɛɛŋ^{4} kind of fish
ŋɛɛŋ^{4} *in* sa^{6} ŋɛɛŋ^{4} kind of vegetable
dɛɛŋ^{3} *in* ka^{6} dɛɛŋ^{3} sterile
tɛɛŋ^{6} to prepare; to dress; to marry

tɛɛŋ^{6} *in* taŋ^{3} tɛɛŋ^{6} to appoint

trɛɛŋ^{4} sharp (of a knife)

trɛɛŋ^{5} to avoid, get out of the way (YG, = OG tlɛɛŋ^{5})

tlɛɛŋ^{5} to avoid, get out of the way (OG, = YG trɛɛŋ^{5})

thɛɛŋ^{2} *in* mɔɔ^{3} thɛɛŋ^{2} frying pan

thɛɛŋ^{4} top of the head

thɛɛŋ^{4} to love

thɛɛŋ^{4} to guard jealously; hate to lose

thɛɛŋ^{5} a bar, e.g., of silver or gold

nɛɛŋ^{1} tooth, teeth

  siik^{6} nɛɛŋ^{1} to bare the teeth

pɛɛŋ^{3} starch, flour

pɛɛŋ^{3} rice boiled in cakes with banana (= Siamese khaaw^{3} tom^{3})

prɛɛŋ^{1} a brush

prɛɛŋ^{1} *in* tɛɛŋ^{6} prɛɛŋ^{1} to marry

phɛɛŋ^{4} expensive

mɛɛŋ^{2} *in* mɔt^{4} mɛɛŋ^{2} clean

mɛɛŋ^{4} insect

  mɛɛŋ^{4} kɔɔk^{6} kind of beetle that digs around the roots of the wild olive tree

  mɛɛŋ^{4} ŋɔɔt^{6} scorpion (= mɛɛŋ^{4} ŋaw^{4})

  mɛɛŋ^{4} yay^{1} insect that makes mud nests in walls

mɛɛŋ^{6} a bite (of food); a small scrap (of cloth)

yɛɛŋ^{4} eaves

yɛɛŋ^{6} howdah (< Lao; = Saek bɛŋ^{4})

ɲɛɛŋ^{4} to look at (a mirror)

ɲɛɛŋ^{6} *in* ɣaw^{6} maa^{2} ɲɛɛŋ^{6} kind of wild rice with very short grains

rɛɛŋ^{6} vulture (clf. thua^{4})

lɛɛŋ^{3} *in* khɔɔk^{5} lɛɛŋ^{3} quiver for arrows

lɛɛŋ^{3} *in* lɯk^{6} lɛɛŋ^{3} worker, employee (< Lao; = Saek lɯk^{6} caaŋ^{3})

lɛɛŋ^{4} evening meal

lɛɛŋ^{5} pen for buffaloes beneath the house

lɛɛŋ^{6} dry (of weather)

vɛɛŋ^{6} having a part out (of the mouth) (= fast speech form vɛŋ^{6})

sɛɛŋ^{2} light

sɛɛŋ^{4} a cluster (of coconuts, areca nuts, etc.)

sɛɛŋ^{6} metal clappers (= fast speech form sɛŋ^{6}; = Siamese chiŋ^{2})

hɛɛŋ^{1} cracked

hɛɛŋ^{3} dry, dried up

hɛɛŋ^{6} of, belonging to

-aŋ

ʔaŋ^{1} *in* van^{4} ʔaŋ^{1} khaan^{4} Tuesday
ʔaŋ^{6} worried, troubled, distressed
kaŋ^{3} to put up (an umbrella)
khaŋ^{4} storehouse; treasury
caŋ^{1} curled up (of leaves); tangled (of rope)
caŋ^{1} a disease with a high fever and with the hands and feet curled up
caŋ^{1} vat^{4} province
caŋ^{3} to stop
daŋ^{1} nose
daŋ^{1} loud
daŋ^{1} in, inside, into, at, during (fast speech form, = daaŋ^{1})
daŋ^{6} lye (water)
taŋ^{1} to partition off (a room)
taŋ^{1} birdlime made from trees such as jackfruit and the banyan
taŋ^{1} ɲɛn^{4} the sun (fast speech form, = taaŋ^{1} ɲɛn^{4})
taŋ^{3} to set up; establish; all
taŋ^{3} tɛɛ^{6} from, since
taŋ^{3} tɛɛŋ^{6} to appoint
taŋ^{3} thrɔɔ^{6} only
taŋ^{6} stool
  taŋ^{6} ʔii^{3} chair (= taŋ^{6} ʔii^{6})
traŋ^{3} kind of fish (YG, = OG tlaŋ^{3})
tlaŋ^{3} kind of fish (OG, = YG traŋ^{3})
thaŋ^{1} bucket, pail; tank
thaŋ^{4} to arrive, reach; even
thaŋ^{5} to ram with a pole (= thraŋ^{5})
thaŋ^{6} anvil
thaŋ^{6} thee^{4} great numbers
  luʔ^{4} laŋ^{3} thaŋ^{6} thee^{4} to move in great numbers
thraŋ^{2} to shut up, imprison
thraŋ^{5} sticklac
thraŋ^{5} to ram with a pole (= thaŋ^{5})
naŋ^{2} skin, hide, leather; the movies
naŋ^{4} sɯɯ^{2} writing, book
naŋ^{5} to sit
baŋ^{1} to obstruct the light or the view
baŋ^{6} bamboo tube
phaŋ^{1} phɛɛt^{6} twins
phaŋ^{4} to listen
phaŋ^{4} *in* caʔ^{6} phaŋ^{4} pail or jug for washing, not drinking

phaŋ^{5} to depend upon (= Siamese phɯŋ^{3})
maŋ^{4} strong, vigorous
maŋ^{5} kind of deer called la^{4} maŋ^{3} in Siamese (= maŋ^{6}; clf. thua^{4})
maŋ^{6} kind of deer called la^{4} maŋ^{3} in Siamese (= maŋ^{5}; clf. thua^{4})
yaŋ^{1} *in* kaʔ^{6} yaŋ^{1} kind of basket with feet
raŋ^{2} to sift; a sieve
laŋ^{2} back; after
laŋ^{2} classifier for houses
laŋ^{2} then
laŋ^{4} some (fast speech form, = laaŋ^{4})
laŋ^{4} *in* kam^{1} laŋ^{4} to be doing, about to
laŋ^{4} *in* kam^{1} laŋ^{4} vaŋ^{4} saa^{4} troops
laŋ^{6} *in* pha^{6} laŋ^{6} Occidental, white person (= fa^{4} laŋ^{6})
laŋ^{6} *in* fa^{4} laŋ^{6} Occidental, white person (= pha^{6} laŋ^{6})
vaŋ^{1} hope; to hope
vaŋ^{3} silent, quiet
vaŋ^{3} vɛɛ^{3} completely silent
vaŋ^{4} pool in a river
vaŋ^{4} palace
vaŋ^{4} *in* kam^{1} laŋ^{4} vaŋ^{4} saa^{4} troops
vaŋ^{6} bank (of a river)
saŋ^{1} ka^{6} sii^{1} tin (= sɯɯn^{4})
saŋ^{1} kaa^{1} dice, a kind of gambling
saŋ^{4} to hate
soŋ^{4} saŋ^{4} hateful, detestable
saŋ^{4} *in* ʔɛt^{4} saŋ^{4} gasoline (= ʔit saŋ^{4})
saŋ^{5} to weigh (cf. tit^{4})
saŋ^{5} ɲia^{2} to cock the ears to try hard to listen
saŋ^{6} to order, give final instruction
saŋ^{6} to blow the nose
haŋ^{3} a fence

-aaŋ

ʔaaŋ^{1} *in* tam^{1} ʔaaŋ^{1} the chest (= taʔ^{6} baaŋ^{1})
ʔaaŋ^{6} basin
ʔaaŋ^{6} to boast
kaaŋ^{1} to open out, set up
kaaŋ^{1} *in* kɯam^{3} kaaŋ^{1} to be a waste of effort
kaaŋ^{3} fish bone
kaaŋ^{3} haam^{4} jaw; chin

kaaŋ^{6} branch, twig
kwaaŋ^{3} poor (eyesight)
khaaŋ^{5} ape (= khaaŋ^{6}; clf. thua^{4})
khaaŋ^{6} ape (= khaaŋ^{5}; clf. thua^{4})
khaaŋ^{6} to be stuck
  praa^{1} khaaŋ^{6} to stare (with amazement)
khwaaŋ^{2} wide (< Siamese)
ɣaaŋ^{4} chin
ɣaaŋ^{4} jaw (= haam^{4})
  ɣaaŋ^{4} thuum^{4} swollen jaws; mumps
caaŋ^{3} to hire
  lɯk^{6} caaŋ^{3} worker, employee (= lɯk^{6} lɛɛŋ^{3} < Lao)
caaŋ^{6} to stand with legs apart
daaŋ^{1} in, inside, into, at, during (= fast speech form daŋ^{1})
daaŋ^{3} mushroom
  daaŋ^{3} ka^{6} tɛl^{6} kind of small mushroom
  daaŋ^{3} la^{6} ŋook^{5} kind of edible mushroom
  daaŋ^{3} het^{4} phɔʔ^{4} kind of mushroom
daaŋ^{3} *in* ka^{6} daaŋ^{3} stiff, motionless, paralyzed
daaŋ^{6} spotted, many colored
taaŋ^{1} money (< Siamese sa^{2} taaŋ^{1})
taaŋ^{1} to substitute
taaŋ^{1} tiʔ^{4} to designate
taaŋ^{1} ɲɛn^{4} the sun (= fast speech form taŋ^{1} ɲɛn^{4})
taaŋ^{3} earring (= Saek taaŋ^{6}, voŋ^{4} vɛɛn^{2}; = tum^{3} huu^{1} < Siamese)
taaŋ^{6} earring (= Saek taaŋ^{3}, voŋ^{4} vɛɛn^{2}; = tum^{3} huu^{1} < Siamese)
taaŋ^{6} to differ, various, strange
taaŋ^{6} packsaddle (< Siamese)
traaŋ^{1} middle (YG, = OG tlaaŋ^{1})
tlaaŋ^{1} middle (OG, = YG traaŋ^{1})
thaaŋ^{2} to clear (e.g., fields)
thaaŋ^{3} *in* kap^{4} thaaŋ^{3} legendary frog that causes eclipses
thaaŋ^{4} road, way, path; side, direction
thaaŋ^{6} to spread (e.g., the legs) apart
thaaŋ^{6} *in* ɲuu^{4} thaaŋ^{6} happy
naaŋ^{4} lady
naaŋ^{4} bamboo shoot
naaŋ^{5} a net; spiderweb
naaŋ^{5} *in* may^{6} thɯɯ^{5} naaŋ^{5} chopsticks (= thuu^{5}, may^{6} ta^{6} khiap^{2})
baaŋ^{1} *in* taʔ^{6} baaŋ^{1} the chest (= tam^{1} ʔaaŋ^{1})
paaŋ^{1} time, period
paaŋ^{1} marian plum (= phaaŋ^{1}; clf. maak^{6})

paaŋ^{1} *in* ka^{6} paaŋ^{1} half a bamboo used as a water pipe, empty can used as a container, lid of an empty oil drum
paaŋ^{3} spleen
paaŋ^{6} flying squirrel (clf. thua^{4})
praaŋ^{1} fragrant (YG, = OG plaaŋ^{1})
praaŋ^{1} jackfruit (YG, = OG plaaŋ^{1}; clf. maak^{6})
praaŋ^{1} *in* phrak^{4} praaŋ^{1} kind of plant called mɛɛŋ^{1} lak^{4} in Siamese
plaaŋ^{1} fragrant (OG, = YG praaŋ^{1})
plaaŋ^{1} jackfruit (OG, = YG praaŋ^{1}; clf. maak^{6})
phaaŋ^{1} marian plum (= paaŋ^{1}; clf. maak^{6})
maaŋ^{4} spirit, ghost; corpse
  paa^{6} reew^{5} maaŋ^{4} cemetery
  maaŋ^{4} phrɔɔŋ^{4} kind of spirit called phii^{5} pɔɔp^{2} in Siamese
yaaŋ^{1} rubber, gum; fibers of lotus stem
yaaŋ^{4} resin
yaaŋ^{4} kind of tree
ɲaaŋ^{1} areca
ɲaaŋ^{5} to walk
raaŋ^{1} *in* rɤɤ^{3} raaŋ^{1} irritated, annoyed
raaŋ^{2} will, about to (= raaŋ^{3})
raaŋ^{3} will, about to (= raaŋ^{2})
raaŋ^{4} to drive, chase
raaŋ^{6} to abandon, desert; to divorce
laaŋ^{1} kind of potato
laaŋ^{4} some (= fast speech form laŋ^{4})
laaŋ^{4} luck
laaŋ^{4} bɛɛn^{1} a skin disease called khii^{3} klɯan^{1} in Siamese
laaŋ^{4} *in* ta^{6} laaŋ^{4} jail
laaŋ^{6} to clear, clean up (out of doors)
lwaaŋ^{1} kind of potato (OG, = YG luaŋ^{1})
vaaŋ^{1} to lay down, set down
vaaŋ^{1} thin (not thick)
vaaŋ^{2} to lie athwart, to block, to obstruct
vaaŋ^{3} spiderweb
vaaŋ^{4} yellow
vaaŋ^{5} to lay (a cloth) across
vaaŋ^{6} between
vaaŋ^{6} *in* sa^{6} vaaŋ^{6} comfortable, comfortably
saaŋ^{1} granary
saaŋ^{2} high, tall
saaŋ^{2} on, on top (of), above
saaŋ^{3} to build, construct
  nam^{6} saaŋ^{3} a well

saaŋ^{5} an artisan, expert; skilled
saaŋ^{6} elephant (clf. thua^{4})
haaŋ^{2} to reheat, warm up (food)
haaŋ^{4} trough, gutter, water pipe
haaŋ^{4} vii^{4} live coals of a fire
haaŋ^{4} *in* ɲɛn^{4} haaŋ^{4} kind of ancient money
hwaaŋ^{3} worried (OG, = YG huaŋ^{3})

-ɔŋ

ʔɔŋ^{3} part of yoke under the neck
ŋɔŋ^{1} erect (of the penis)
cɔŋ^{1} crippled (of the arm)
cɔŋ^{6} to send; to see (someone) off, accompany
dɔŋ^{1} big forest
dɔŋ^{1} sa^{6} mɔɔ^{4} name of a Saek village in Thailand
(= doŋ^{1} su^{6} mɔɔ^{4}, doŋ^{1} sa^{6} mɔɔ^{4}, dɔɔn^{1} suʔ^{6} mɔɔ^{4})
tɔŋ^{3} must, have to (fast speech form, = tɔɔŋ^{3} < Siamese)
tɔŋ^{3} to box
thɔŋ^{2} a shoulder bag
thɔŋ^{5} area of fields
pɔŋ^{1} *in* ka^{6} pɔŋ^{1} can, tin
pɔŋ^{3} shadow
pɔŋ^{3} *in* tum^{6} pɔŋ^{3} a toy balloon
plɔŋ^{1} to lower, put down, take down
phrɔŋ^{5} not full, half empty, partly gone (fast speech form, = phrɔɔŋ^{5})
yɔŋ^{4} to stand
lɔŋ^{2} to forget
lɔŋ^{4} to descend, go down, down
lɔŋ^{4} *in* tɔk^{4} lɔŋ^{4} to agree
lɔŋ^{6} to be pierced through
vɔŋ^{5} a cradle; a swing for children
vɔŋ^{6} caterpillar (clf. thua^{4})

-ɔɔŋ

ʔɔɔŋ^{1} *in* plaa^{1} pha^{6} ʔɔɔŋ^{1} water tortoise (= plaa^{1} via^{3}; clf. thua^{4})
ʔɔɔŋ^{1} *in* phɔɔ^{5} ʔɔɔŋ^{1} old man, old fellow
ʔɔɔŋ^{1} *in* luŋ^{5} tha^{6} nii^{4} ʔɔɔŋ^{1} kind of banana

kɔɔŋ^{1} a heap, pile; to heap up, pile up

kɔɔŋ^{3} kɛɛw^{3} bottle

kɔɔŋ^{5} ɣeeŋ^{5} the foot 'goes to sleep'

kɔɔŋ^{6} to pull down (a branch)

khɔɔŋ^{2} the Mekong River

khɔɔŋ^{2} *see* ʔaat^{6} saa^{1} maat^{5}

khɔɔŋ^{4} to wait, hope, expect

khɔɔŋ^{4} *in* khɔɔp^{5} khɔɔŋ^{4} to rule, govern

khɔɔŋ^{4} *in* ta^{6} khɔɔŋ^{4} ditch

khɔɔŋ^{4} *in* pok^{4} khɔɔŋ^{4} to govern

khɔɔŋ^{4} *in* hiit^{5} thɯk^{6} khɔɔŋ^{4} traditions

khɔɔŋ^{6} gong

  cuum^{1} khɔɔŋ^{6} ankle bone

ɣɔɔŋ^{6} to lasso; to put over the head

ŋɔɔŋ^{6} *in* nɔɔy^{3} ŋɔɔŋ^{6} to be unable to speak

cɔɔŋ^{1} hɔɔŋ^{1} arrogant

cɔɔŋ^{6} to pull, hold firm by pulling

dɔɔŋ^{1} to pickle (< Siamese; = Saek bɔɔŋ^{1})

tɔɔŋ^{3} must, have to (< Siamese, = fast speech form tɔŋ^{3})

tɔɔŋ^{3} the santol fruit (clf. maak^{6})

trɔɔŋ^{1} drum (YG, = OG tlɔɔŋ^{1})

trɔɔŋ^{1} related by the marriage of children

  kin^{1} trɔɔŋ^{1} to get married; to have a wedding feast

trɔɔŋ^{4} eye (YG, = OG tlɔɔŋ^{4})

tlɔɔŋ^{1} drum (OG, = YG trɔɔŋ^{1})

tlɔɔŋ^{4} eye (OG, = YG trɔɔŋ^{4})

tlɔɔŋ^{6} to put around (the neck) (= thrɔɔŋ^{6}, thlɔɔŋ^{6})

  tlɔɔŋ^{6} ɣɔɔ^{4} to put (a scarf, necklace, etc.) around the neck (= thrɔɔŋ^{6} ɣɔɔ^{4}, thlɔɔŋ^{6} ɣɔɔ^{4})

thɔɔŋ^{4} brass, bronze, copper, gold (in certain expressions)

thɔɔŋ^{6} to admonish

thɔɔŋ^{6} to greet

thrɔɔŋ^{6} to put around (the neck) (YG, = OG thlɔɔŋ^{6}; tlɔɔŋ^{6})

  thrɔɔŋ^{6} ɣɔɔ^{4} to put (a scarf, necklace, etc.) around the neck (YG, = OG thlɔɔŋ^{6} ɣɔɔ^{4}; tlɔɔŋ^{6} ɣɔɔ^{4})

thlɔɔŋ^{6} to put around (the neck) (OG, = YG thrɔɔŋ^{6}; tlɔɔŋ^{6})

  thlɔɔŋ^{6} ɣɔɔ^{4} to put (a scarf, necklace, etc.) around the neck (OG, = YG thrɔɔŋ^{6} ɣɔɔ^{4}; tlɔɔŋ^{6} ɣɔɔ^{4})

nɔɔŋ^{1} khaay^{4} Nong Khai, a city in Northeast Thailand

nɔɔŋ^{2} lake

nɔɔŋ^{2} pus

nɔɔŋ^{4} noise, noisy
  nɔɔŋ^{4} nɛn^{4} noisy
bɔɔŋ^{1} to pickle (= dɔɔŋ^{1} < Siamese)
bɔɔŋ^{1} *in* ka^{6} bɔɔŋ^{1} torch
bɔɔŋ^{3} cut section of bamboo
bɔɔŋ^{6} to pierce a hole
bɔɔŋ^{6} *in* pak^{4} tuu^{1} bɔɔŋ^{6} window
pɔɔŋ^{3} praa^{1} to shade the eyes
prɔɔŋ^{3} *in* ca^{6} prɔɔŋ^{3} rice husks (YG, = OG ca^{6} plɔɔŋ^{3})
prɔɔŋ^{6} hollow tube, as of bamboo (YG, = OG plɔɔŋ^{6})
prɔɔŋ^{6} *in* priaŋ^{1} prɔɔŋ^{6} cucumber (YG, = OG priaŋ^{1} plɔɔŋ^{6})
plɔɔŋ^{3} *in* ca^{6} plɔɔŋ^{3} rice husks (OG, = YG ca^{6} prɔɔŋ^{3})
plɔɔŋ^{6} hollow tube, as of bamboo (OG, = YG prɔɔŋ^{6})
plɔɔŋ^{6} *in* priaŋ^{1} plɔɔŋ^{6} cucumber (OG, = YG priaŋ^{1} prɔɔŋ^{6})
phɔɔŋ^{2} to put rice into a bamboo tube to cook
phɔɔŋ^{3} to bring a lawsuit (= fɔɔŋ^{3})
phɔɔŋ^{4} blistered (= phooŋ^{4})
phɔɔŋ^{4} waves in water
phɔɔŋ^{4} foam, bubbles (< Lao)
phɔɔŋ^{4} *in* sii^{1} phɔɔŋ^{4} face powder
phrɔɔŋ^{4} *in* maaŋ^{4} phrɔɔŋ^{4} kind of spirit called phii^{5} pɔɔp^{2} in Siamese
phrɔɔŋ^{5} not full, half empty, partly gone (= fast speech form phrɔŋ^{5})
yɔɔŋ^{1} to take, lead
yɔɔŋ^{3} *in* naŋ^{5} yɔɔŋ^{3} yɔɔ^{6} to squat down (= naŋ^{5} yɔɔŋ^{3} yɔɔ^{3})
ɲɔɔŋ^{1} mussed, disheveled (of hair)
ɲɔɔŋ^{5} to crumple up (paper) (= ɲɔɔŋ^{6})
ɲɔɔŋ^{5} to squeeze clothes when washing them (= ɲɔɔŋ^{6})
ɲɔɔŋ^{6} to crumple up (paper) (= ɲɔɔŋ^{5})
ɲɔɔŋ^{6} to squeeze clothes when washing them (= ɲɔɔŋ^{5})
rɔɔŋ^{2} big leaf, especially a banana leaf
rɔɔŋ^{4} nest of a bird (= rɔɔk^{5})
rɔɔŋ^{4} a beam
rɔɔŋ^{4} vaa^{6} shoulder
rɔɔŋ^{4} *in* ŋuak^{5} rɔɔŋ^{4} rainbow
rɔɔŋ^{4} *in* rap^{6} rɔɔŋ^{4} to receive; to sustain (= lap^{6} lɔɔŋ^{4})
rɔɔŋ^{5} light, bright; dawn; clear
lɔɔŋ^{1} loose-fitting
lɔɔŋ^{3} to sing
lɔɔŋ^{4} to try
lɔɔŋ^{4} *in* lap^{6} lɔɔŋ^{4} to receive; to sustain (= rap^{6} rɔɔŋ^{4})
lɔɔŋ^{5} to go downstream

lɔɔŋ^{6} *in* laay^{4} lɔɔŋ^{6} striped
vɔɔŋ^{1} to roof
vɔɔŋ^{4} couplet used with saaŋ^{2} 'tall, high (of people, elephants, etc.)'
thaŋ^{4} saaŋ^{2} thaŋ^{4} vɔɔŋ^{4} tall (of elephants, people)
sɔɔŋ^{2} two
sɔɔŋ^{4} envelope
sɔɔŋ^{4} couplet used with baan^{3} 'house' and luaŋ^{5} 'space under a house'
rim^{2} luaŋ^{5} rim^{2} sɔɔŋ^{4} filling the space under the house
sɔɔŋ^{4} name of abandoned Saek town in Vietnam
sɔɔŋ^{5} hole; pit; crack; chasm
sɔɔŋ^{6} to look
fɔɔŋ^{3} to bring a lawsuit (= phɔɔŋ^{3})
hɔɔŋ^{1} *in* cɔɔŋ^{1} hɔɔŋ^{1} arrogant
hɔɔŋ^{2} things, possessions
hɔɔŋ^{2} of, belonging to
hɔɔŋ^{6} a room

-il

lil^{5} pangolin (OG, = YG lin^{5}; also recorded as lil^{6} and lin^{6}; nin^{6}; clf. thua^{4})
lil^{6} pangolin (OG, = YG lin^{6}; also recorded as lil^{5} and lin^{5}; nin^{6}; clf. thua^{4})

-iil

ŋiil^{6} turmeric (OG, = YG ŋiin^{6})
thiil^{4} wasp (OG, = YG thiin^{4}; clf. thua^{4})
riil^{2} stone (OG, = YG riin^{2})
ŋɤɤp^{5} riil^{2} blocks of stone on a mountain (OG, = YG ŋɤɤp^{5} riin^{2})
viil^{6} having a piece torn off the corner or edge

-ial

khial^{4} cockscomb (OG, = YG khian^{4})
tial^{3} *in* tuŋ^{6} tial^{3} cricket (OG, = YG tuŋ^{6} tian^{3}; clf. thua^{4})
plial^{1} ɣaa^{4} a flat of woven thatchgrass for roofing (OG, = YG plian^{1} ɣaa^{4})

-ɯl

dɯl^{6} a pond or marsh in the forest with soft clay into which one sinks (OG, = YG dɯn^{6})
bɯl^{1} to fly (OG, = YG bɯn^{1})
vɯl^{1} firewood (OG, = YG vɯn^{1})

-ɯɯl

mlɯɯl^{5} slippery (OG, = YG mlɯɯn^{5})

-ul

kul^{3} kul^{3} descriptive of the earth rising with a heaving motion
pul^{1} body hair (OG, = YG pun^{1})
mul^{4} dust; crushed or smashed to small pieces (OG, = YG mun^{4}; = phun^{5} < Lao)
mul^{5} flesh on the seeds of jackfruit
mul^{6} to force one's way into or through (OG, = YG mun^{6})

-uul

muul^{6} lime (eaten with betel or used for plaster, etc.) (OG, = YG muun^{6})
ruul^{6} hot (OG, = YG ruun^{6})

-ual

tual^{3} top for spinning (OG, = YG tuan^{3}; clf. maak^{6})
trual^{1} worm (OG, = YG truan^{1}; clf. thua^{4})
thual^{6} forest (OG, = YG thuan^{6})
yual^{5} to hand to someone (OG, = YG yuan^{5})
ɲual^{6} gnat, gadfly (OG, = YG ɲuan^{6}; clf. thua^{4})
sual^{6} part; while; as for (OG, = YG suan^{6})

-eel

keel^{6} hard, solid, firm (OG, = YG keen^{6})
kheel^{6} a splinter (OG, = YG kheen^{6})

theel^{5} *in* vaay^{2} theel^{5} broom (OG, = YG vaa^{2} theen^{5})
reel^{4} *in* ʔee^{5} kaʔ^{6} reel^{4} ʔee^{5} sound of rooster crowing
(OG, = OG ʔek^{4} kaʔ^{6} reel^{4} ʔeek^{4}, YG ʔee^{5} kaʔ^{6} reen^{4} ʔee^{5},
YG ʔek^{4} kaʔ^{6} reen^{4} ʔeek^{4})
heel^{3} pillow (OG, = YG heen^{3})

-ool

mool^{4} base of a plant (OG, = YG moon^{4})
yool^{6} trellis (as for cucumbers) (OG, = YG yoon^{6})
ɲool^{6} *in* pa^{6} ɲool^{6} small bits of rubbish

-ɛl

tɛl^{6} *in* daaŋ^{3} ka^{6} tɛl^{6} kind of small mushroom
tlɛl^{1} to snore (OG, = YG trɛn^{1})
thɛl^{6} loud (noise) (OG, = YG thɛn^{6})
blɛl^{3} to protrude (as a body part or something in the pocket) (OG, = YG blɛn^{3})
mlɛl^{4} body louse (OG, = YG mlɛn^{4}; clf. thua^{4})
ɲɛl^{2} civet cat (OG, = YG ɲɛn^{2}; clf. thua^{4})
ɲɛl^{2} housefly (OG, = YG ɲɛn^{2}; clf. thua^{4})
sɛl^{3} classifier for long thin objects (OG, = YG sɛn^{3})
sɛl^{6} to shake (e.g., a bottle, fruit from a tree)

-ɛɛl

vɛɛl^{6} left (hand) (OG, = YG vɛɛn^{6})

-al

ʔal^{1} classifier for things (OG, = YG ʔan^{1})
khal^{4} classifier for spoons, pencils, saws (OG, = YG khan^{4})
khal^{6} to squeeze juice out (OG, = YG khan^{6})
ɣal^{4} dike between fields, bank of a river
ɣal^{4} ɣaak^{5} toad (clf. thua^{4})
ɣal^{4} *in* ɣum^{4} ɣal^{4} to itch (= YG ɣum^{4} ɣan^{4})
bal^{1} dirt, earth, ground (OG, = YG ban^{1})

bal^{1} bluŋ^{6} mud (OG, = YG ban^{1} buŋ^{6})
peen^{6} bal^{1} the earth (OG, = YG peen^{6} ban^{1})
pal^{1} to spin (cotton) (OG, = YG pan^{1}; = pan^{6})
phal^{4} to be, become; to have a disease (OG, = YG phan^{4})
val^{1} to slash, cut (OG, = YG van^{1})
val^{3} to twist, wring; to form (rice) into a ball (OG, = YG pan^{3})
hal^{2} to crow (OG, = YG han^{2})

-aal

khaal^{2} to fasten (a button) (OG, = YG khaan^{2})
ŋaal^{3} the medicinal plant called waan^{3} in Siamese (OG, = YG ŋaan^{3})
caal^{3} the *Pandanus* tree (OG, = YG caan^{3}; = tɤɤy^{1})
baal^{6} nicked, chipped (OG, = YG baan^{6})
paal^{3} to dam up water (OG, = YG paan^{3})
yaal^{4} slack (OG, = YG yaan^{4})
laal^{6} kind of tree called ben^{1} ca^{2} phan^{1} in Siamese
vaal^{2} sweet (OG, = YG vaan^{2})
vaal^{4} kind of deer (OG, = YG vaan^{4}; clf. thua^{4})
vaal^{6} to throw, cast, sow (OG, = YG vaan^{6})
saal^{2} *in* ɣaw^{6} saal^{2} white rice
haal^{1} kind of poisonous caterpillar (OG, = YG haan^{1}; = OG haal^{2}, YG haan^{2}; clf. thua^{4})
haal^{2} kind of poisonous caterpillar (OG, = YG haan^{2}; = OG haal^{1}, YG haan^{1}; clf. thua^{4})

-ɔl

kɔl^{6} stump, stubble (OG, = YG kɔn^{6})

-ɔɔl

khɔɔl^{4} to carry on one end of a pole over the shoulder (OG, = YG khɔɔn^{4})
khɔɔl^{5} to slip loose, fall off, fall out (OG = YG khɔɔn^{5})
ɣɔɔl^{6} hammer, club (OG, = YG ɣɔɔn^{6})
tɔɔl^{6} to scrape off (fish scales) (OG, = YG tɔɔn^{6}; cf. trɛk^{4}, tlɛk^{4})
nɔɔl^{2} worm (OG, = YG nɔɔn^{2}; clf. thua^{4})
yɔɔl^{5} to hide (OG, = YG yɔɔn^{5})
ɲɔɔl^{4} to dig out (the ear) (OG, = YG ɲɔɔn^{4})

sɔɔl^{2} to teach (OG, = YG sɔɔn^{2})
sɔɔl^{3} kind of fish trap (OG, = YG sɔɔn^{3})

-ip

kip^{4} to pick up, to gather, put away
kip^{4} bobby pin
cip^{4} *in* nɔk^{6} ka^{6} cip^{4} kind of bird
tip^{4} round basket with cover for glutinous rice
thip^{6} divine
thrip^{4} *in* ca^{6} thrip^{4} centipede (clf. thua^{4})
pip^{4} large can for water (= pip^{6})
pip^{6} large can for water (= pip^{4})
yip^{4} to pick up with the fingers
ɲip^{4} to close (the eyes), blink (the eyes)
  ɲip^{4} kɛɛp^{6} to close the eyes a moment and then open them
ɲip^{6} to sew
rip^{4} raw, unripe
  hun^{4} rip^{4} man who's never been a monk
rip^{4} a tick (clf. thua^{4})
rip^{6} to confiscate
lip^{4} to bury in the ground
lip^{4} to disappear
lip^{4} very (far)
lip^{4} lip^{4} (to walk or ride) fast
sip^{4} ʔiit^{4} sip^{4} ʔɔɔy^{5} a little
sip^{6} a salad of bamboo shoots
sip^{6} ten
  rɔk^{4} sip^{6} sixty
  rɔk^{4} sip^{6} haa^{3} sixty-five
  sip^{6} saam^{2} thirteen

-iip

ŋiip^{5} a nap
tiip^{6} constricted, pressed together
triip^{6} petal; section of orange or garlic (YG, = OG tliip^{6})
triip^{6} Lao unit of money (YG, = OG tliip^{6})
tliip^{6} petal; section of orange or garlic (OG, = YG triip^{6})
tliip^{6} Lao unit of money (OG, = YG triip^{6})
thiip^{5} continent; place

thiip^{5} *in* pa^{6} thiip^{5} incense stick
thiip^{6} to pedal (a bicycle)
niip^{6} to pinch, as a crab's claw (< Lao; = Saek khɛɛp^{5})
niip^{6} to carry under the arm (< Lao; = Saek khɛɛp^{5})
niip^{6} to pick up with chopsticks (< Lao; = Saek khɛɛp^{5})
  maak^{5} niip^{6} tweezers
biip^{6} to squeeze; to massage
liip^{5} fingernail, toenail; hoof
liip^{5} (rice) without full kernel
liip^{6} to fold up neatly; to arrange in tidy order
siip^{5} *in* ʔaa^{1} siip^{5} occupation
hiip^{6} box, trunk, suitcase

-iap

khiap^{2} custard apple (clf. maak^{6}; cf. lot^{6})
khiap^{2} *in* ɣaw^{6} khiap^{2} crisp rice
khiap^{2} *in* may^{6} ta^{6} khiap^{2} chopsticks (= thuu^{5}, may^{6} thɯɯ^{5} naaŋ^{5})
thiap^{5} to compare
biap^{6} loufah gourd (clf. maak^{6})
piap^{6} advantage
phiap^{5} (full) to the brim
yiap^{6} to step on, tread on
yiap^{6} to run over (of a car)
ɲiap^{6} coarse, tough (of meat, food)
liap^{5} to make a circuit, go around
liap^{5} of good quality
  liap^{5} lɔɔy^{5} proper
siap^{6} to impale

-ɯp

kɯp^{4} to gang up, get together in a gang (slang)
khɯp^{6} khɯp^{6} sound of a cart in motion
khɯp^{6} khɯp^{6} sound of drunkards in a group at a distance
thɯp^{6} to pile a lot of felled trees in a road to block it
pɯp^{6} to blaze up suddenly (= phɯp^{6})
  pɯp^{6} pap^{6} to blaze up suddenly
pɯp^{6} pup^{6} to get up suddenly from a sitting or lying position (= pup^{6} pap^{6})
phɯp^{6} to blaze up suddenly (= pɯp^{6})

lɯp^{4} to bury
lɯp^{6} to erase, rub out

-ɯɯp

khɯɯp^{5} a finger span
khɯɯp^{5} to measure as a measuring worm does
thɯɯp^{5} to stomp
lɯɯp^{6} a layer, stratum (as of rocks on a mountain) (= lɤɤp^{6})
sɯɯp^{6} to trace a secret, investigate

-ɯap

ʔɯap^{6} to salt (fish, meat)
kɯap^{6} almost, nearly
khɯap^{5} to enamel, enameled
phɯap^{5} action of many people getting up all at once
lɯap^{6} gadfly (clf. thua^{4})

-up

ʔup^{4} to brood, incubate
ʔup^{4} pa^{6} thaak^{6} to wait on, serve
ʔup^{6} sound of beating, of fruit falling (= tup^{6})
ŋup^{4} ŋup^{4} action of trudging along not paying attention
cup^{4} to dip in water
cup^{4} to dye
cup^{6} to be stuck in the flesh (of a knife)
tup^{4} shack, hut, temporary shelter
tup^{6} sound of beating, of fruit falling (= ʔup^{6})
thrup^{6} to pounce upon
pup^{6} action of getting up suddenly
pup^{6} pap^{6} to get up suddenly from a sitting or lying position (= pɯp^{6} pup^{6})
yup^{4} to pick up with the tips of all five fingers
ɲup^{6} to break, cancel (e.g., a contract)
lup^{4} to duck, dodge
lup^{4} thɯn^{4} to lose one's investments
sup^{4} to place by inserting or impaling
sup^{4} to put on (a hat, a ring)

hup^{4} to close (the mouth)

hup^{4} to carry off one's belongings

-uup

cuup^{6} to kiss

duup^{6} to smoke (tobacco)

tuup^{2} having a long muzzle (of a dog) (= tuup^{6})

tuup^{2} bruised and swollen from a blow (of the face) (= tuup^{6})

tuup^{6} having a long muzzle (of a dog) (= tuup^{2})

tuup^{6} bruised and swollen from a blow (of the face) (= tuup^{2})

thuup^{5} a clump of bamboo

thuup^{5} an incense stick

muup^{2} to crouch down (= muup^{6})

muup^{6} to crouch down (= muup^{2})

ruup^{5} a picture

luup^{5} to stroke, wipe

luup^{6} to make a dash

suup^{6} to pump (water)

-uap

ʔuap^{5} a frog (in talking to children)

khuap^{6} year

cuap^{5} sound of frog jumping into the water

buap^{5} sound of chewing

buap^{5} sound of cars colliding

phuap^{5} *in* lam^{6} phuap^{5} to fall down, fall flat (= lam^{6} phuak^{5})

suap^{5} to eat with a snapping action, as a dog, tiger, or fish

-ep

sep^{6} figure, shape (of a person) (< English)

thep^{6} recording tape (< English)

-eep

ɣeep^{5} narrow; small; tight-fitting

theep^{5} *in* kuŋ^{1} theep^{5} Bangkok, capital of Thailand

meep^{2} *in* nuun^{4} meep^{2} to lie flat on one's face
seep^{6} to smart (of a wound)
seep^{6} to play (music)

-ɤp

tɤp^{6} tɤp^{6} sound of people walking barefoot

-ɤɤp

kɤɤp^{6} shoe, shoes
  kɤɤp^{6} tɛʔ^{6} sandals
khɤɤp^{6} afraid when looking down from a height
ŋɤɤp^{5} gill slit of a fish
ŋɤɤp^{5} riil^{2} blocks of stone on a mountain (OG, = YG ŋɤɤp^{5} riin^{2})
cɤɤp^{6} lightning
thɤɤp^{5} a stack of small dry sticks
lɤɤp^{6} a layer, stratum (as of rocks on a mountain) (= lɯɯp^{6})

-op

ʔop^{4} *in* nam^{6} ʔop^{4} perfume
kop^{4} a plane (the tool)
khop^{4} to bite (< Lao)
khop^{6} to associate with
khop^{6} complete, all
ŋop^{4} *in* sa^{6} ŋop^{4} quiet
cop^{4} good
  cop^{4} cɯa^{1} good, proper
top^{4} *in* phrak^{4} top^{4} name of an edible plant called phak^{2} top^{2} in Siamese
top^{6} sound of string breaking when pulled
thop^{4} sound of switch striking a child
thop^{6} to fold double
lop^{6} to fight, make war

-oop

ʔoop^{6} to put the arms around something to measure circumference

ʔoop^{6} to cut a cutting and plant it in the ground

ʔoop^{6} to put earth around the base of a plant

koop^{6} to curl up (of a leaf)

khoop^{5} sound of leaves or fruit falling

tloop^{5} to cover with a lid (= throop^{5})

throop^{5} to cover with a lid (= tloop^{5})

boop^{5} crunching sound

poop^{6} bubbles, foam, lather

ɲoop^{5} to sit down, lower oneself to a sitting position

ɲoop^{5} to shrivel from heat (of leaves)

ɲoop^{5} ɲoop^{5} ɲaap^{5} ɲaap^{5} descriptive of a house shaking

roop^{5} bundle, sheaf, faggot

roop^{5} *in* ta^{6} roop^{5} eggshell; matchbox; sheath

roop^{6} to carry large things

roop^{6} *in* yu^{4} roop^{6} Europe

-ɛp

cɛp^{6} sound of chewing noisily

tɛp^{6} a snap fastener

nɛp^{4} to tuck (something) into the waist, into the wall, or behind the ear (= nɛɛp^{5})

-ɛɛp

kɛɛp^{6} *in* ɲip^{4} kɛɛp^{6} to close the eyes for a moment and then open them

khɛɛp^{5} to pinch, as a crab's claw (Saek; = niip^{6} < Lao)

khɛɛp^{5} to carry under the arm (Saek; = niip^{6} < Lao)

khɛɛp^{5} to pick up with chopsticks (Saek; = niip^{6} < Lao)

cɛɛp^{6} close, tight (as of boards joined together)

nɛɛp^{5} to tuck into the wall (= nɛp^{4})

bɛɛp^{6} way, manner

bɛɛp^{6} rian^{4} textbook

pɛɛp^{6} *in* thua^{5} pɛɛp^{6} kind of bean called thua^{2} pɛɛp^{2} in Siamese

phɛɛp^{6} *in* praay^{1} phɛɛp^{6} a cursing expression

lɛɛp^{6} to stack up or fold neatly

lɛɛp^{6} to stick (e.g., money) between things (e.g., books) stacked up
vɛɛp^{5} flat (of a tire)

-ap

kap^{4} with, and
kap^{4} frog (clf. thua^{4})
  kap^{4} thaaŋ^{3} legendary frog that causes eclipses
kap^{4} kɛɛ^{5} gecko (= kak^{4} kɛɛ^{5}; clf. thua^{4})
kap^{4} pheet^{5} to transform oneself
kap^{6} sudden, suddenly (of grabbing, seizing, embracing)
khap^{4} to drive a car
ɣap^{6} to bite
cap^{4} to catch; to seize, grasp; to take hold of
dap^{4} to go out (of a fire)
dap^{4} to extinguish (a light or fire)
dap^{4} to die
dap^{4} to destroy
dap^{4} *in* pa^{6} dap^{4} to decorate
tap^{4} liver
tap^{4} to slap; to clap (the hands)
tap^{4} a stack (of paper)
trap^{4} small box (YG, = OG tlap^{4})
tlap^{4} small box (OG, = YG trap^{4})
thap^{6} to pound, batter (= Siamese thup^{4})
thap^{6} to run over (= Siamese thap^{4})
thrap^{6} to fold up (e.g., clothes) (= phap^{6}, phlap^{6})
nap^{4} scab on a wound
nap^{4} nɤɤ^{4} fontanelle
nap^{6} to count
nap^{6} thɯɯ^{4} to revere
pap^{4} to fine, impose a fine
pap^{6} *in* pɯp^{6} pap^{6} to blaze up suddenly
pap^{6} *in* pup^{6} pap^{6} to get up suddenly from a sitting or lying position (= pɯp^{6} pup^{6})
phap^{6} to fold up (e.g., clothes) (= thrap^{6}, phlap^{6})
phlap^{6} to fold up (e.g., clothes) (= thrap^{6}, phap^{6})
map^{4} *in* kha^{6} map^{4} temples of the head
map^{6} *in* praay^{1} map^{6} to die
yap^{6} to chop up (e.g., papaya)
ɲap^{4} to shift, move
rap^{4} yaa^{4} a spit for roasting

rap^{6} to receive (= lap^{6})
lap^{4} dark
lap^{6} to sharpen
lap^{6} a cast-net
lap^{6} to receive (= rap^{6})
lap^{6} last day in a twenty-nine-day lunar month
sap^{4} to squeeze, force
sap^{4} to twist (strands to make rope)
sap^{4} to chop fine
sap^{4} to rap with the knuckles
sap^{4} phaʔ^{6} phiʔ^{4} every sort
sap^{6} beautiful
hap^{4} to sing

-aap

ʔaap^{6} to bathe
kaap^{6} husk, rind, (banana) peel
khaap^{5} to hold in the jaws
ɣaap^{5} a meal (= thraap^{5})
daap^{6} sword (< Lao; = Saek raaw^{2})
taap^{6} to patch (a garment)
thraap^{5} a meal (= ɣaap^{5})
thraap^{5} discarded snake skin
thraap^{5} corpse
naap^{5} close together
naap^{5} to subjugate, bring under control (= phaap^{6})
baap^{5} sound of fish jumping in water
baap^{6} sin
phaap^{6} to conquer, put down (= naap^{5})
ɲaap^{5} to sparkle (= ɲaap^{5} ɲaap^{5})
ɲaap^{5} slightly numb as from an insect bite (= ɲaap^{5} ɲaap^{5})
ɲaap^{5} descriptive of many people streaming along or chicks behind a hen (= ɲaap^{5} ɲaap^{5})
ɲaap^{5} *in* ɲoop^{5} ɲoop^{5} ɲaap^{5} ɲaap^{5} descriptive of a house shaking
raap^{6} to carry on the two ends of a shoulder pole
laap^{5} a dish made of chopped meat called laap^{3} in Siamese
laap^{5} wealth
laap^{6} *in* kuʔ^{4} laap^{6} rose
saap^{6} cockroach (clf. thua^{4})
haap^{6} haaw^{2} to yaw

-ɔɔp

kɔɔp^{6} frame (as of a picture)
khɔɔp^{5} to report (to), inform
khɔɔp^{5} khɔɔŋ^{4} to govern
khɔɔp^{5} cɯɯ^{1} thank you
khɔɔp^{6} edge, rim
cɔɔp^{6} to watch
tɔɔp^{6} to answer, reply
mɔɔp^{5} to give, hand over, turn over
mɔɔp^{5} to level, make smooth and level
rɔɔp^{5} around
lɔɔp^{6} *in* kha^{6} lɔɔp^{6} quilt, blanket, coverlet
hɔɔp^{6} to fly in circles (= huʔ^{4} hɔɔp^{6})

-it

ʔit^{4} tired
ʔit^{4} brick (= din^{1} cii^{6})
ʔit^{4} purple
ʔit^{4} saa^{1} to envy
ʔit^{4} saŋ^{4} gasoline (= ʔɛt^{4} saŋ^{4})
ʔit^{4} sa^{6} raʔ^{4} independent
khit^{6} *in* lak^{6} khit^{6} lak^{6} khay^{4} (to ask) indirectly
cit^{4} heart
cit^{6} *in* mit^{6} cit^{6} silent
tit^{4} fastened, attached
tit^{4} to weigh (= saŋ^{5})
  tit^{4} praa^{1} to weigh fish
thit^{4} cɯɯ^{1} to breathe (less frequent, = more frequent thɯt^{4} cɯɯ^{1})
thit^{6} *in* van^{4} ʔaa^{1} thit^{6} Sunday (= van^{4} ʔa^{6} thit^{6}, van^{4} thit^{6})
nit^{4} say^{1} character, personality, disposition
bit^{4} to twist
  phan^{4} bit^{4} to have dysentery (YG, = OG phal^{4} bit^{4})
  phal^{4} bit^{4} to have dysentery (OG, = YG phan^{4} bit^{4})
pit^{4} duck (clf. thua^{4})
pit^{4} *in* ram^{1} pit^{4} completely black
phit^{4} wrong, incorrect
phit^{4} caa^{1} la^{6} naa^{4} to consider (= phit^{6} caa^{1} la^{6} naa^{4}, phiʔ^{4} caa^{1} la^{6} naa^{4}, phiʔ^{6} caa^{1} la^{6} naa^{4})
phit^{6} poison

phit^{6} caa^{1} la^{6} naa^{4} to consider (= phit^{4} caa^{1} la^{6} naa^{4}, phiʔ^{4} caa^{1} la^{6} naa^{4}, phiʔ^{6} caa^{1} la^{6} naa^{4})
phit^{6} *in* thot^{6} sa^{6} phit^{6} laat^{5} sa^{6} tham^{4} the ten royal precepts
mit^{6} quiet
  mit^{6} cit^{6} silent
mit^{6} *in* nii^{4} mit^{6} to create (= ni^{6} mit^{6})
lit^{6} power
vit^{4} penis
vit^{4} tha^{6} yuʔ^{6} radio (= vit^{4} tha^{6} ɲuʔ^{6})
sit^{6} to shake something off
hit^{4} impetigo
hit^{6} to do, make

-iit

ʔiit^{4} a little
  sip^{4} ʔiit^{4} sip^{4} ʔɔɔy^{5} a little
ʔiit^{6} kind of very small fish
khiit^{6} to scratch, draw a line
diit^{6} to kick (of a horse, a spring) (YG, = OG bliit^{6})
bliit^{6} to kick (of a horse, a spring) (OG, = YG diit^{6})
bliit^{6} to snap the fingers (OG, = YG diit^{6})
miit^{5} knife (< Lao)
riit^{5} to hide oneself
riit^{5} ceremony, tradition
riit^{6} sunshine
liit^{5} to iron (clothes)
hiit^{5} customs, traditions
hiit^{5} to milk (a cow)
hiit^{5} to have an abortion

-iat

niat^{5} *in* pha^{6} niat^{5} a birdcage with a bird in it, used as a decoy
biat^{6} to oppress, crowd (= biat^{6} bian^{1})
piat^{6} to squirm as when dying
phiat^{5} to open up, uncover
viat^{5} wing
viat^{6} astringent in taste
siat^{5} vagina, female organ

-ɯt

khɯt^{6} to think
ŋɯt^{6} amazed, surprised
thɯt^{4} cɯɯ^{1} to breathe (more frequent, = less frequent thit^{4} cɯɯ^{1})
thɯt^{6} thɯt^{6} sound of gongs and drums
phɯt^{6} used as a couplet with mul^{4} 'small pieces'
  phal^{4} mul^{4} phal^{4} phɯt^{6} to become fine pieces
phɯt^{6} *in* ta^{6} phɯt^{6} ta^{6} phɯɯ^{4} all around
rɯt^{6} to pull
rɯt^{6} to snap or break when pulled

-ɯɯt

ʔɯɯt^{6} bloated, uncomfortable (of the stomach) (= Siamese thɔɔŋ^{4} ʔɯɯt^{2})
nɯɯt^{5} *in* la^{6} nɯŋ^{6} la^{6} nɯɯt^{5} in disorder
phɯɯt^{6} not smooth
hɯɯt^{6} tobacco

-ɯat

ŋɯat^{5} to hold up threateningly
thɯat^{6} a stopper of clay for a skyrocket
thɯat^{6} to paw the ground in anger when about to attack (of buffalo)
phɯat^{5} to spill, overflow, slop over
hɯat^{6} dry

-ut

khut^{6} to dig
tut^{4} *in* pii^{1} tut^{4} eleventh year in the Saek twelve-year cycle
nut^{6} *in* ma^{6} nut^{6} human being
but^{4} *in* thee^{4} va^{6} but^{4} angel, divine child
put^{6} *in* kaat^{6} put^{6} to break apart
phut^{6} Buddhist
phut^{6} thiʔ^{6} the Buddha
phut^{6} *in* van^{4} phut^{6} Wednesday
mut^{4} *in* sa^{6} mut^{4} ocean
mut^{6} *in* koo^{1}mut^{6} kind of flower

yut^{4} to stop
ɲut^{6} ti^{4} tham^{4} just (= ɲot^{6} ti^{4} tham^{4})
ɲut^{6} *in* phɯan^{4} ɲut^{6} to sway, as a house in the wind
sut^{4} most
sut^{4} end
sut^{6} set (of furniture)
hut^{4} to scoop up (rice)
hut^{4} to dig or scratch (the earth) with the hands
hut^{4} to search (e.g., in a box or trunk)

-uut

ʔuut^{6} very smoky
ʔuut^{6} hot and airless (of a room)
kuut^{6} caŋ^{1} curled up (of feet and hands in certain illnesses)
kuut^{6} *in* phrak^{4} kuut^{6} an edible fern
khuut^{5} to scratch as a cat does
khuut^{6} to scrape
duut^{6} to suck
truut^{6} a wart
thuut^{5} *in* ka^{6} thuut^{5} leprosy (= ruan^{5}; cf. ruan^{6})
thuut^{6} to remove (garments, shoes, etc.)
thruut^{5} to push
puut^{6} a bump (e.g., a knot in a tree)
pruut^{6} to spit (YG, = OG pluut^{6})
pluut^{6} to spit (OG, = YG pruut^{6})
phuut^{5} a part, portion (especially of fish or meat when cut)
phuut^{6} luk^{6} phuut^{6} naŋ^{5} to get up and sit down suddenly
muut^{5} to beat (e.g., an ox) to death
yuut^{5} to sip (a hot liquid)
ɲuut^{5} highest point, tip
ɲuut^{5} to have sexual intercourse (modern slang; cf. suut^{5}, sam^{2})
ruut^{5} to strip off (leaves)
ruut^{5} to move (e.g., a curtain along a rod)
ruut^{6} to roast
luut^{6} to slip loose, slip from the hand
luut^{6} spindle, spool
luut^{6} light bulb
suut^{5} to have sexual intercourse (modern slang; cf. ɲuut^{5}, sam^{2})

-uat

kuat^{6} to inspect
kuat^{6} to sweep (YG, = OG kwaat^{6})
khuat^{5} to carry on the shoulder
nuat^{5} lip salve used by betel chewers
buat^{6} to take orders as a novice or monk
  buat^{6} kee^{3} baʔ^{4} to become a monk to fulfill a promise
ruat^{6} bedbug (clf. thua^{4})
ruat^{6} vessel for steaming glutinous rice
luat^{5} blood
luat^{5} wire
luat^{5} overly full, as a container of water or other liquid (YG, = OG lwaat^{5})
luat^{5} *in* hit^{6} luat^{5} luat^{5} to do a hasty job of something
vuat^{6} the waist (=ʔɛɛw^{1})
  thaa^{6} khat^{4} vuat^{6} knife put in the waist at back
suat^{5} *in* khɯt^{6} suat^{5} to remember something which one had forgotten
suat^{5} *in* pii^{1} suat^{5} Year of the Rat, first year in the twelve-year cycle

-et

khet^{4} efficacious, effective (of a magic spell, of an official order)
det^{4} *in* ka^{6} det^{4} ka^{6} dɔɔ^{3} really, very (late, much)
phet^{4} spicy hot (< Siamese; cf. thaat^{5})
het^{4} mushroom (< Siamese, Lao)
  daaŋ^{3} het^{4} phɔʔ^{4} kind of mushroom

-eet

keet^{6} to hurt, pain, ache
kheet^{6} territory; boundary
deet^{6} power
teet^{6} name of an annual festival similar to Chinese New Year (Tet ?)
theet^{5} sermon
theet^{5} foreign *in* maa^{6} theet^{5} a foreign horse
theet^{5} *in* pa^{6} theet^{5} country
beet^{6} to lie down
peet^{6} eight
pheet^{5} *in* kap^{4} pheet^{5} to transform oneself
pheet^{6} spirit, ghost (= Siamese phii^{5} preet^{2})
ɲeet^{5} to stuff, push in

veet^{5} *in* pha^{6} veet^{5} su^{4} kam^{1} name of the gods' architect
veet^{6} *in* bun^{1} phaʔ^{6} veet^{6} name of a merit-making ceremony
seet^{5} to slice thin
seet^{6} fish hook
  tɯk^{4} seet^{6} to fish with hook and line
seet^{6} thii^{2} rich man
seet^{6} *in* phrak^{4} ka^{6} seet^{6} an edible plant called phak^{2} ka^{2}cheet^{2} in Siamese

-ɤɤt

kɤɤt^{6} to be born
cɤɤt^{6} to throw (e.g., a stone)
cɤɤt^{6} *in* bɯn^{1} cɤɤt^{6} to fly zigzag
dɤɤt^{6} *in* plaa^{1} ka^{6} dɤɤt^{6} kind of freshwater fish called plaa^{1} ka^{2}dii^{2} in Siamese
dɤɤt^{6} *in* sa^{6} dɤɤt^{6} to be startled
tɤɤt^{6} flat, flattened; crushed
thɤɤt^{6} chopping board
thrɤɤt^{5} to slip and fall (YG, = OG thlɤɤt^{5})
thlɤɤt^{5} to slip and fall (OG, = YG thrɤɤt^{5})
bɤɤt^{2} *in* la^{6} bɤɤt^{2} a bomb
bɤɤt^{6} to hold the head high proudly and arrogantly
pɤɤt^{6} to be tired of something
lɤɤt^{6} *in* phrak^{4} lɤɤt^{6} an edible plant called bay^{1} chaʔ^{4} phluu^{1} in Siamese

-ot

ʔot^{4} to go without (food, water); to endure
ʔot^{4} saʔ^{4} to persevere
kot^{4} *in* khan^{4} kot^{4} cloth umbrella
khot^{4} (to sleep) curled up
khot^{6} crooked, not straight
cot^{4} maay^{2} letter
thot^{6} to dam up (water)
thot^{6} sa^{6} phit^{6} laat^{5} sa^{6} tham^{4} the ten royal precepts
not^{4} *in* kam^{1} not^{4} limit, period (= kam^{1} not^{6})
not^{6} *in* kam^{1} not^{6} limit, period (= kam^{1} not^{4})
bot^{4} overcast (of the sky)
phot^{6} heat rash
ɲot^{6} rank

ɲot^{6} ti^{4} tham^{4} just (= ɲut^{6} ti^{4} tham^{4})
lot^{4} *in* plaa^{1} lot^{4} kind of fish called plaa^{1} lot^{2} in Siamese
lot^{6} car, bicycle, vehicle
lot^{6} custard apple (clf. maak^{6}; cf. khiap^{2})
hot^{4} to shrink
hot^{4} to sprinkle

-oot

koot^{6} a very large number (= Siamese koot^{2})
khoot^{5} family, clan
  caw^{3} khoot^{5} voŋ^{4} taa^{1} the elder who is an arranger at a wedding
doot^{6} to jump, leap
thoot^{5} guilt, punishment, penalty
  nak^{6} thoot^{5} a convict
poot^{6} (to come) in a flock
phoot^{5} too, too much
phoot^{6} to help, rescue, release (= Siamese proot^{2})
yoot^{6} to fall
yoot^{6} to fall when overripe (of fruit)
yoot^{6} to fall in, cave in (of the bank of a stream)
ɲoot^{5} a furlong (= Siamese yoot^{3})
ɲoot^{6} *in* pa^{6} ɲoot^{6} use
loot^{5} to shed the skin (of a snake)
loot^{5} and so, then (expresses finality, = Siamese lɤɤy^{1})
voot^{6} a bamboo toy whirled on the end of a string

-ɛt

ʔɛt^{4} saŋ^{4} gasoline (= ʔit^{4} saŋ^{4})
ʔɛt^{4} one *in* sip^{6} ʔɛt^{4} eleven
ʔɛt^{4} one *in* saaw^{4} ʔɛt^{4} twenty-one
ʔɛt^{4} one *in* rɔɔy^{6} ʔɛt^{4} 101
cɛt^{4} seven
dɛt^{4} phram^{2} to have a permanent wave
thɛt^{4} pay^{1} next
thɛt^{6} *in* ban^{1} thɛt^{6} ruler
nɛt^{4} to move the hips in sexual intercourse (= Siamese ka^{2} daw^{3})
nɛt^{6} pineapple (clf. maak^{6})
blɛt^{4} to bend or straighten as desired

prɛt^{4} to remove, take down (YG, = OG plɛt^{4})
prɛt^{4} to remove (a yoke) (YG, = OG plɛt^{4})
prɛt^{4} to undo (a button) (YG, = OG plɛt^{4})
plɛt^{4} to remove, take down (OG, = YG prɛt^{4})
plɛt^{4} to remove (a yoke) (OG, = YG prɛt^{4})
plɛt^{4} to undo (a button) (OG, = YG prɛt^{4})
mlɛt^{6} a grain (= mlɛk^{6})
rɛt^{4} to break wind
rɛt^{6} to tie or bind tightly
sɛt^{4} animal (= sat^{4}; clf. thua^{4})
sɛt^{4} *in* ka^{6} sɛt^{4} king (= ka^{6} sat^{4})
sɛt^{6} to wipe
sɛt^{6} to hurl down

-ɛɛt

ʔɛɛt^{5} to carry (a child) in a cloth on the back
ʔɛɛt^{6} instrument for removing seeds from cotton
khɛɛt^{6} unpleasantly pungent
phɛɛt^{5} to compare
phɛɛt^{6} siaŋ^{2} to roar (as an elephant)
phɛɛt^{6} *in* phaŋ^{1} phɛɛt^{6} twins
phɛɛt^{6} *in* ɲua^{3} phɛɛt^{6} kind of grass called yaa^{3} phrɛɛk^{3} in Siamese
rɛɛt^{5} rhinoceros (clf. thua^{4})
lɛɛt^{5} to paint, paint on, smear
vɛɛt^{5} short-handled sickle (= vɛɛk^{5}; clf. maak^{5}, maak^{6})
sɛɛt^{6} orange (color)

-at

ʔat^{4} sa^{6} cɛn^{1} strange, amazing
kat^{4} to bite
kat^{4} *in* nam^{6} man^{4} kat^{4} kerosene
khat^{4} unwilling, to object
khat^{4} to feel slightly feverish
khat^{4} to stop (e.g., the flow of blood)
  khat^{4} luat^{5} to stop the flow of blood
  lay^{4} khat^{4} pak^{4} tuu^{1} wooden bar for a door
khat^{4} *in* thaa^{6} khat^{4} vuat^{6} knife put in the waist at back

khat^{6} *in* khem^{1} khat^{6} belt (< Lao; = tɔɔy^{3} ʔɛɛw^{1}, trɔɔy^{3} ʔɛɛw^{1},
taay^{3} ʔɛɛw^{1}, saay^{3} ʔɛɛw^{1})
ŋat^{6} to pry
cat^{4} *in* ka^{6} cat^{4} ka^{6} caay^{1} scattered about
tat^{4} to cut
bat^{4} *in* pat^{4} ti^{4} bat^{4} to serve
bat^{4} *in* som^{1} bat^{4} property
pat^{4} ti^{4} bat^{4} to serve
pat^{4} sum^{4} to meet, have a meeting
phat^{2} and then, so, but
phat^{4} to polish
phat^{4} to stir fry, sauté
phat^{4} to ask for a delay
phat^{6} lum^{4} electric fan
phat^{6} *in* saa^{1} laʔ^{6} phat^{6} saa^{1} laʔ^{6} phaa^{4} every sort of thing
mat^{4} flea (clf. thua^{4})
mat^{6} tɤɤ^{5} say^{4} motorcycle
vat^{4} *in* caŋ^{1} vat^{4} province
vat^{4} *in* pra^{6} vat^{4} story, history
vat^{4} *in* phal^{4} vat^{4} to have a cold
vat^{6} monastery
sat^{4} animal (= sɛt^{4}; clf. thua^{4})
sat^{4} ta^{4} ʔaa^{1} kaat^{6} air, atmosphere
sat^{4} *in* ka^{6} sat^{4} king (= ka^{6} sɛt^{4})
hat^{4} to practice, learn
hat^{4} *in* van^{4} phaʔ^{6} hat^{4} Thursday

-aat

ʔaat^{6} saa^{1} maat^{5} name of a Saek village in Thailand (=ʔaa^{6} saa^{1},
ʔa^{6} saa^{1}, ʔaa^{1} saa^{1} maat^{5}, ʔaa^{1} sa^{6} maat^{5}, ʔa^{4} sa^{6} maat^{5},
ʔaat^{6} sa^{6} maat^{5}, old name ʔeek^{6} ʔaa^{1} saa^{1}, alternate name khɔɔŋ^{2})
ʔaat^{6} sa^{6} maat^{5} *see* ʔaat^{6} saa^{1} maat^{5}
kaat^{6} to break; broken, torn
kaat^{6} put^{6} to break apart
kaat^{6} *in* ʔaa^{1} kaat^{6} sky, air, atmosphere
kwaat^{6} to sweep (OG, = YG kuat^{6})
khaat^{5} to rake, a rake (= phia^{3})
daat^{6} to scorch, burn
daat^{6} *in* ka^{6} daat^{6} paper
daat^{6} *in* saʔ^{4} ʔaʔ^{6} noo^{4} daat^{6} name of a pool

thaat^5 spicy hot (cf. phet^4 < Siamese)
  maak^6 thaat^5 peppers
thaat^5 stupa, pagoda
thaat^5 *in* thuu^4 thaat^5 descriptive of dragging
naat^6 *in* kha^6 naat^6 size
baat^6 time, now, when
  baat^6 nii^6 now
baat^6 to wound
baat^6 monk's begging bowl
paat^4 thoo^4 exclamation (= thoo^4, paa^4 thoo^4)
paat^6 *in* nak^6 paat^6 scholar
phaat^5 *in* phin^4 phaat^5 music, orchestra
maat^5 *in* ʔa^4 sa^6 maat^5 *see* ʔaat^6 saa^1 maat^5
maat^5 *in* ʔaa^1 sa^6 maat^5 *see* ʔaat^6 saa^1 maat^5
maat^5 *in* ʔaa^1 saa^1 maat^5 *see* ʔaat^6 saa^1 maat^5
maat^5 *in* ʔaat^6 sa^6 maat^5 *see* ʔaat^6 saa^1 maat^5
maat^6 slightly damp
mlaat^5 insipid, flavorless
yaat^6 nam^6 to perform the rite after merit-making called
  truat^2 nam^4 in Siamese
raat^5 *in* vian^4 raat^5 very much, excessively (= vɛɛn^4 raat^5)
laat^5 kingdom
laat^5 sa^6 dɔɔn^1 people
laat^5 sa^6 tham^4 royal precepts
laat^5 sa^6 sii^2 lion
laat^5 sa^6 vaŋ^4 royal palace
laat^5 *in* kay^1 laat^5 name of a mythical mountain
laat^6 *in* ta^6 laat^6 market
lwaat^5 overly full, as a container of water or other liquid (OG, = YG luat^5)
saat^2 *in* phaa^1 saat^2 palace (= phaa^1 saat^6)
saat^5 existence; race
saat^5 body
saat^5 *in* taa^1 saat^5 of poor quality
saat^6 to splash out, scoop out (water)
saat^6 a festival at the end of the ninth lunar month
saat^6 sa^6 naa^2 religion
saat^6 *in* phaa^1 saat^6 palace (= phaa^1 saat^2)
haat^6 beach, sandbar
haat^6 to desire, want
haat^6 hungry

-ɔt

ʔɔt^{4} to close (a door)
ʔɔt^{4} to cover (the face)
ʔɔt^{4} to plug (a hole)
bɔt^{4} to dive or swim under water
mɔt^{4} clean; smooth

-ɔɔt

kɔɔt^{6} to hug, embrace, clasp
  kɔɔt^{6} kum^{6} to embrace
ŋɔɔt^{6} *in* mɛɛŋ^{4} ŋɔɔt^{6} scorpion (= mɛɛŋ^{4} ŋaw^{4})
cɔɔt^{5} to dig a small hole
cɔɔt^{6} to touch
cɔɔt^{6} to repair, mend; to solder
cɔɔt^{6} to stop
cɔɔt^{6} to moor (a boat)
cɔɔt^{6} to park (a car)
tɔɔt^{6} to sting (of an insect)
tɔɔt^{6} to bite, nibble (of a fish)
thɔɔt^{5} to fry
thɔɔt^{5} ka^{6} thin^{2} Buddhist ceremony of giving robes to the monks
pɔɔt^{2} *in* phrak^{4} pɔɔt^{2} edible plant called phak^{2} buay^{1} naam^{4} in Siamese (= phrak^{4} pɔɔt^{6})
pɔɔt^{6} *in* phrak^{4} pɔɔt^{6} edible plant called phak^{2} buay^{1} naam^{4} in Siamese (= phrak^{4} pɔɔt^{2})
phɔɔt^{6} traces (e.g., broken branches) of an animal having passed
phɔɔt^{6} bubble nest of a fish
mɔɔt^{5} termite (clf. thua^{4})
mɔɔt^{6} to eat every last bit of something, spend every last bit of one's money
mlɔɔt^{6} kind of fruit (clf. maak^{6})
yɔɔt^{6} to drip; a drop
rɔɔt^{6} to pour
lɔɔt^{5} to go under (a fence, house, table)
lɔɔt^{6} to put something under (e.g., leg of bed or table) to raise it
lɔɔt^{6} to line (a basket) with banana leaves
lɔɔt^{6} great-great grandchild
lɔɔt^{6} *in* ta^{6} lɔɔt^{6} continuously
sɔɔt^{5} to come to an end, be finished

sɔɔt^{5} youngest (child); last (oxcart)
sɔɔt^{6} to insert
hɔɔt^{5} to arrive (< Lao)
hɔɔt^{6} a knot; to tie a knot; to do up the hairknot

-ik

dik^{4} to press down
dik^{4} to dive in headfirst
tik^{4} *in* ka^{6} tik^{4} thermos bottle
yik^{4} to pinch
ɲik^{6} *in* paak^{6} ɲik^{6} paak^{6} ɲɛɛk^{5} to make faces to tease children
sik^{4} to leave orders (of a monk)

-iik

khiik^{5} uneven, odd, without a mate, not a pair
triik^{6} lazy (YG, = OG tliik^{6})
tliik^{6} lazy (OG, = YG triik^{6})
viik^{5} having a piece torn off
siik^{6} to tear
siik^{6} nɛɛŋ^{1} to bare the teeth

-iak

khiak^{5} war; enemy
tiak^{6} to regret the loss of something
phiak^{5} vii^{4} a stove, fireplace (= phriak^{5} vii^{4}, phrɯak^{5} vii^{4})
phiak^{6} *in* saak^{5} phiak^{6} a long rope (e.g., as a clothesline)
phriak^{5} vii^{4} a stove, fireplace (= phiak^{5} vii^{4}, phrɯak^{5} vii^{4})
riak^{6} lead (the metal)
viak^{5} work (noun)

-ɯk

khɯk^{6} khɯk^{6} sound of oxcarts
dɯk^{4} late at night
dɯk^{4} dam^{1} ban^{1} olden times
tɯk^{4} displeased with each other, at outs; to argue

tɯk^{4} building
tɯk^{4} (with various objects) to fish, go fishing
  tɯk^{4} plaa^{1} to go fishing
  tɯk^{4} seet^{6} to fish with hook and line
thɯk^{6} correct
thɯk^{6} cheap
thɯk^{6} to hit, touch
bɯk^{4} big
  plaa^{1} bɯk^{4} kind of big fish
bɯk^{4} naa^{4} tɤɤ^{3} name of abandoned Saek village in Vietnam
bɯk^{4} *in* mee^{5} bɯk^{4} girl, woman
pɯk^{4} stupid, dull-witted
mɯk^{6} ink
lɯk^{6} child, offspring
  lɯk^{6} khooy^{4} son-in-law
  lɯk^{6} caaŋ^{3} worker, employee (= lɯk^{6} lɛɛŋ^{3} < Lao)
  lɯk^{6} taw^{3} one's children
  lɯk^{6} thraa^{6} orphan (= Saek thraa^{6}; = kam^{1} phaa^{3} < Lao)
lɯk^{6} used in names of various objects
  lɯk^{6} diŋ^{6} plumb line with weight on the end

-ɯɯk

kɯɯk^{6} unable to speak, dumb, mute

-ɯak

phɯak^{6} white, albino
phrɯak^{5} vii^{4} a stove, fireplace (= phiak^{5} vii^{4}, phriak^{5} vii^{4})
mɯak^{5} wet and muddy (of a road)
lɯak^{6} staring wide open (of the eyes)
lɯak^{6} to open one's eyes wide
lɯak^{6} to turn back the eyelid

-uk

ʔuk^{4} worried, troubled
kuk^{4} *in* mlɛk^{6} kuk^{4} button (= mɛk^{6} kuk^{4})
kuk^{6} sad and gloomy

cuk^{4} to light a fire; to set fire to; to burn; to cremate
cuk^{4} to have a sharp pain in the stomach
thuk^{6} to make a hole with a stick
thuk^{6} every
thuk^{6} poor; to have hardship, trouble
thuk^{6} thraw^{3} kɔɔ^{6} to kneel down
nuk^{4} *in* sa^{6} nuk^{4} happy, merry
  sa^{6} nuk^{4} sa^{6} naan^{1} happily
puk^{4} strong-smelling (of tobacco)
pruk^{4} bamboo strip for tying or weaving (YG, = OG pluk^{4})
pruk^{4} *in* ca^{6} pruk^{4} white ant (YG, = OG ca^{6} pluk^{4}; clf. thua^{4})
pluk^{4} to awaken (someone)
pluk^{4} bamboo strip for tying or weaving (OG, = YG pruk^{4})
pluk^{4} *in* ca^{6} pluk^{4} white ant (OG, = YG ca^{6} pruk^{4}; clf. thua^{4})
phuk^{4} *in* ka^{6} phuk^{4} kind of wild plant
phuk^{6} pomelo, grapefruit (clf. maak^{6})
muk^{6} pearl, mother-of-pearl
ɲuk^{6} to raise up, establish
ruk^{4} to pull (whiskers, feathers)
ruk^{4} to be startled
luk^{6} to get up (from sleep); to stand up; to raise, lift
luk^{6} to blaze up (of fire)
suk^{4} happy
suk^{4} *in* van^{4} suk^{4} Friday
suk^{6} cooked, ripe

-uuk

ʔuuk^{6} brains
kuuk^{6} tiger (clf. thua^{4})
tuuk^{6} to wrap, wrap up a package; a package
nuuk^{6} deaf
muuk^{5} mucus of the nose, snot
ruuk^{5} raan^{4} home, house
ruuk^{6} tadpole (clf. thua^{4})
huuk^{6} grey (of hair); grey-haired
huuk^{6} *in* tam^{3} huuk^{6} to weave

-uak

ʔuak^{5} ɲuak^{5} (to pile) in a heap
kuak^{6} to send (a present) (YG, = OG kwaak^{6})
khuak^{5} sound of tearing (e.g., paper) (YG, = OG khwaak^{5})
ŋuak^{5} mythical water creature (clf. thua^{4})
ŋuak^{5} to turn the head to look (YG, = OG ŋwaak^{5}; ŋɛɛk^{5}, ŋwɛɛk^{5})
ŋuak^{5} rɔɔŋ^{4} rainbow
truak^{6} to boil, be boiling (of water) (YG, = OG tluak^{5})
tluak^{6} to boil, be boiling (of water) (OG, = YG truak^{5})
phuak^{5} group
phuak^{5} *in* lam^{6} phuak^{5} to fall down, fall flat (= lam^{6} phuap^{5})
muak^{2} hat, cap (= muak^{6})
muak^{6} hat, cap (= muak^{2})
yuak^{6} hungry, to go hungry
ɲuak^{5} *in* ʔuak^{5} ɲuak^{5} (to pile) in a heap
ruak^{5} to vomit
ruak^{5} beeswax
luak^{5} to scald
suak^{6} elbow; a cubit

-ek

ʔek^{4} kaʔ^{6} reel^{4} ʔeek^{4} sound of rooster crowing (OG, = OG ʔee^{5} kaʔ^{6} reel^{4} ʔee^{5}, YG ʔek^{4} kaʔ^{6} reen^{4} ʔeek^{4}, YG ʔee^{5} kaʔ^{6} reen^{4} ʔee^{5})
khek^{6} cake
cek^{6} Chinese
phek^{6} *in* traaw^{1} phek^{6} morning star

-eek

ʔeek^{4} *in* ʔek^{4} kaʔ^{6} reel^{4} ʔeek^{4} sound of crowing (OG, = OG ʔee^{5} kaʔ^{6} reel^{4} ʔee^{5}, YG ʔek^{4} kaʔ^{6} reen^{4} ʔeek^{4}, YG ʔee^{5} kaʔ^{6} reen^{4} ʔee^{5})
ʔeek^{6} ʔaa^{1} saa^{1} *see* ʔaat^{6} saa^{1} maat^{5}
deek^{6} to eat (slang)
preek^{6} to break, be broken, burst
phleek^{5} all, all gone, completely
reek^{5} to call, summon; to be called (so-and-so)
yeek^{6} *in* may^{6} yooŋ^{1} yeek^{6} teeter-totter
heek^{5} guest

-ɤɤk

khɤɤk^{5} to be a waste of time
ŋɤɤk^{5} to fall over backwards
ŋɤɤk^{5} to pry (something) up
thɤɤk^{6} bald-headed
bɤɤk^{6} to cash, take out (money)
plɤɤk^{5} skinned, having the skin abraded (= lɤɤk^{5})
lɤɤk^{5} skinned, having the skin abraded (= plɤɤk^{5})
  lɤɤk^{5} saak^{5} to take skin and flesh off bones
lɤɤk^{5} to stop, stop work

-ok

cok^{4} hoe, mattock (clf. maak^{5}, maak^{6})
dok^{4} thick, abundant (of hair, fruit)
thok^{4} to pull, tug
bok^{4} *in* ka^{6} bok^{4} kind of tree called may^{4} ca^{2} bok^{2} in Siamese
pok^{4} to cover; a cover (e.g., of a book) (= pɔk^{4})
pok^{4} khɔɔŋ^{4} to rule, govern
pok^{6} sound of something falling (= pɔk^{6})

-ook

ʔook^{6} snail, mollusk (clf. thua^{4})
kook^{5} sound of a tiger roaring
kook^{5} sound of stomach rumbling when hungry (= kook^{5} kaak^{5})
khook^{5} lump, piece, classifier
  khook^{5} phraa^{2} rocky cliff
  khook^{5} maaŋ^{4} corpse, body
khook^{5} log, big piece of wood
khook^{5} deep forest
ŋook^{5} to crane the neck to look
ŋook^{5} *in* daaŋ^{3} la^{6} ŋook^{5} kind of edible mushroom
cook^{5} sound of water falling or being poured (= cɔɔk^{5})
thook^{6} to make or force one's way through (a forest)
book^{2} a kind of gambling game (= book^{6})
book^{5} a place
book^{5} sound of elephant chewing up a coconut
book^{6} a kind of gambling game (= book^{2})

pook^{5} sound of rapping the head of a child with the knuckles
prook^{6} rotten (of wood underground at the base of a pillar or post) (YG, = OG plook^{6})
prook^{6} loose in the ground (YG, = OG plook^{6})
plook^{6} rotten (of wood underground at the base of a pillar or post) (OG, = YG prook^{6})
plook^{6} loose in the ground (OG, = YG prook^{6})
mook^{6} kind of long gourd used in curry (clf. maak^{6})
mook^{6} *in* tɔk^{4} mook^{6} moldy (e.g., of food)
yook^{6} to pull up (a plant)
ɲook^{5} to rock a post back and forth
look^{5} the world
sook^{5} luck
sook^{6} sad

-ɛk

kɛk^{4} *in* phrak^{4} kɛk^{4} mustard plant
dɛk^{4} child
tɛk^{4} to cut
trɛk^{4} fish scales (YG, = OG tlɛk^{4}; cf. tɔɔl^{6}, tɔɔn^{6})
tlɛk^{4} fish scales (OG, = YG trɛk^{4}; cf. tɔɔl^{6}, tɔɔn^{6})
thɛk^{4} sii^{2} taxi
nɛk^{4} cool, cold
pɛk^{4} to sweep, dust off
pɛk^{4} to blow (of the wind)
prɛk^{4} vii^{4} matches (YG, = OG plɛk^{4} vii^{4}; YG prak^{4} vii^{4}, OG plak^{4} vii^{4})
plɛk^{4} vii^{4} matches (OG, = YG prɛk^{4} vii^{4}; YG prak^{4} vii^{4}, OG plak^{4} vii^{4})
mɛk^{6} ant (clf. thua^{4})
  mɛk^{6} nɔɔy^{1} kind of ant called mot^{4} ta^{2} nɔɔy^{1} in Siamese
  mɛk^{6} ŋaam^{5} kind of ant
mɛk^{6} kuk^{4} button (= mlɛk^{6} kuk^{4})
mlɛk^{6} seed, grain, small round object
  mlɛk^{6} kuk^{4} button (= mɛk^{6} kuk^{4})
  mlɛk^{6} tuy^{5} hail
  mlɛk^{6} tum^{3} beads
rɛk^{4} to pick, pluck flowers (= rak^{4})
rɛk^{4} side (of the body, of a house); beside
rɛk^{6} to water (plants); to sprinkle (water)
lɛk^{6} small
sɛk^{4} to jump, dance

-ɛɛk

ʔɛɛk^{1} *in* mooŋ^{6} ʔɛɛk^{1} the moon (in talking to children)
ʔɛɛk^{6} yoke
khɛɛk^{6} an Indian; a Muslim
thaa^{5} khɛɛk^{6} a place name
khwɛɛk^{5} sound of tearing (= khwaak^{5})
ŋɛɛk^{5} to turn the head to look (= ŋwɛɛk^{5}, ŋuak^{5}, ŋwaak^{5})
ŋwɛɛk^{5} to turn the head to look (= ŋɛɛk^{5}, ŋuak^{5}, ŋwaak^{5})
cɛɛk^{6} to distribute, hand out
dɛɛk^{6} *in* plaa^{1} dɛɛk^{6} fermented fish paste
thɛɛk^{5} to measure (length)
thrɛɛk^{6} the Saek people
phrɛɛk^{5} *in* ɲua^{3} phrɛɛk^{5} kind of grass called yaa^{3} phrɛɛk^{3} in Siamese (= ɲua^{3} phɛɛk^{6})
ɲɛɛk^{5} *in* paak^{6} ɲik^{6} paak^{6} ɲɛɛk^{5} to make faces to tease children
rɛɛk^{5} to cut (cloth)
vɛɛk^{5} short-handled sickle (= vɛɛt^{5}; clf. maak^{5}, maak^{6})
hɛɛk^{6} frying pan (used only as a couplet of mɔɔ^{3} ‘pot’)

-ak

ʔak^{4} a device onto which silk or cotton thread is wound as it comes from the pot in which it is boiled
kak^{4} kɛɛ^{5} gecko (= kap^{4} kɛɛ^{5}; clf. thua^{4})
kwak^{4} to beckon with the hand
khak^{6} certain
khak^{6} excellent, very good
cak^{4} sewing machine
cak^{4} *in* rɔɔ^{6} cak^{4} to know
dak^{4} asleep
dak^{4} far, far away
tak^{4} to dip up, dip out, draw (water)
thak^{4} to knit; to braid
thak^{4} male (animal) (= thak^{6})
thak^{6} male (animal) (= thak^{4})
thak^{6} *in* ka^{6} thak^{6} couplet of ka^{6} thɔɔ^{4} ‘basket’
nak^{4} heavy
nak^{4} *in* kha^{6} nak^{4} grasshopper (clf. thua^{4})
nak^{6} one skilled in something
nak^{6} thoot^{5} a convict

nak^{6} paat^{6} scholar
nak^{6} rian^{4} student
nak^{6} *in* pha^{6} nak^{6} railing
bak^{2} *in* ta^{6} poʔ^{4} bak^{2} thraw^{3} skull
pak^{4} to plant (a stake)
pak^{4} to embroider
pak^{4} tuu^{1} door
pak^{4} tuu^{1} bɔɔŋ^{6} window
pak^{6} vit^{4} the penis
prak^{4} vii^{4} matches (YG, = OG plak^{4} vii^{4}; YG prɛk^{4} vii^{4}, OG plɛk^{4} vii^{4})
plak^{4} vii^{4} matches (OG, = YG prak^{4} vii^{4}; YG prɛk^{4} vii^{4}, OG plɛk^{4} vii^{4})
phak^{6} difficult
phak^{6} phɤɤ^{5} difficult
phrak^{4} vegetable
mak^{6} to like, be fond of
yak^{6} to wash (clothes)
yak^{6} angry (cf. bɯn^{3}, man^{3} thuu^{3}, lɤɤ^{1})
ɲak^{4} to speak of, mention
ɲak^{6} giant
ɲak^{6} to wind or bind a cord around
rak^{4} to break, be broken (a stick, bone, etc.)
rak^{4} to pick, pluck flowers (= rɛk^{4})
rak^{6} saa^{2} to take care of, guard
lak^{4} a stake, post
lak^{4} pra^{6} cam^{1} basic, regular
lak^{4} a large amount of money (in folktales)
lak^{6} to steal
lak^{6} deep
lak^{6} khit^{6} lak^{6} khay^{4} (to ask) indirectly
vak^{4} sheath (of a knife), pod (of beans, etc.)
vak^{4} to wear over one shoulder and diagonally across the chest
vak^{4} thaa^{6} fish basket
vak^{6} kind of gourd called fak^{4} in Siamese (clf. maak^{6})
vak^{6} part
vak^{6} a phrase, clause
sak^{4} to plant (a stake)
sak^{4} to tattoo
sak^{4} laay^{4} to tattoo, tattoo designs
sak^{4} to split (bamboo strips)
sak^{4} one or so; about, approximately; (not) even one
hak^{2} ɣaa^{5} but (= haak^{5} ɣaa^{5})

-aak

kaak^5 *in* kook^5 kaak^5 sound of the stomach rumbling with hunger (= kook^5)
kwaak^6 to send (a present) (OG, = YG kuak^6)
khaak^6 to cough up phlegm
khwaak^5 sound of tearing (= khwɛɛk^5)
khwaak^6 sharpened stake
khwaak^6 to scratch, claw (= khwaa^4, khwaaw^4)
ɣaak^5 *in* ɣal^4 ɣaak^5 toad (clf. thua^6)
ŋaak^5 *in* sa^6 ŋaak^5 to look up
ŋwaak^5 to turn the head to look (OG, = YG ŋuak^5; ŋɛɛk^5, ŋwɛɛk^5)
daak^6 the anus
taak^4 *in* ka^6 taak^4 to cackle (of a hen)
thaak^5 land leech (clf. thua^4)
thaak^6 to cut a piece off the side of a tree or log
thaak^6 *in* ʔup^4 pa^6 thaak^6 to wait upon, serve
thraak^5 food swallowed returns to the mouth (YG, = OG thlaak^5)
thlaak^5 food swallowed returns to the mouth (OG, = YG thraak^5)
naak^5 otter (clf. thua^4)
naak^5 large serpent in stories (clf. thua^4)
naak^5 alloy of gold and copper
naak^5 *in* sa^6 naak^5 shears used to cut areca nuts (clf. maak^5, maak^6)
baak^5 albino (buffalo, elephant)
baak^6 to cut a blaze in a tree to mark it
paak^6 mouth
  paak^6 ɲik^6 paak^6 ɲɛɛk^5 to make faces to tease children
praak^6 to expose to the sun
praak^6 rind, peel, bark (YG, = OG plaak^6)
plaak^6 rind, peel, bark (OG, = YG praak^6)
phraak^6 forehead
maak^5 classifier for tools, implements, knives, and other sharp tools (= maak^6)
maak^5 *in* nam^6 maak^5 high water (< Lao)
maak^6 classifier for tools, implements, knives, and other sharp tools (= maak^5)
maak^6 classifier for fruit and certain other round objects, frequent in names of fruit and fruit-bearing trees and plants
maak^6 *in* ŋaam^5 maak^6 ka^6 thun^1 slingshot
yaak^6 spade, shovel (clf. maak^5)
raak^5 rust (noun)
raak^5 root (= raak^6)
raak^5 saʔ^4 name of soŋ^1 kaan^1 day when it falls on Tuesday
raak^6 root (= raak^5)
laak^6 ringworm
vaak^5 split bamboo for flooring

saak^{5} rope, cord
  saak^{5} phiak^{6} long rope, as a clothesline
saak^{5} vine
saak^{5} to wake up, get up
saak^{5} corpse, carcass
saak^{6} pestle
haak^{5} ɣaa^{5} but (= hak^{2} ɣaa^{5})

-ɔk

cɔk^{4} to dip down into
tɔk^{4} to fall, drop
tɔk^{4} lɔŋ^{4} to agree
nɔk^{6} bird (clf. thua^{4})
nɔk^{6} luŋ^{5} a bunch of bananas
bɔk^{4} dry land
pɔk^{4} to cover; a cover (e.g., of a book) (= pok^{4})
pɔk^{6} sound of something falling (= pok^{6})
pɔk^{6} pɔk^{6} sound of knocking
phɔk^{6} to carry tucked in the waist
mɔk^{4} dɛɛk^{6} fish paste wrapped and cooked in the fire
mɔk^{4} *in* sɯɯn^{5} mɔk^{4} sɯɯn^{5} cɯɯ^{1} happy, cheerful
mɔk^{6} to strike, hit, beat, pound; to fight
mɔk^{6} to thresh (rice)
ɲɔk^{6} to pick fruit with a pole
ɲɔk^{6} to poke an animal out of its hole with a stick
rɔk^{4} six
  rɔk^{4} sip^{6} sixty
  rɔk^{4} sip^{6} haa^{3} sixty-five
rɔk^{4} catfish (clf. thua^{4})
vɔk^{6} bruised, swollen
sɔk^{6} chalk

-ɔɔk

ʔɔɔk^{6} to go out
kɔɔk^{6} *in* maak^{6} kɔɔk^{6} knuckles
kɔɔk^{6} *in* maak^{6} kɔɔk^{6} wild olive
kɔɔk^{6} *in* mɛɛŋ^{4} kɔɔk^{6} kind of beetle that digs around the roots of the wild olive tree

khɔɔk^{5} bamboo tube to hold water, rice, various objects
khɔɔk^{5} ŋiaŋ^{5} spittoon (= ŋiaŋ^{5}, ka^{6} thoon^{1})
khɔɔk^{5} tam^{1} phun^{6} small mortar for betel
khɔɔk^{5} lɛɛŋ^{3} quiver for arrows
ɣɔɔk^{5} a pen (for animals)
ŋɔɔk^{5} to sprout
cɔɔk^{5} sound of water falling or being poured (= cook^{5})
cɔɔk^{6} cup, glass
dɔɔk^{6} raan^{4} beam in a house
tɔɔk^{6} to pound
tɔɔk^{6} scraps of wood
thɔɔk^{5} tomorrow (= mɯɯ^{6} thɔɔk^{5} nii^{6})
thɔɔk^{5} name of a Saek village in Laos
thɔɔk^{6} to pour out
thɔɔk^{6} *in* ɣaw^{6} thɔɔk^{6} unhusked rice, paddy
thrɔɔk^{5} to stab
nɔɔk^{6} hump on the back of an ox or buffalo (< Lao; = Saek lam^{1})
nɔɔk^{6} *in* phrak^{4} nɔɔk^{6} kind of plant called ton^{3} bua^{1} bok^{2} in Siamese
blɔɔk^{6} flower (= blɔɔk^{6} may^{6})
prɔɔk^{6} to plant (plants); to build (a house) (YG, = OG plɔɔk^{6})
plɔɔk^{6} to plant (plants); to build (a house) (OG, = YG prɔɔk^{6})
phɔɔk^{5} to plaster on (e.g., mud)
phɔɔk^{5} kind of fruit (clf. maak^{6})
mɔɔk^{6} fog
mɔɔk^{6} to ferment, pickle
mɔɔk^{6} water in which glutinous rice has been cooked
yɔɔk^{5} to seek, search
ɲɔɔk^{5} to poke a stick into a gunbarrel, a hole, or a tube to clean it
rɔɔk^{5} nest of a bird (= rɔɔŋ^{4})
rɔɔk^{5} squirrel (clf. thua^{4})
rɔɔk^{5} a litter (of young); family, clan
rɔɔk^{6} bone
lɔɔk^{5} outside
lɔɔk^{5} hot
lɔɔk^{6} to lie, deceive
lɔɔk^{6} to scare, frighten (someone)
vɔɔk^{5} *in* pii^{1} vɔɔk^{5} Year of the Monkey, ninth year in the twelve-year cycle
sɔɔk^{6} elbow; cubit (= suak^{6})
hɔɔk^{6} husband

-iʔ

kiʔ^4 miʔ^6 nii^4 name of soŋ^1 kaan^1 day when it falls on Friday (= ki^4 mi^6 nii^4)
kiʔ^4 liʔ^6 thaa^4 name of soŋ^1 kaan^1 day when it falls on Thursday (= ki^4 li^6 thaa^4)
ciʔ^2 so, then (= ci^2)
ciʔ^6 thooy^2 never mind, let it be, no matter
diʔ^4 final particle (= di^4)
tiʔ^4 to criticize
raw^2 ɲiim^5 kin^1 tiʔ^4 hiiŋ^4 They whisper together criticizing us.
tiʔ^4 *in* taan^1 tiʔ^4 to designate
thiʔ^6 *in* ka^6 thiʔ^6 coconut cream
thiʔ^6 *in* phut^6 thiʔ^6 the Buddha
niʔ^4 thaan^4 story (= niʔ^6 thaan^4)
niʔ^6 this
niʔ^6 final particle (= nih^6)
tuaŋ^1 ɣaa^5 niʔ^6 I presume it was like that.
niʔ^6 thaan^4 story (= niʔ^4 thaan^4)
niʔ^6 mon^4 to invite (monks)
niʔ^6 mon^4 phaʔ^6 to invite a monk
biʔ^4 to break off a piece (e.g., of a cake)
piʔ^4 *in* ka^6 piʔ^4 shrimp paste
phiʔ^4 to try, make an effort
tɔɔŋ^3 khɯt^6 phiʔ^4 kaa^3 must think and try to find a way to kill (him)
phiʔ^4 nɔɔy^3 to try to speak
phiʔ^4 hit^6 to try to do
phiʔ^4 caa^1 la^6 naa^4 to consider (= phiʔ^6 caa^1 la^6 naa^4, phit^4 caa^1 la^6 naa^4, phit^6 caa^1 la^6 naa^4)
phiʔ^4 *in* sap^4 phaʔ^6 phiʔ^4 every sort
phiʔ^6 caa^1 la^6 naa^4 to consider (= phiʔ^4 caa^1 la^6 naa^4, phit^4 caa^1 la^6 naa^4, phit^6 caa^1 la^6 naa^4)
miʔ^6 *in* kiʔ^4 miʔ^6 nii^4 name of soŋ^1 kaan^1 day when it falls on Friday (= ki^4 mi^6 nii^4)
liʔ^6 *in* ʔaʔ^6 mee^4 liʔ^6 kaa^1 America (= ʔa^6 mee^4 li^4 kaa^1)
liʔ^6 *in* kiʔ^4 liʔ^6 thaa^4 name of soŋ^1 kaan^1 day when it falls on Thursday (= ki^4 li^6 thaa^4)

-iaʔ

phiaʔ^{4} phiaŋ^{6} sound of an elephant trumpeting

-ɯʔ

khɯʔ^{6} to shove someone in the back, push
cɯʔ^{4} to swarm on fruit, pastry (of ants, flies) (= ɲɯʔ^{4} ɲɯʔ^{4})
mɯʔ^{4} *in* daŋ^{1} mɯʔ^{4} term applied to a person who curries favor
ɲɯʔ^{4} ɲɯʔ^{4} to swarm on fruit, pastry (of ants, flies) (= cɯʔ^{4})
sɯʔ^{6} sɯɯ^{4} nii^{6} now

-uʔ

ʔuʔ^{4} container for drinking water
ʔuʔ^{4} dɔɔn^{1} Udorn, city in Northeast Thailand (= ʔu^{4} dɔɔn^{1})
kuʔ^{4} kuan^{1} to disturb
kuʔ^{4} laap^{6} rose
kuʔ^{6} maan^{4} boy (= ku^{6} maan^{4})
khuʔ^{4} to strike something to free it of mud or the like
khuʔ^{6} a waterproof basket
cuʔ^{4} to reach to, come very near, almost touch
duʔ^{4} diligent, industrious
thuʔ^{4} term used to tell children to make a gesture of obeisance
thuʔ^{6} thaa^{4} what, anything (= thaa^{4})
thuʔ^{6} lian^{4} durian (= thu^{6} lian^{4}; clf. maak^{6})
buʔ^{6} lii^{4} cigar, cigarette (= bu^{6} lii^{4})
phuʔ^{6} blowgun
phuʔ^{6} rotten (of wood)
phuʔ^{6} to grow bigger (of a child)
yuʔ^{6} *in* vit^{4} tha^{6} yuʔ^{6} radio (= vit^{4} tha^{6} ɲuʔ^{6})
ɲuʔ^{6} *in* ʔaa^{1} ɲuʔ^{6} age (= ʔa^{6} ɲuʔ^{6})
ɲuʔ^{6} *in* vit^{4} tha^{6} ɲuʔ^{6} radio (= vit^{4} tha^{6} yuʔ^{6})
luʔ^{4} laŋ^{3} thaŋ^{6} thee^{4} to move in great numbers
suʔ^{6} to poke an ant nest to make the eggs fall out
suʔ^{6} *in* dɔɔn^{1} suʔ^{6} mɔɔ^{4} *see* dɔŋ^{1} sa^{6} mɔɔ^{4}
suʔ^{6} *in* ɣay^{6} suʔ^{6} diarrhea
huʔ^{4} hɔɔp^{6} to fly in circles

-eʔ

teʔ^{4} to kick
leʔ^{4} then, and then, so, and so, therefore (= lee^{4}, le^{4}, lɤɤy^{4})
leʔ^{6} soft and mushy (of fruit)
seʔ^{6} exclamation used to chase a dog away

-ɤʔ

ŋɤʔ^{4} awkward, as country folk coming to the city
ŋɤʔ^{4} to think
thɤʔ^{4} mild final imperative particle
phrɤʔ^{6} (to speak) obscenely

-oʔ

koʔ^{4} *in* maak^{6} thaa^{6} koʔ^{4} cleaver-like knife with big blade curved on top
coʔ^{4} to stop
toʔ^{4} table (= toʔ^{6})
toʔ^{6} table (= toʔ^{4})
poʔ^{4} *in* ka^{6} poʔ^{4} coconut shell
poʔ^{4} *in* ta^{6} poʔ^{4} bak^{2} thraw^{3} skull
phoʔ^{6} to spend a lot of money on something (slang)
moʔ^{4} small cloth bib on strings covering the genitalia of a small child
moʔ^{4} vagina, female organ
moʔ^{6} *in* tɛɛ^{6} moʔ^{6} at first
loʔ^{6} to lose, be defeated
loʔ^{6} to throw away

-ɛʔ

kɛʔ^{4} to undo, open (= ŋɛʔ^{6})
khɛʔ^{6} tired of (e.g., food)
ŋɛʔ^{6} to undo, open (= kɛʔ^{4})
cɛʔ^{4} to touch with the tongue in order to taste
tɛʔ^{4} *in* vaa^{1} ka^{6} tɛʔ^{4} wall of woven bamboo
tɛʔ^{6} *in* kɤɤp^{6} tɛʔ^{6} sandals

phɛʔ^{6} goat (< Siamese; clf. thua^{4})
mɛʔ^{6} to stand leaning against (e.g., a wall)
lɛʔ^{4} final interrogative particle
hɛʔ^{4} or

-aʔ

ʔaʔ^{6} mee^{4} liʔ^{6} kaa^{1} America (= ʔa^{6} mee^{4} li^{4} kaa^{1})
ʔaʔ^{6} *in* saʔ^{4} ʔaʔ^{6} noo^{4} daat^{6} name of a pool
kaʔ^{6} yaŋ^{1} kind of basket with feet
kaʔ^{6} *in* ʔee^{5} kaʔ^{6} reel^{4} ʔee^{5} sound of rooster crowing
(OG, = OG ʔek^{4} kaʔ^{6} reel^{4} ʔeek^{4}, YG ʔee^{5} kaʔ^{6} reen^{4} ʔee^{5},
YG ʔek^{4} kaʔ^{6} reen^{4} ʔeek^{4})
khaʔ^{6} *in* khoo^{4} laa^{4} khaʔ^{6} thee^{4} vii^{4} name of soŋ^{1} kaan^{1} day when it falls
on Monday
khwaʔ^{4} to peel off (of paint)
caʔ^{6} trɛn^{6} skink (YG, = OG caʔ^{6} tlɛn^{6}; OG ca^{6} tlɛn^{6}, YG ca^{6} trɛn^{6}; clf. thua^{4})
caʔ^{6} tlɛn^{6} skink (OG, = YG caʔ^{6} trɛn^{6}; OG ca^{6} tlɛn^{6}, YG ca^{6} trɛn^{6}; clf. thua^{4})
caʔ^{6} phaŋ^{4} pail or jug for washing, not drinking
taʔ^{6} baaŋ^{1} the chest (= tam^{1} ʔaaŋ^{1})
thaʔ^{6} bian^{1} registry (= tha^{6} bian^{1})
naʔ^{6} *in* saa^{1} thaa^{4} laʔ^{6} naʔ^{6} public
baʔ^{4} *in* buat^{6} kee^{3} baʔ^{4} to become a monk to fulfill a promise
paʔ^{6} hun^{4} people (= pa^{6} hun^{4})
paʔ^{6} vɔɔ^{4} la^{6} naa^{4} old term for the end of Buddhist Lent (= vɔɔ^{4} la^{6} naa^{4})
phaʔ^{6} title denoting royalty (= pha^{6})
phaʔ^{6} phom^{4} a Brahma divinity
phaʔ^{6} a monk
phaʔ^{6} ʔooŋ^{1} simple ladder made of a bamboo pole
phaʔ^{6} *in* bun^{1} phaʔ^{6} veet^{6} name of a merit-making ceremony
phaʔ^{6} *in* van^{4} phaʔ^{6} hat^{4} Thursday
phaʔ^{6} *in* sap^{4} phaʔ^{6} phiʔ^{4} every sort
maʔ^{6} *in* tham^{4} maʔ^{6} baan^{1} personal name (= tham^{4} ma^{6} baan^{1})
maʔ^{6} *in* sam^{6} maʔ^{6} almost, about to, will
ɲaʔ^{6} broken, cracked open
raʔ^{6} *in* ʔit^{4} sa^{6} raʔ^{6} independent
raʔ^{6} *in* ma^{6} raʔ^{6} bitter gourd (clf. maak^{6})
laʔ^{6} final particle

laʔ6 *in* ka6 bin1 laʔ6 phom4 name of a Brahma divinity (= ka6 bin1 la6 phom4)

laʔ6 *in* naa4 laʔ6 vaay4 *see* naa4 laʔ6 vaay4

laʔ6 *in* saa1 thaa4 laʔ6 naʔ6 public

laʔ6 *in* saa1 laʔ6 phat6 saa1 laʔ6 phaa4 every sort of thing

vaʔ4 *in* ka6 vaʔ4 having a side or corner broken off

saʔ4 pond

  saʔ4 ʔaʔ6 noo4 daat6 name of a pool

saʔ4 *in* ʔot4 saʔ4 to persevere

saʔ4 *in* thuŋ4 saʔ4 thee4 vii4 name of soŋ1 kaan1 day when it falls on Sunday

saʔ4 *in* raak5 saʔ4 name of soŋ1 kaan1 day when it falls on Tuesday

saʔ6 saʔ6 descriptive of plodding along

-aaʔ

ʔaaʔ6 hesitation particle (= ʔaa6)

-ɔʔ

ʔɔʔ4 to make a particular kind of curry

kɔʔ4 to take hold of

khɔʔ4 to scrape out (e.g., rice out of a pot)

khɔʔ4 to spend all one's money

khɔʔ6 to knock (e.g., on a door)

ŋɔʔ6 rambutan (clf. maak6)

ŋɔʔ6 paralyzed and curled up (of an arm or leg)

cɔʔ4 to pierce a hole

tɔʔ4 to strike, knock

tɔʔ4 *in* luŋ5 ʔii6 tɔʔ4 kind of banana (clf. maak6)

tɔʔ6 *in* ka6 tɔʔ6 small basket used for marketing

thɔʔ2 final imperative particle

thɔʔ4 *in* pii1 thɔʔ4 Year of the Rabbit, fourth year in the twelve-year cycle

thrɔʔ6 luck (good or bad)

  thrɔʔ6 raay6 bad luck

nɔʔ4 final particle of invitation

bɔʔ4 cushion

phɔʔ4 *in* daaŋ3 het4 phɔʔ4 kind of mushroom

yɔʔ4 to add condiments to food

rɔʔ^{6} *in* boo^{6} rɔʔ^{6} I don't know (= rɔɔ^{6})
lɔʔ^{6} to seek, search
lɔʔ^{6} to make a circuit of
lɔʔ^{6} to use a knife to cut away and make smooth a knot in wood (= sɔʔ^{6})
sɔʔ^{6} to use a knife to cut away and make smooth a knot in wood (= lɔʔ^{6})
sɔʔ^{6} to plane wood
sɔʔ^{6} to use a spade to make the sides of a hole even and smooth
hɔʔ^{4} to fly through the air

Reduced Short Vowels in Final Position

-i

ki^{4} mi^{6} thaa^{4} name of soŋ^{1} kaan^{1} day when it falls on Friday
(= kiʔ^{4} miʔ^{6} thaa^{4})
ki^{4} li^{6} nii^{4} name of soŋ^{1} kaan^{1} day when it falls on Thursday
(= kiʔ^{4} liʔ^{6} nii^{4})
ci^{2} so, then (= ciʔ^{2})
ti^{4} *in* pat^{4} ti^{4} bat^{4} to serve
ti^{4} *in* ɲut^{6} ti^{4} tham^{4} just (= ɲot^{6} ti^{4} tham^{4})
ni^{6} mit^{6} to create (= nii^{4} mit^{6})
phi^{6} thuun^{4} a gem (= phiʔ^{6} thuun^{4})
mi^{6} *in* ki^{4} mi^{6} thaa^{4} name of soŋ^{1} kaan^{1} day when it falls on Friday
(= kiʔ^{4} miʔ^{6} thaa^{4})
li^{4} *in* ʔa^{6} mee^{4} li^{4} kaa^{1} America (= ʔaʔ^{6} mee^{4} liʔ^{6} kaa^{1})
li^{4} *in* naa^{4} li^{4} kaa^{1} watch, clock
li^{6} *in* bɔɔ^{1} li^{6} veen^{4} area
li^{6} *in* ki^{4} li^{6} nii^{4} name of soŋ^{1} kaan^{1} day when it falls on Thursday
(= kiʔ^{4} liʔ^{6} nii^{4})
si^{2} will

-ɯ

sɯ^{6} sɯɯ^{4} time (= sɯɯ^{4}, sɤɤ^{4})
sɯ^{6} sɯɯn^{4} now

-u

ʔu^{4} dɔɔn^{1} Udorn, city in Northeast Thailand (= ʔuʔ^{4} dɔɔn^{1})
yu^{4} roop^{6} Europe
su^{4} meen^{4} Mt. Meru (= su^{6} meen^{4})
su^{4} *in* pha^{6} veet^{5} su^{4} kam^{1} name of the gods' architect
ku^{6} maan^{4} boy (= kuʔ^{4} maan^{4})
thu^{6} lian^{4} durian (= thuʔ^{6} lian^{4}; clf. maak^{6})
thu^{6} *in* khan^{4} tha^{6} thu^{6} lii^{1} name of a cave
bu^{6} lii^{4} cigar, cigarette (= buʔ^{6} lii^{4})
su^{6} meen^{4} Mt. Meru (= su^{4} meen^{4})
su^{6} *in* doŋ^{1} su^{6} mɔɔ^{4} *see* dɔŋ^{1} sa^{6} mɔɔ^{4}

-e

le^{4} then, and then, so, and so, therefore (= lee^{4}, leʔ^{4}, lɤɤy^{4})

-ɛ

mɛ^{4} final emphatic particle

-a

ɣa^{3} *in* khan^{4} ɣa^{3} if
ɣa^{3} *in* sɔɔ^{5} ɣa^{3} named
ʔa^{4} sa^{6} maat^{5} *see* ʔaat^{6} saa^{1} maat^{5}
ma^{4} at
fa^{4} laŋ^{6} Occidental, white person (= pha^{6} laŋ^{6}, fa^{6} laŋ^{6})
ʔa^{6} thit^{6} *in* van^{4} ʔa^{4} thit^{6} Sunday (= van^{4} ʔaa^{1} thit^{6}, van^{4} thit^{6})
ʔa^{6} mee^{4} li^{4} kaa^{1} America (= ʔaʔ^{6} mee^{4} liʔ^{6} kaa^{1})
ʔa^{6} ɲuʔ^{6} age (= ʔaa^{1}ɲuʔ^{6})
ʔa^{6} rii^{6} this one
ʔa^{6} saa^{1} *see* ʔaat^{6} saa^{1} maat^{5}
ka^{6} to
ka^{6} cat^{4} ka^{6} caay^{1} scattered about
ka^{6} diŋ^{1} name of a river, name of a wind
ka^{6} dɛɛŋ^{3} sterile
ka^{6} daaŋ^{3} stiff, motionless, paralyzed
ka^{6} det^{4} ka^{6} dɔɔ^{3} really, very

ka^{6} daat^{6} paper
ka^{6} taa^{6} basket
ka^{6} tɔɔ^{6} small basket used for marketing
ka^{6} taay^{6} rabbit (clf. thua^{4})
ka^{6} tɔɔy^{3} old-fashioned lower garment
ka^{6} tik^{4} thermos bottle
ka^{6} taak^{4} to cackle (of a hen)
ka^{6} thɔɔ^{4} basket
ka^{6} thɔm^{5} small hut (< Siamese)
ka^{6} thɛn^{4} guava (clf. maak^{6})
ka^{6} thoon^{1} spittoon (= ŋiaŋ^{5}, khɔɔk^{5} ŋiaŋ^{5})
ka^{6} thuut^{5} leprosy (= ruan^{5})
ka^{6} thak^{6} couplet paired with ka^{6} thɔɔ^{4} 'basket'
ka^{6} thiʔ^{6} coconut cream
ka^{6} bɯaŋ^{3} tile
ka^{6} baw^{1} kind of tree called ka^{2} baw^{1} in Siamese
ka^{6} bɔɔŋ^{1} torch
ka^{6} bok^{4} kind of tree called may^{4} ca^{2} bok^{2} in Siamese
ka^{6} paw^{1} bag, suitcase
ka^{6} poʔ^{4} coconut shell
ka^{6} pooŋ^{1} skirt
ka^{6} paaŋ^{1} half a bamboo used as a water pipe
ka^{6} paaŋ^{1} empty can used as a container
ka^{6} paaŋ^{1} lid of an empty oil drum
ka^{6} pɔŋ^{1} can, tin
ka^{6} piʔ^{4} shrimp paste
ka^{6} poʔ^{4} coconut shell
ka^{6} phuk^{4} kind of wild plant
ka^{6} bin^{1} la^{6} phom^{4} name of a Brahma divinity (= ka^{6} bin^{1} laʔ^{6} phom^{4})
ka^{6} lɛŋ^{6} small metal bell
ka^{6} vaʔ^{4} having a side or corner broken off
ka^{6} soo^{3} basket for scooping up water
ka^{6} sɛt^{4} king (= ka^{6} sat^{4})
ka^{6} sat^{4} king (= ka^{6} sɛt^{4})
ka^{6} *in* ʔek^{4} ka^{6} reel^{4} ʔeek^{4} sound of rooster crowing (*see* ʔee^{5} kaʔ^{6} reel^{4} ʔee^{5})
ka^{6} *in* ŋaam^{5} maak^{6} ka^{6} thun^{1} slingshot
ka^{6} *in* daaŋ^{3} ka^{6} tɛl^{6} kind of small mushroom
ka^{6} *in* thɔŋ^{2} ka^{6} thiaw^{4} kind of bag
ka^{6} *in* thɔɔt^{5} ka^{6} thin^{2} Buddhist ceremony of giving robes to the monks
ka^{6} *in* nɔk^{6} ka^{6} cip^{4} kind of bird
ka^{6} *in* plaa^{1} ka^{6} dɤɤt^{6} kind of fish called plaa^{1} ka^{2} dii^{2} in Siamese
ka^{6} *in* phrak^{4} ka^{6} seet^{6} kind of edible plant called phak^{2} ka^{2} cheet^{2} in Siamese

ka^{6} *in* yaaŋ^{1} ka^{6} tiw^{3} rubber band
ka^{6} *in* vaa^{1} ka^{6} tɛʔ^{4} wall of woven bamboo
ka^{6} *in* saŋ^{1} ka^{6} sii^{1} tin
kha^{6} naat^{6} size
kha^{6} nak^{4} grasshopper
kha^{6} maa^{3} bathing cloth
kha^{6} mooy^{4} thief
kha^{6} moom^{4} pubic mound
kha^{6} map^{4} temples of the head
kha^{6} ɲɛŋ^{3} afterbirth
kha^{6} lɔɔp^{6} quilt, blanket, coverlet
kha^{6} *in* pha^{6} kha^{6} va^{6} dii^{1} name of a hall
ca^{6} kooy^{1} kind of red-headed lizard (clf. thua^{4})
ca^{6} trɛn^{6} skink (YG, = OG ca^{6} tlɛn^{6}; OG caʔ^{6} tlɛn^{6}, YG caʔ^{6} trɛn^{6}; clf. thua^{4})
ca^{6} tlɛn^{6} skink (OG, = YG ca^{6} trɛn^{6}; OG caʔ^{6} tlɛn^{6}, YG caʔ^{6} trɛn^{6}; clf. thua^{4})
ca^{6} thrip^{4} centipede (clf. thua^{4})
ca^{6} prɔɔŋ^{3} rice husks (YG, = OG ca^{6} plɔɔŋ^{3})
ca^{6} plɔɔŋ^{3} rice husks (OG, = YG ca^{6} prɔɔŋ^{3})
ca^{6} pruk^{4} white ant (YG, = OG ca^{6} pluk^{4}; clf. thua^{4})
ca^{6} pluk^{4} white ant (OG, = YG ca^{6} pruk^{4}; clf. thua^{4})
ca^{6} phrɤɤ^{4} lemongrass (= ca^{6} thrɤɤ^{4})
ta^{4} *in* sat^{4} ta^{4} ʔaa^{1} kaat^{6} air, atmosphere
ta^{6} kiaŋ^{1} lamp
ta^{6} khɛɛŋ^{4} (to lie) on the side
ta^{6} khɔɔŋ^{4} ditch
ta^{6} khiap^{2} *in* may^{6} ta^{6} khiap^{2} chopsticks (= thuu^{5}, may^{6} thɯɯ^{5} naaŋ^{5})
ta^{6} bay^{1} a file (the tool)
ta^{6} puu^{1} nail
ta^{6} poʔ^{6} bak^{2} thraw^{3} skull
ta^{6} phɯt^{6} ta^{6} phɯɯ^{4} all around
ta^{6} mooy^{1} big spoon, ladle (= ta^{6} mooy^{4})
ta^{6} mooy^{4} big spoon, ladle (= ta^{6} mooy^{1})
ta^{6} roop^{5} eggshell, matchbox, sheath
ta^{6} laaŋ^{4} jail
ta^{6} laat^{6} market
ta^{6} lɔɔt^{6} continuously
ta^{6} *in* ʔɛŋ^{3} ta^{6} ʔɤɤn^{1} kind of potato
tha^{6} nii^{4} gibbon (clf. thua^{4})
tha^{6} nuu^{4} bow, arrow
tha^{6} bian^{1} registry (= thaʔ^{6} bian^{1})
tha^{6} raay^{3} really (= thraay^{3})
tha^{6} vaay^{2} to offer, present

tha^6 haan^2 soldier
tha^6 *in* khan^4 tha^6 thu^6 lii^1 name of a cave
tha^6 *in* luŋ^5 tha^6 nii^6 kind of banana
tha^6 *in* luŋ^5 tha^6 nii^6 ʔɔɔŋ^1 kind of banana
tha^6 *in* vit^4 tha^6 yuʔ^6 radio (= vit^4 tha^6 ɲuʔ^6)
na^6 khɔɔn^4 city
na^6 khɔɔn^4 pha^6 nom^4 Nakhon Phanom, city in Northeast Thailand (= la^6 khɔɔn^4)
pa^6 dap^4 to decorate
pa^6 thiip^5 incense stick
pa^6 theet^5 country
pa^6 maan^4 approximately
pa^6 ɲool^6 small bit of rubbish
pa^6 ɲoot^6 use
pa^6 hun^4 people (= paʔ^6 hun^4)
pa^6 *in* ʔup^4 pa^6 thaak^6 to wait on, serve
pra^6 cam^1 regular, usual
  lak^4 pra^6 cam^1 basic, regular
pra^6 vat^4 story, history
pha^6 title denoting royalty (= phaʔ^6)
pha^6 kha^6 va^6 dii^1 name of a hall
pha^6 niat^5 bird cage with a bird in it, used as a decoy
pha^6 nak^6 railing
pha^6 ɲaa^4 king, prince, chief, lord
pha^6 laŋ^6 Occidental, white person (= fa^4 laŋ^6, fa^6 laŋ^6)
pha^6 veet^5 su^4 kam^1 name of the gods' architect
pha^6 *in* na^6 khɔɔn^4 pha^6 nom^4 Nakhon Phanom, city in Northeast Thailand (= la^6 khɔɔn^4)
pha^6 *in* plaa^1 pha^6 ʔɔɔŋ^1 water tortoise (= plaa^1 via^3)
pha^6 *in* plaa^1 pha^6 lay^4 kind of fish (= plaa^1 pha^6 lay^5)
ma^6 kii^4 until (= kii^4, maʔ^6 kii^4)
ma^6 nut^6 human being
ma^6 raʔ^6 bitter gourd (clf. maak^6)
ma^6 haa^1 great (used in various expressions)
  ma^6 haa^1 phom^4 great Brahma
  ma^6 haa^1 sa^6 mut^4 ocean (= sa^6 mut^4)
ma^6 hoo^1 thɔɔn^4 name of soŋ^1 kaan^1 day when it falls on Saturday
ma^6 *in* tham^4 ma^6 daa^1 ordinary, usual
ma^6 *in* tham^4 ma^6 baan^1 personal name (= tham^4 maʔ^6 baan^1)
ma^6 *in* pii^1 ma^6 mia^4 Year of the Horse, seventh year in the twelve-year cycle
ma^6 *in* pii^1 ma^6 mɛɛ^4 Year of the Goat, eighth year in the twelve-year cycle
ma^6 *in* pii^1 ma^6 looŋ^4 Year of the Dragon, fifth year in the twelve-year cycle

ma^{6} *in* pii^{1} ma^{6} seŋ^{1} Year of the Snake, sixth year in the twelve-year cycle
ma^{6} *in* him^{1} ma^{6} phaan^{4} name of a mythical forest
la^{6} khɔɔn^{4} Nakhon Phanom, city in Northeast Thailand
(= na^{6} khɔɔn^{4} pha^{6} nom^{4})
la^{6} duu^{1} season
la^{6} nɯŋ^{4} la^{6} nɯɯt^{5} in disorder
la^{6} nɯŋ^{4} la^{6} naat^{5} in disorder
la^{6} bɤɤt^{2} a bomb
la^{6} mɛɛ^{4} final particle (= mɛɛ^{4})
la^{6} vaay^{4} really, truly
la^{6} *in* ka^{6} bin^{1} la^{6} phom^{4} name of a Brahma divinity (= ka^{6} bin^{1} laʔ^{6} phom^{4})
la^{6} *in* daaŋ^{3} la^{6} ŋook^{5} kind of edible mushroom
la^{6} *in* pii^{1} la^{6} kaa^{1} Year of the Cock, tenth year in the twelve-year cycle
la^{6} *in* paʔ^{6} vɔɔ^{4} la^{6} naa^{4} old term for the end of Buddhist Lent (= vɔɔ^{4} la^{6} naa^{4})
la^{6} *in* phit^{4} caa^{1} la^{6} naa^{4} to consider (= phit^{6} caa^{1} la^{6} naa^{4}, phiʔ^{4} caa^{1} la^{6} naa^{4},
phiʔ^{6} caa^{1} la^{6} naa^{4})
la^{6} *in* vɔɔ^{4} la^{6} naa^{4} old term for the end of Buddhist Lent (= paʔ^{6} vɔɔ^{4} la^{6} naa^{4})
va^{6} *in* thee^{4} va^{6} daa^{1} divinity, god
va^{6} *in* thee^{4} va^{6} but^{4} angel, divine child
va^{6} *in* pha^{6} kha^{6} va^{6} dii^{1} name of a hall
sa^{6} nɛɛn^{4} bamboo frame on which people sit in a boat
sa^{6} naan^{1} *in* sa^{6} nuk^{4} sa^{6} naan^{1} happily
sa^{6} nuk^{4} happy, merry
sa^{6} nuk^{4} sa^{6} naan^{1} happily
sa^{6} naak^{5} shears used to cut areca nuts (clf. maak^{5}, maak^{6})
sa^{6} ŋɛɛŋ^{4} kind of fish
sa^{6} ŋɛɛŋ^{4} kind of vegetable
sa^{6} ŋop^{4} quiet
sa^{6} ŋaak^{5} to look up
sa^{6} duŋ^{3} kind of square fishnet
sa^{6} dɤɤt^{6} to be startled
sa^{6} buu^{1} soap (< Siamese)
sa^{6} mut^{4} ocean (= ma^{6} haa^{1} sa^{6} mut^{4})
sa^{6} roo^{3} the So people (= soo^{3})
sa^{6} rɔɔy^{4} mortar
sa^{6} rooŋ^{3} sarong (= sa^{6} looŋ^{2})
sa^{6} lii^{4} Indian corn, maize
sa^{6} looŋ^{2} sarong (= sa^{6} rooŋ^{3})
sa^{6} vɤɤy^{1} to rule over (a kingdom)
sa^{6} vaaŋ^{6} comfortable, comfortably
sa^{6} *in* ʔa^{4} sa^{6} maat^{5} *see* ʔaat^{6} saa^{1} maat^{5}
sa^{6} *in* ʔaa^{1} sa^{6} maat^{5} *see* ʔaat^{6} saa^{1} maat^{5}

sa^6 *in* ʔit^4 sa^6 raʔ^4 independent

sa^6 *in* ʔat^4 sa^6 cɛn^1 amazing

sa^6 *in* ʔaat^6 sa^6 maat^5 *see* ʔaat^6 saa^1 maat^5

sa^6 *in* doŋ^1 sa^6 mɔɔ^4 *see* dɔŋ^1 sa^6 mɔɔ^4

sa^6 *in* dɔŋ^1 sa^6 mɔɔ^4 *see* dɔŋ^1 sa^6 mɔɔ^4

sa^6 *in* thot^6 sa^6 phit^6 laat^5 sa^6 tham^4 the ten royal precepts

sa^6 *in* pii^1 sa^6 luu^1 Year of the Ox, second year in the twelve-year cycle

sa^6 *in* laat^5 sa^6 dɔɔn^1 people

sa^6 *in* laat^5 sa^6 tham^4 royal precepts

sa^6 *in* laat^5 sa^6 vaŋ^4 royal palace

sa^6 *in* laat^5 sa^6 sii^2 lion

sa^6 *in* soŋ^6 sa^6 kaan^1 to have a funeral (< Lao)

sa^6 *in* saat^6 sa^6 naa^2 religion

fa^6 laŋ^6 Occidental, white person (= pha^6 laŋ^6, fa^4 laŋ^6)

ha^6 lii^6 still, yet (= haʔ^6 lii^6, lii^6)

English-Saek

A

abandon, desert, divorce raaŋ^{6}
abduct; capture, arrest kum^{1}
able; get, obtain; past tense marker day^{3}
  get more than others vɛɛn^{4}
able (to be); worthy of taa^{1}
abortion (to have); milk a cow hiit^{5}
about, approximately pa^{6} maan^{4}
  about, approximately, one or so, not even one sak^{4}
about to, be doing kam^{1} laŋ^{4}
  about to, will raaŋ^{2}, raaŋ^{3}
  about to, will, would daa^{1}
above, on, on top of; high, tall saaŋ^{2}
  above, on, upper, north khɯn^{4}
abundant (of hair, fruit), thick dok^{4}
accompany, follow; go in search of; with; from; along nam^{4}
  accompany; see (someone) off, send cɔŋ^{6}
according to; follow; search for; along taam^{1}
ache ciw^{3}, ciiw^{3}
  ache, hurt, pain keet^{6}
across, away phɔn^{6}
act, action, work kaan^{1}
Adam's apple ɣɔɔ^{4} hɔɔy^{1}
add tɯɯm^{6}
admonish, greet thɔɔŋ^{6}
adorn, ornament ʔee^{5}
advantage piap^{6}
affected, flirtatious khiaw^{4}
afraid, cured by bad experience trɯa^{4}
  afraid looking down from a height khɤɤp^{6}
after; back; classifier for houses laŋ^{2}
afterbirth kha^{6} ɲɛŋ^{3}
afternoon, nightfall baay^{6}
again, also loo^{5}
again, new, another mɔɔ^{6}

age ʔaa^{1} ɲuʔ^{6}, ʔa^{6} ɲuʔ^{6}
agree tɔk^{4} lɔŋ^{4}
aim, intend; make a mark, mark maay^{2}
air, atmosphere ʔaa^{1} kaat^{6}, sat^{4} ta^{4} ʔaa^{1} kaat^{6}
albino baak^{5}, phɯak^{6}
algae ɣii^{4}
algae (green) lay^{4}
edible green algae pham^{1}, pham^{2}
all, all gone sin^{6}
all, all gone, completely phleek^{5}
all around, scattered about ta^{6} phɯt^{6} ta^{6} phɯɯ^{4}
all, complete khop^{6}
to eat all lɔɔn^{2}
all, both, together with; even though thɯŋ^{4}
all; set up, establish taŋ^{3}
allow, consent, yield, submit ɲɔɔm^{4}
alloy of gold and copper naak^{5}
almost, nearly kɯap^{6}, thram^{3}
almost, almost to, will sam^{5} maʔ^{6}
alms thaan^{4}
alone (to do), do stubbornly ʔɯa^{1}
along; follow, search for, according to taam^{1}
along; with; from; accompany, follow; go in search of nam^{4}
already; be finished; then lɛɛw^{1}, lɛɛw^{6}
also, again loo^{5}
also; repeat yam^{6}
altogether, together phrɔɔm^{6}
always, continually maay^{5}
amazing, strange ʔat^{4} sa^{6} cɛn^{1}
amazed, surprised ŋɯt^{6}
America ʔaʔ^{6} mee^{4} liʔ^{6} kaa^{1}, ʔa^{6} mee^{4} li^{4} kaa^{1}
amount, time; like paan^{1}
amusing, fun muan^{5}
and, with kap^{4}
and so, then (expresses finality) loot^{5}
and then, so, but phat^{2}
and then, then, and so, so, therefore lee^{4}, leʔ^{4}, le^{4}, lɤɤy^{4}
angel, divine child thee^{4} va^{6} but^{4}
angle, corner, edge liam^{5}
at an angle cɤɤy^{3}, pɤɤy^{3}
angry bɯn^{3}, man^{3} thuu^{3}, yak^{6}, lɤɤ^{1}
animal sɛt^{4}, sat^{4}

animal; meat nɯa^{3}
  animal varieties ʔom^{3}, trɛɛ^{1}, bɯŋ^{3}, ɲɛn^{2}
  classifier for animals; body thua^{4}
  male animal thak^{4}, thak^{6}
ankle bone cuum^{1} khɔɔŋ^{6}
announce paaw^{6}
annoy, crowd, oppress biat^{6} bian^{1}
  annoyed, irritated, excited rɤɤ^{3} raaŋ^{1}
another, new, again mɔɔ^{6}
answer, reply ŋaan^{2}, tɔɔp^{6}
  term used in answer to a call kuu^{3}
ant mɛk^{6}
  ant varieties mɛk^{6} ŋaam^{5}, mɛk^{6} nɔɔy^{1}
  white ant ca^{6} pruk^{4}, ca^{6} pluk^{4}
anus daak^{6}, troon^{1} tree^{1}, tloon^{1} tlee^{1},
anvil khook^{5} leen^{5} thaŋ^{6}, thaŋ^{6}
any, which, what nɤɤ^{4}
anybody, who, everybody dɤɤ^{1}
anything, what; why thaa^{4}, thrɤɤ^{4}
ape khaaŋ^{5}, khaaŋ^{6}
appendix say^{3} tiŋ^{6}
appoint taŋ^{3} tɛɛŋ^{6}
approximately doo^{5} ɣaa^{5}
  approximately, about pa^{6} maan^{4}
  approximately, about, one or so, not even one sak^{4}
arch, archway (of gate) sum^{3}
  arched gateway at monastery khoŋ^{1}
architect of the gods pha^{6} veet^{5} su^{4} kam^{1}
area bɔɔ^{1} li^{6} veen^{4}
  area, district ɲaan^{5}
  area of fields thɔŋ^{5}
areca phun^{6}, ɲaaŋ^{1}
argue thiaŋ^{2}
  argue, displeased with each other tɯk^{4}
arm keen^{1}
  carry under the arm; pinch, as a crab; pick up with chopsticks khɛɛp^{5}, niip^{6}
  hold or carry in the arms ʔuum^{3}
  put arms around to measure circumference ʔoop^{6}
  take up in both arms ʔoom^{1}
armpit khɛɛ^{5} haa^{2}, khɛŋ^{5} haa^{2}

armspread, fathom, measure with armspread   vaa^{4}

around   rɔɔp^{5}

all around, scattered about   ta^{6} phɯt^{6} ta^{6} phɯɯ^{4}

around (to go), make a circuit   liap^{5}

arrange tidily, fold neatly   liip^{6}

arrest, capture; abduct   kum^{1}

arrive   hɔɔt^{5}

arrive, reach; even   thaŋ^{4}

arrogant   ʔoŋ^{6}, cɔɔŋ^{1} hɔɔŋ^{1}

hold the head high, proudly or arrogantly   bɤɤt^{6}

arrow, bow   tha^{6} nuu^{4}

arrow of crossbow   naa^{6}

artisan, expert; skilled   saaŋ^{5}

as for; part; while   suan^{6}, sual^{6}

ascend, rise, go up, come up, up   hɯn^{3}

ascetic, hermit   rɯɯ^{4} sii^{2}, lɯɯ^{4} sii^{2}

ashamed, embarrassed   trɤɤy^{1}, tlɤɤy^{1}

ashes   thaw^{5}

ashes of dead fire, dead coals   plɔɔ^{6} mii^{3}

ask   thaam^{1}, thaam^{2}

ask for a delay   phat^{4}

ask indirectly   lak^{6} khit^{6} lak^{6} khay^{4}

ask, pray   vay^{6} vɔɔn^{4}

asleep   dak^{4}

assemble   sum^{4}

associate with   khop^{6}

assume, guess, estimate   tuaŋ^{1}

astringent in taste   viat^{6}

at   ma^{4}

at, in, inside, into, during   daŋ^{1}, daaŋ^{1}

at, in, there   nɛɛn^{1}, nɛɛn^{2}

athwart (to lie), block, obstruct   vaaŋ^{2}

atmosphere, air   ʔaa^{1} kaat^{6}, sat^{4} ta^{4} ʔaa^{1} kaat^{6}

attached, fastened   tit^{4}

aunt, older sister of either parent   paa^{3}

automobile (sedan)   lot^{6} keŋ^{1}

avoid   blian^{3}

avoid, get out of the way   trɛɛŋ^{5}, tlɛɛŋ^{5}

awaken someone   pluk^{4}

away, across   phɔn^{6}

away; to flee   theew^{4}

awkward, as country folks ŋɤʔ^{4}
axe vaan^{2}

B

back; after; classifier for houses laŋ^{2}
back of a knife sɛn^{2}
back of the head ŋɔɔn^{5}
carry (a child) in a cloth on the back ʔɛɛt^{5}
lie flat on the back; open (the hand) bɛɛ^{1}
back up thɔɔy^{1}
bad raay^{6}, sua^{6}
bad luck thrɔʔ^{6} raay^{6}
bad (of a person) khuaŋ^{2}
bad, wicked phaan^{4}
baffled ʔan^{3} tuu^{3}
bag, pocket day^{5}
bag, suitcase ka^{6} paw^{1}
bag varieties ka^{6} thiaw^{4}, thɔŋ^{2}
bait ɲɯa^{2}, ɲɯa^{6}
balance, scales siŋ^{4}
bald laan^{3}
bald-headed thɤɤk^{6}
ball of sugar piaŋ^{6}
form (rice) into a ball; twist, wring van^{3}, val^{3}
balloon (toy) tum^{6} pɔŋ^{3}
balustrade koŋ^{1}
bamboo traa^{3}, tlaa^{3}
bamboo bell for buffaloes reeŋ^{6}
bamboo frame on which people sit in a boat sa^{6} nɛɛn^{4}
bamboo shoot naaŋ^{4}
bamboo shoot before cut vay^{4} naaŋ^{4}
bamboo star to ward off spirits vaa^{1} leew^{2}
bamboo strip for tying or weaving pruk^{4}, pluk^{4}
bamboo toy whirled on the end of a string voot^{6}
bamboo tube baŋ^{6}
bamboo tube for water, rice, etc. khɔɔk^{5}
bamboo varieties may^{6} phray^{6} thual^{5}, ree^{6}
clump of bamboo kɔɔ^{1}, thuup^{5}
cut section of bamboo bɔɔŋ^{3}

half of bamboo used as water pipe; empty can used as container; lid of empty oil drum   ka^{6} paaŋ^{1}
put rice in a bamboo tube to cook   phɔɔŋ^{2}
split bamboo for flooring   vaak^{5}
wall of woven bamboo   vaa^{1} ka^{6} tɛʔ^{4}
banana   luŋ^{5}
banana blossom   plii^{1}
banana varieties   luŋ^{5} ʔii^{6} tɔʔ^{4}, luŋ^{5} ŋaaw^{6}, luŋ^{5} tha^{6} nii^{4}, luŋ^{5} tha^{6} nii^{4} ʔɔɔŋ^{1}
bunch of bananas   nɔk^{6} luŋ^{5}
line (a basket) with banana leaves; put something under (e.g., leg of bed or table) to raise it   lɔɔt^{6}
rice boiled in cakes with a banana; starch, flour   pɛɛŋ^{3}
bandit   coon^{1}
Bangkok   kuŋ^{1} theep^{5}
bank (of a river)   vaŋ^{6}
bank of a river, dike between fields   ɣan^{4}, ɣal^{4}
bank of a river; side, direction; classifier for one of a pair   viaŋ^{3}
banyan tree   khoo^{6} hay^{4}, hay^{4}
bar (wooden and for a door)   lay^{4}
bar of silver or gold   thɛɛŋ^{5}
bare the teeth   siik^{6} nɛɛŋ^{1}
bark (of a dog)   haw^{6}
bark, rind, peel   praak^{6}, plaak^{6}
base of a plant   moon^{4}, mool^{4}
base of a tree; foot   tiin^{1}
base; tree, plant; first part   khoo^{6}
basin   ʔaaŋ^{6}
basin, bowl, dish   saam^{4}
basket varieties   kaʔ^{6} taa^{6}, ka^{6} thaa^{6}, ka^{6} thɔɔ^{4}, lɯan^{4}
basket, container (for betel)   khay^{2}
basket for scooping water   ka^{6} soo^{3}
basket with feet   kaʔ^{6} yaŋ^{1}
couplet paired with ka^{6} thɔɔ^{4} 'basket'   ka^{6} thak^{6}
round basket for glutinous rice   tip^{4}
small basket used for marketing   ka^{6} tɔʔ^{6}
waterproof basket   khuʔ^{6}
weave a basket   saan^{2}
winnowing basket   thuŋ^{3} vii^{6}
bat (the animal)   kia^{1}, cia^{1}
bat variety   biŋ^{3}
bathe   ʔaap^{6}
bathing cloth   kha^{6} maa^{3}

batter, beat, strike   thap^{6} thoo^{4}
   batter, pound   thap^{6}
be, become; have a disease   phan^{4}, phal^{4}
   be in a place   yuu^{6}
beach, sandbar   haat^{6}
beads   mlɛk^{6} tum^{3}
beam   dɔɔk^{6} raan^{4}, pɛɛ^{1}, rɔɔŋ^{4}
bean   thua^{5}
   bean variety   pɛɛp^{6}
   pod (of beans, etc.); sheath (of knife)   vak^{4}
bear   mii^{2}, mɯay^{2}, mɤɤy^{2}
beat, batter, strike   thap^{6} thoo^{4}
   beat, strike, hit, pound; fight; thresh (rice)   mɔk^{6}
   beat to death   muut^{5}
   sound of beating   tup^{6}
   sound of beating; fruit falling   ʔup^{6}
beater, comb-like part of a loom   via^{1}, via^{4}
beautiful   sap^{6}, hay^{1}
because   kham^{3}, kham^{5}
beckon with the hand   kwak^{4}
become, be; have a disease   phan^{4}, phal^{4}
bed   tiaŋ^{1}
   garden bed   naan^{1}
bedbug   ruat^{6}
bee   rooy^{2}
   carpenter bee; person; male   phuu^{6}
   small bee variety   sɯŋ^{4}
beehive   ruaŋ^{4}
beer   bia^{1}
beeswax   ruak^{5}
beetle variety   mɛɛŋ^{4} kɔɔk^{6}
   dung beetle   kuŋ^{6} khuu^{4}
before, first   kɔɔn^{6}
beg   thrɔɔ^{2}
belch   ʔɯam^{3}
believe   sɯa^{5}
bell (small metal)   ka^{6} lɛŋ^{6}
   bamboo bell for buffaloes   reeŋ^{6}
belly   phuŋ^{4}
   belly, stomach   thuŋ^{6}
belonging to, of   hɛɛŋ^{6}
   belonging to, of; things, possessions   hɔɔŋ^{2}

below, under, south   tɤɤ^{3}

belt   khem^{1} khat^{6}, taay^{3} ʔɛɛw^{1}, tɔy^{3} ʔɛɛw^{1}, tɔɔy^{3} ʔɛɛw^{1}, trɔɔy^{3} ʔɛɛw^{1}, saay^{2} ʔɛɛw^{1}

bend, straighten   blɛt^{4}

  bend backwards   ʔɛɛn^{1}

  bend into a curve   kɔɔm^{1}

  bend over, bow   kam^{3}

bent; curved; a coil; to bow   khooŋ^{3}

beside; edge, side   thrɛɛm^{4}

  beside; side (of the body, of house)   rɛk^{4}

betel   phluu^{4}

  basket, container (for betel)   khay^{2}

between   vaaŋ^{6}

bicycle, car, vehicle   lot^{6}

big   bɯk^{4}, ɲɤɤ^{6}; ɲay^{6}

  big (of a heap)   soon^{3} soon^{3}

bird   nɔk^{6}

  bird varieties   thua^{1}, nɔk^{6} ka^{6} cip^{4}

  mynah bird   ʔiaŋ^{3}, ʔiaŋ^{6}

  nest of a bird   rɔɔŋ^{4}, rɔɔk^{5}

birdlime   taŋ^{1}

birth (to give)   rooy^{2}

  birthmark   paan^{1}

bite   kat^{4}, khop^{4}, ɣap^{6}

  bite, nibble (of a fish); sting (of an insect)   tɔɔt^{6}

  bite (of food); small scrap (of cloth)   mɛɛŋ^{6}

bitter   ɣam^{4}

black   ram^{1}

  completely black   ram^{1} pit^{4}

blanket, quilt, coverlet   kha^{6} lɔɔp^{6}

  cover with a blanket   ham^{6}

blaze, cut in a tree to mark it   baak^{6}

blaze up suddenly   pɯp^{6}, pɯp^{6} pap^{6}, phɯp^{6}

  blaze up (a fire)   luk^{6}

blessing   khuun^{4}, phɔɔn^{4}

blind   lɔɔ^{4}

blink (the eyes), close (the eyes)   ɲip^{4}

blistered   phooŋ^{4}, phɔɔŋ^{4}

bloated (of a stomach)   ʔɯɯt^{6}

block, lie athwart, obstruct   vaaŋ^{2}

blocks of stone on a mountain   ŋɤɤp^{5} riin^{2}, ŋɤɤp^{5} riil^{2}

blood   luat^{5}
stop the flow of blood   khat^{4} luat^{5}
bloom   baan^{1}
blow (of the wind)   pɛk^{4}
blow away   priw^{1}, pliw^{1}
blow (a wind instrument), play   phɔɔ^{6}
blow the nose; order, give final instructions   saŋ^{6}
blowgun   phuʔ^{6}
blue   muuy^{4}, sii^{2} phaa^{3}, sii^{2} faa^{3}
Bo tree   phoo^{4}
board   peen^{3}
boast   ʔaaŋ^{6}
boat   rua^{1}
classifier for boats, books, knives, oxcarts, various sharp objects   lɛm^{3}
bobby pin   kip^{4}
body   too^{1}, tuu^{6} thua^{4}, tua^{6} thua^{4}, tuŋ^{6} thua^{4}, thua^{6} thua^{4}, saat^{5}
body, corpse   khook^{5} maaŋ^{4}
classifier for animals; body   thua^{4}
side (of the body, house); beside   rɛk^{4}
sides (of the body), ribs   hooŋ^{2}
body hair   pun^{1}, pul^{1}
boil, boiling   truak^{6}, tluak^{6}, rɔɔm^{6}
boil; cook rice; distil   ruŋ^{2}
boil (a)   sii^{5}
bold, brave   kaa^{3}, traa^{3}, tlaa^{3}
bomb   la^{6} bɤɤt^{2}
bone   rɔɔk^{6}
book, writing   naŋ^{4} sɯɯ^{2}
classifier for books, knives, boats, oxcarts, various sharp objects   lɛm^{3}
border, frontier post   daan^{6}
bored with; dislike, hate   cee^{1}
born   kɤɤt^{6}
borrow   kham^{6}
borrow; ask for help   maan^{6}
boss, master   naay^{4}
both, all, together with; even though   thɯŋ^{4}
bottle   kɔɔŋ^{3} kɛɛw^{3}
bottle; glass, drinking glass   kɛɛw^{3}
water bottle   nam^{6} taw^{3}
boundary, territory   kheet^{6}, dɛɛn^{1}
bow, arrow   tha^{6} nuu^{4}

bow, bend over kam^{3}
bow; curved; bent; a coil khooŋ^{3}
bowl, basin, dish saam^{4}
metal water bowl ʔoo^{1}
monk's begging bowl baat^{6}
old-fashioned Chinese earthen bowl; big cup, glass caʔ^{6} ʔɤɤŋ^{1}
box (to) tɔŋ^{3}, muay^{4}
box, trunk, suitcase hiip^{6}
small box trap^{4}, tlap^{4}
boy ku^{6} maan^{4}, kuʔ^{4} maan^{4}
bracelet phram^{1}, phlam^{1}, phlam^{4}
Brahma phom^{4}
Brahma divinity phom^{4}, phaʔ^{6} phom^{4}
great Brahma ma^{6} haa^{1} phom^{4}
name of a Brahma divinity ka^{6} bin^{1} laʔ^{6} phom^{4}, ka^{6} bin^{1} la^{6} phom^{4}
braid pia^{1}
braid, knit thak^{4}
brains ʔuuk^{6}
bran ram^{4}
branch kiiŋ^{6}, ŋaa^{5}
branch, twig kaaŋ^{6}
brass, bronze; in certain expressions copper or gold thɔɔŋ^{4}
brass, bronze, copper luaŋ^{4}
brave, bold kaa^{3}, traa^{3}, tlaa^{3}
break, broken, torn kaat^{6}
break apart kaat^{6} put^{6}
break, be broken rak^{4}
break, be broken, burst preek^{6}
break off a piece biʔ^{4}
break a contract, cancel ɲup^{6}
break wind rɛt^{4}
breast cuu^{3}
breathe thit^{4} cɯɯ^{1}, thɯt^{4} cɯɯ^{1}
hold the breath kan^{3}
brick ʔit^{4}, din^{1} cii^{6}
bridge khaw^{4}
bright, gleaming (red, yellow) rɤɤ^{5} rɤɤ^{5}
bright, light; dawn, clear rɔɔŋ^{5}
brinjals (small variety) veeŋ^{3}
brittle, tender, crisp cɔɔn^{1}
broad, wide rooŋ^{6}
broken, cracked open ɲaʔ^{6}

broken, break, torn kaat^{6}
be broken, break rak^{4}
be broken, break, burst preek^{6}
bronze, brass; in certain expressions copper or gold thɔɔŋ^{4}
bronze, brass, copper luaŋ^{4}
brood, incubate ʔup^{4}
broom vaa^{2} theen^{5}, vaay^{2} theel^{5}
brother (older) ʔɛɛŋ^{1}
father's younger brother ʔaaw^{5}
bruised sam^{6}
bruised, swollen vɔk^{6}
bruised and swollen from a blow; having a long muzzle tuup^{6}
brush prɛɛŋ^{1}
bubbles, foam, lather poop^{6}
bubble nest of fish phɔɔt^{6}
bucket, pail; tank thaŋ^{1}
bud, sprout caaw^{1}
be in bud cuum^{1}
Buddha phut^{6} thiʔ^{6}
Buddhist phut^{6}
Buddhist ceremony of giving robes to the monks thɔɔt^{5} ka^{6} thin^{2}
Buddhist Law, Dharma tham^{4}
Buddhist Lent phan^{4} saa^{2}
old term for leaving Buddhist Lent paʔ^{6} vɔɔ^{4} la^{6} naa^{4}, vɔɔ^{4} la^{6} naa^{4}
buffalo vaay^{4}
buffalo hide cut into strips naŋ^{2} niiw^{4}; naŋ^{2} liw^{4}
edible, partially digested contents of buffalo intestines phia^{3}
fight (of buffaloes) seew^{2}
hump on the back of an ox or buffalo nɔɔk^{6}, lam^{1}
male buffalo with short horns vaay^{4} tuu^{3}
build, construct, erect kɔɔ^{6}, saaŋ^{3}
build (a house); plant (plants) prɔɔk^{6}, plɔɔk^{6}
building tɯk^{4}
building, hall rooŋ^{4}
official building saan^{1}
bulb (light); spindle, spool luut^{6}
bullfrog ʔɯɯŋ^{6}
bump, knot on tree puut^{6}
bump on skin nuun^{3}
bundle, faggot lɯm^{4}
bundle, sheaf, faggot roop^{5}

bundle, tie in bundles   pɔɔ^{3}
tie in bundles   phay^{4}
burn (intransitive)   ham^{2}
burn (transitive)   phraw^{2}
burn, cremate, light a fire, set fire   cuk^{4}
burn, scorch   daat^{6}
burst, break, be broken   preek^{6}
bury   lip^{4}, lɯp^{4}
bus   lot^{6} mee^{4}
but   tɛɛ^{6} ɣaa^{3}, hak^{2} ɣaa^{5}, haak^{5} ɣaa^{5}
but; from, since   tɛɛ^{6}
but, so, and then   phat^{2}
butt, end; heel   sɔn^{3}
butter, cheese   nɣɣy^{4}
butterfly   buŋ^{6} baa^{3}
buttocks   troon^{1}, tloon^{1}
curving of the buttocks   ŋeen^{4}
button   mɛk^{6} kuk^{4}, mlɛk^{6} kuk^{4}
fasten (a button)   khaan^{2}, khaal^{2}
undo a button; remove, take down; remove (a yoke)   prɛt^{4}, plɛt^{4}
buy   sɯɯ^{6}
by, with   dooy^{1}

C

cackle (of a hen)   ka^{6} taak^{4}
cage; trap for frogs   tum^{3}
bird cage with bird in it used as a decoy   pha^{6} niat^{5}
chicken cage; fish trap   sum^{6}
cake   khek^{6}
cake, dessert   ɣaw^{6} nom^{1}
rice boiled in cakes with a banana; starch, flour   pɛɛŋ^{3}
calf of the leg   kuaŋ^{6}, blii^{1}
call, summon; be called (so-and-so)   reek^{5}
can, tin   ka^{6} pɔŋ^{1}
can for water   pip^{4}, pip^{6}
empty can used as a container; half of bamboo used as water pipe; lid of empty oil drum   ka^{6} paaŋ^{1}
cancel, break a contract   ɲup^{6}
cancer   heŋ^{4}
candle   thian^{4}

cap, hat muak^{2}, muak^{6}
  knitted cap for cold weather mooŋ^{3}
capital, investment thɯn^{4}
  lose investments lup^{4} thɯn^{4}
capture, arrest; abduct kum^{1}
car, bicycle, vehicle lot^{6}
  park (a car); stop; moor (a boat) cɔɔt^{6}
  run over (of a car); step on, tread yiap^{6}
  sound of cars colliding; sound of chewing buap^{5}
  turn (a car) around ʔuay^{6}, ʔwaay^{6}
carcass, corpse saak^{5}
care for, treat (the ill) pua^{1}, pin^{6} pua^{1}
  take care of, guard rak^{6} saa^{2}
careful; whisper ɲiim^{5} ɲia^{2}
carry, hold thɯɯ^{4}
  carry (a child) in a cloth on the back ʔɛɛt^{5}
  carry an infant against the side in a cloth ʔam^{6}
  carry big things roop^{6}
  carry hanging down from the hand riw^{3}, riiw^{3}, hiiw^{5}
  carry in a procession, have a procession rɛɛ^{6}
  carry in the arms ʔuum^{3}
  carry off one's belongings hup^{4}
  carry on one end of a pole over the shoulder khɔɔn^{4}, khɔɔl^{4}
  carry on the shoulder khuat^{5}
  carry on two ends of a shoulder pole raap^{6}
  carry slung over the shoulder phaa^{6}
  carry, transport khun^{2}
  carry tucked in the waist phɔk^{6}
  carry under the arm; pick up with chopsticks; pinch, as a crab khɛɛp^{5}, niip^{6}
  carrying pole ɣaan^{4}
  descriptive of carrying or dragging thiʔ^{4} thuu^{1} thiʔ^{4} thay^{1}
  two or more carry raam^{2}
cart; wheel lɔɔ^{3}
  sound of cart in motion khɯp^{6} khɯp^{6}
cash, take out money bɤɤk^{6}
cast, throw, sow vaan^{6}, vaal^{6}
cast-net lap^{6}
castrate; part, section tɔɔn^{1}
cat mɛɛw^{4}
catch, seize, grasp, take hold of cap^{4}
caterpillar vɔŋ^{6}
  poisonous caterpillar haan^{1}, haal^{1}, haan^{2}, haal^{2}

catfish rɔk^{4}
cause; give; for hɣɣ^{3}
  cause, create nii^{4} mit^{6}, ni^{6} mit^{6}
cave tham^{3}
  name of a cave khan^{4} tha^{6} thu^{6} lii^{1}
ceiling thrɣɣŋ^{6}
cemetery paa^{6} reew^{5} maaŋ^{4}
centipede ca^{6} thrip^{4}
  coil up (of a centipede) pɔɔm^{3}
ceremony, tradition riit^{5}
certain; excellent, very good khak^{6}
certain, sure nɛɛ^{5}
chain soo^{3}, soo^{6}
  chain, necklace saay^{1}
chair taŋ^{6} ʔii^{3}, taŋ^{6} ʔii^{6}
chalk sɔk^{6}
challenge too^{3}
chance (take a), risk; make a wish siaŋ^{5}, siaŋ^{6}
change, exchange pian^{6}
  make change (money) thɔɔn^{4}
character, personality, disposition nit^{4} say^{1}
characterized by khii^{2}
charcoal thaan^{6}, riaw^{4}
chase lay^{5}
  chase, drive raaŋ^{4}
chasm; crack; hole; pit sɔɔŋ^{5}
chat, converse khuy^{4}, khuuy^{4}
cheap; correct; hit; touch thɯk^{6}
cheek keem^{3}
cheerful, happy sɯɯn^{5} cɯɯ^{1}, sɯɯn^{5} mɔk^{4}, sɯɯn^{6} cɯɯ^{1}
cheese, butter nɣɣy^{4}
chest tam^{1} ʔaaŋ^{1}, ta^{6} baaŋ^{1}
chevrons on a uniform ŋɛŋ^{5}
chew ɲam^{3}
  sound of chewing; cars colliding buap^{5}
  sound of chewing noisily cɛp^{5}
chicken kay^{6}
  chicken cage; fish trap sum^{6}
  chicken louse rii^{4}
  scratch (of chickens) khia^{6}
  scratch (of chickens); dip a ball of rice in food and take it up khuy^{3}

chief, king, prince, lord pha^{6} ɲaa^{4}
  chief, prince, lord caw^{3}
child dɛk^{4}
  child, offspring lɯk^{6}
  divine child, angel thee^{4} va^{6} but^{4}
  one's children lɯk^{6} taw^{3}
  term used with a small child similar to ʔay^{3} nuu^{5} in Siamese tɤŋ^{3}
  term used with children to raise hands in obeisance thuʔ^{4}
chin ɣaaŋ^{4}
  chin, jaw kaaŋ^{3} haam^{4}
Chinese cek^{6}
chipped; torn hian^{2}
  chipped, nicked baan^{6}, baal^{6}
chisel siw^{6}, siiw^{6}
choose lee^{5}
chop up yap^{6}
  chop fine pham^{3}, sap^{4}
  chopped meat dish laap^{5}
  chopping board thɤɤt^{6}
chopsticks thɯɯ^{5}, thuu^{5}, may^{6} thɯɯ^{5} naaŋ^{5}, may^{6} thɯɯ^{5} ta^{6} khiap^{2}
  one chopstick; twig kiŋ^{6}
  pick up with chopsticks; pinch, as a crab; carry under the arm khɛɛp^{5}, niip^{6}
cigar, cigarette buʔ^{6} lii^{4}, bu^{6} lii^{4}
cigarette, cigar buʔ^{6} lii^{4}, bu^{6} lii^{4}
circle (go in) von^{4}
  circle dancing lam^{4} voŋ^{4}
circuit (make a), go around liap^{5}, vian^{4}
  make a circuit lɔʔ^{6}
city na^{6} khɔɔn^{4}
  city name peeŋ^{1} caan^{1}
city; country, kingdom phiaŋ^{4}
civet cat ɲɛn^{2}, ɲɛl^{2}
clan, family khoot^{5}
  clan, family; litter rɔɔk^{5}
  elder who arranges at weddings caw^{3} khoot^{5} voŋ^{4} taa^{1}
clap (the hands); slap tap^{4}
clappers (of metal) sɛŋ^{6}, sɛɛŋ^{6}
clasp, hug, embrace kɔɔt^{6}
classifier
  for animals; body thua^{4}
  for books, knives, boats, oxcarts, various sharp objects lɛm^{3}
  for fruit, round objects maak^{6}

for houses; back; after laŋ^{2}
for long, thin objects sɛn^{3}, sɛl^{3}
for mats, cloth phɯn^{4}, phɯɯn^{4}
for one of a pair; side, direction; bank of a river viaŋ^{3}
for piece, length; a lump thɔɔn^{5}
for royal persons ʔoŋ^{1}
for spoons, pencils, saws khan^{4}, khal^{4}
for things ʔan^{1}, ʔal^{1}
for tools, knives, sharp implements maak^{5}, maak^{6}
clause, phrase; part vak^{6}
claw, scratch khwaa^{4}, khuaw^{4}, khwaaw^{4}, khwaak^{6}
clean mɔt^{4} mɛɛŋ^{2}
clean; smooth prian^{3}, plian^{3}, mɔt^{4}
clean up outdoors, clear laaŋ^{6}
clear, dawn; light, bright rɔɔŋ^{5}
clear fields, etc. thaaŋ^{2}
clear, clean up outdoors laaŋ^{6}
cleaver-like knife maak^{6} thaa^{6} koʔ^{4}
clever, intelligent khuun^{2}
clever, skilled keŋ^{6}, keeŋ^{6}
cliff (rocky) khook^{5} phraa^{2}, phraa^{2}
climb (a tree) piin^{1}
clitoris tiw^{6}, tiiw^{6}
clock, watch naa^{4} li^{4} kaa^{1}
close a door; cover the face ʔɔt^{4}
close (the eyes), blink ɲip^{4}
close one eye liiw^{6}
close the eyes for a moment and then open them ɲip^{4} kɛɛp^{6}
close the mouth hup^{4}
close together nɛɛp^{5}, naap^{5}
close, tight cɛɛp^{6}
closely spaced, finely woven; miserly thii^{5}
cloth umbrella khan^{4} kot^{4}
clothesline; pole for picking fruit yaaw^{6}
clothing; things, possessions; food; utensils thrɯaŋ^{5}
cloth to cover the genitalia of a small child moʔ^{4}
cover with a cloth hum^{6}
squeeze clothes when washing them; crumple up (paper) ɲɔɔŋ^{5}, ɲɔɔŋ^{6}
wash (clothes) yak^{6}
cloud via^{3}
club, hammer ɣɔɔn^{6}, ɣɔɔl^{6}
clump of bamboo kɔɔ^{1}, thuup^{5}

cluster (of coconuts, areca nuts)   sɛɛŋ^{4}

  cluster of fruit   phua^{3}, phuaŋ^{4}

coals (live)   haaŋ^{4} vii^{4}

  dead coal, ashes of a dead fire   plɔɔ^{6} mii^{3}

coarse, coarsely woven; far apart, widely spaced   saa^{6}

coarse, tough (of meat, food)   ɲiap^{6}

cockroach   saap^{6}

cockscomb   khian^{4}, khial^{4}, hɔɔn^{1}

cockspur   traa^{1}, praa^{1}

coconut   phraaw^{6}, phlaaw^{6}

  coconut cream   ka^{6} thiʔ^{6}

  coconut grub   duaŋ^{3}

  coconut shell   ka^{6} poʔ^{4}

coffin   looŋ^{4}

coil up, roll up   muan^{6}

coil up a rope   kuan^{3}, khuan^{3}, khwaan^{3}, tlooŋ^{1}

  a coil; curved; bent; to bow   khooŋ^{3}

  coil up (of a centipede)   pɔɔm^{3}

coin, medal   lian^{1}

cold (have a)   phan^{4} vat^{4}, phal^{4} vat^{4}

cold   seeŋ^{2}

  cold, cool   nɛk^{4}

collide, fight (of buffaloes)   seew^{2}

  collide; stab, pierce; pound   tam^{1}

color; paint   sii^{2}

column, row   thɛɛw^{2}, lian^{4}

comb, to comb   hɔɔy^{2}

come, return   maa^{2}, hun^{4}

  come up, go up, up; rise, ascend   hɯn^{3}

comfortable, comfortably   sa^{6} vaaŋ^{6}

commune   tam^{1} bon^{1}

comparative, more than   kua^{6}, kwaa^{6}

compare   thiap^{5}, phɛɛt^{5}

compel, force   cam^{1}, khuu^{1}

compete   khɛɛŋ^{6}, khɛɛŋ^{6} khan^{1}

complain, grumble   thraam^{4}

complete, all   khop^{6}

  completely, all, all gone   phleek^{5}

conceal   ʔam^{1}

condiments (to add)   yɔʔ^{4}

confiscate   rip^{6}

confused ɲuŋ^{6}

confused, disheveled, entangled ɲuŋ^{6} ɲaaw^{2}

conquer, put down phaap^{6}

conscript keen^{1}

consider phit^{4} caa^{1} la^{6} naa^{4}, phiʔ^{4} caa^{1} la^{6} naa^{4}, phit^{6} caa^{1} la^{6} naa^{4}, phiʔ^{6} caa^{1} la^{6} naa^{4}

consider, weigh a matter ŋii^{5}

constrict, pucker up ɲum^{3}

constricted, pressed together tiip^{6}

construct, build, erect kɔɔ^{6}, saaŋ^{3}

consult baan^{4}

container for drinking water ʔuʔ^{4}

container, basket (for betel) khay^{2}

continent; place thiip^{5}

a mythical continent chom^{4} phuu^{4} thiip^{5}

continually, always maay^{5}

continually, steadily lɯay^{3}, lɯay^{5}

continue; join tɔɔ^{6}

continuously ta^{6} lɔɔt^{6}

contract; promise sɛn^{3} ɲaa^{4}

make a contract maw^{2}

converse, chat khuy^{4}, khuuy^{4}

convict nak^{6} thoot^{5}

cook, stew for a long time ʔɔɔm^{6}

cooked, ripe suk^{6}

put rice in a bamboo tube to cook phɔɔŋ^{2}

cool, cold nɛk^{4}

copper, brass, bronze luaŋ^{4}

in certain expressions copper and gold; brass, bronze thɔɔŋ^{4}

cord, rope saak^{5}

cord, string saay^{2}

wind or bind a cord around ɲak^{6}

core (hard) kɛɛn^{1}

corn (Indian), maize sa^{6} lii^{4}

corner lɛɛ^{1}

corner, angle, edge liam^{5}

corner or side broken off ka^{6} vaʔ^{4}

corpse, carcass saak^{5}

corpse, body khook^{5} maaŋ^{4}

corpse; discarded snake skin thraap^{5}

corpse; spirit, ghost maaŋ^{4}

correct; cheap; hit; touch thɯk^{6}

cotton, cotton cloth paay^{1}
instrument to remove seeds from cotton ʔɛɛt^{6}
spin cotton thray^{4}, pan^{1}, pan^{6}, pal^{1}
cough ʔay^{1}
cough up phlegm khaak^{6}
could not, do not bay^{3}, boo^{6} day^{3}
count nap^{6}
country pa^{6} theet^{5}
country, kingdom; city phiaŋ^{4}
couple, pair tooy^{1}
court, woo; play sɤɤn^{6}
cover, to cover pok^{4}, pɔk^{4}
cover of a book loom^{4}
cover the face, close a door ʔɔt^{4}
cover with a big lid kuam^{1}
cover with a blanket ham^{6}
cover with a cloth hum^{6}
cover, as with a lid ŋam^{4}, tloop^{5}, throop^{5}
cover with the hand ŋum^{5}
cover, wrap up hum^{3}
coverlet, quilt, blanket kha^{6} lɔɔp^{6}
crab paw^{1}
pinch, as a crab; carry under the arm; pick up with chopsticks khɛɛp^{5}, niip^{6}
crack; chasm; hole; pit sɔɔŋ^{5}
cracked hɛɛŋ^{1}
cracked open, broken ɲaʔ^{6}
cradle ʔuu^{6}
cradle, swing for children vɔŋ^{5}
crane the neck to look ŋook^{5}
crave ŋɛɛn^{3}
crawl luan^{4}
crawl, creep tay^{6}
crazy, mad kua^{3}, kwaa^{3}
create, cause nii^{4} mit^{6}, ni^{6} mit^{6}
creature (mythical water) ŋuak^{5}
creep, crawl tay^{6}
cremate; light a fire; set fire; burn cuk^{4}
cricket tuŋ^{6} tian^{3}, tuŋ^{6} tial^{3}
crippled, weak, tired pia^{3}
crippled, lame khee^{4}
crippled (of the arm) cɔŋ^{1}

crisp, tender, brittle cɔɔn^{1}
criticize tiʔ^{4}
crocodile khɛɛ^{6}
crooked, not straight khot^{6}, vii^{5}
  crooked, twisted biaw^{3}
cross khway^{6}
  cross, go across haam^{3}
crossbow nua^{3}
crouch down muup^{2}, muup^{6}
crow kaa^{1}
  to crow han^{2}, hal^{2}
crowd, annoy, oppress biat^{6} bian^{1}
  crowded; stuffed neen^{3}
crowing sound of rooster ʔek^{4} kaʔ^{6} reen^{4} ʔeek^{4}, ʔek^{4} kaʔ^{6} reel^{4} ʔeek^{4}, ʔee^{5} kaʔ^{6} reen^{4} ʔee^{5}, ʔee^{5} kaʔ^{6} reel^{4} ʔee^{5}
crucible baw^{3}
crumple up (paper); squeeze clothes when washing them ɲɔɔŋ^{5}, ɲɔɔŋ^{6}
crunching sound boop^{5}
crushed, flatten, smashed raa^{5}
  crushed; flat, flattened tɤɤt^{6}
cry, weep tay^{3}
cry out vaan^{1}
cubit, elbow suak^{6}, sɔɔk^{6}
cucumber priaŋ^{1} prɔɔŋ^{6}, priaŋ^{1} plɔɔŋ^{6}
  cucumber, melon priaŋ^{1}
cup, glass cɔɔk^{6}
  big cup, glass; old-fashioned Chinese earthen bowl caʔ^{6} ʔɤɤŋ^{1}
  cup, dish, bowl thooy^{6}
cupboard tuu^{3}
cured by a bad experience, be afraid trɯa^{4}
curl up (of a leaf) koop^{6}
  curled up (of hands and feet in a disease) caŋ^{1}, kuut^{6} caŋ^{1}
  curled up (of leaves); tangled (of rope) caŋ^{1}
  (sleep) curled up khot^{4}
curry keeŋ^{1}
  to make a particular curry ʔɔʔ^{4}
cursing expression praay^{1} phɛɛp^{6}, praay^{1} haa^{6}
curtain maan^{3}
  move (e.g., a curtain) along a rod; strip off (leaves) ruut^{5}
curved; bent; a coil; to bow khooŋ^{3}
  curving of the buttocks ŋeen^{4}
cushion bɔʔ^{4}

custard apple khiap^{2}, lot^{6}
customs, traditions praʔ^{6} phee^{4} nii^{4}, hiit^{5}
cut tat^{4}, tɛk^{4}, ban^{3}, ban^{6}
cut a blaze in a tree to mark it baak^{6}
cut a cutting, put earth around the base of a plant ʔoop^{6}
cut a piece off the side of a tree or log thaak^{6}
cut cloth rɛɛk^{5}
cut into pieces, trim a tree after it is felled rɛɛm^{3}
cut or pull up grass; disappear; spoil; die; pay ʔiin^{3}
cut up a slaughtered animal khua^{4}
cut, slash van^{1}, val^{1}

D

dam khan^{4}, khan^{4} thɛɛ^{4}, phaay^{1}
dam up thot^{6}, paan^{3}, paal^{3}
damaged, spoiled hɯɯ^{2}
damp (slightly) maat^{6}
dance yɔɔn^{3}, saay^{2}
dance, jump sɛk^{4}
danger phooy^{4} phay^{4}
dark lap^{4}
dark (of color) khem^{3}
dark (of color), old, ripe kee^{6}
dash luup^{6}
daughter-in-law khwɤɤ^{6}, phɤɤ^{6}, fɤɤ^{6}
dawn, clear; light, bright rɔɔŋ^{5}
day mɯɯ^{6}, van^{4}
day after tomorrow rɯɯ^{1}
day before yesterday phɔɔn^{4}
day, daytime, the sun ɲɛn^{4}
dead sua^{3}
dead coals, ashes of a dead fire plɔɔ^{6} mii^{3}
deaf nuuk^{6}
debt say^{6}
decayed, soft yuay^{3}, ɲuay^{3}
deceive, lie; scare, frighten lɔɔk^{6}
decorate pa^{6} dap^{4}
deeds (good); merit, favor khun^{4}
do a favor for mii^{4} khun^{4} mii^{4} noo^{4}
deep lak^{6}

deer varieties maŋ^{5}, maŋ^{6}, vaan^{4}, vaal^{4}, vuaŋ^{4}

defeat, win, be victorious phɛɛ^{5}

  defeat, hold one's own (in idiomatic phrases) laay^{6}

defeated sua^{2}

  defeated, lose loʔ^{6}

degree, equal, quantity leeŋ^{4}

delicious, enjoy one's food ŋɔɔn^{2}, nua^{2}, bua^{1}

demolish, dismantle thaaw^{3}

dented bum^{3}

depend upon phaŋ^{5}

  depending upon, up to lɛɛw^{3} tɛɛ^{6}

descend, go down, down lɔŋ^{4}

desert, divorce, abandon raaŋ^{6}

design, stripe, mark, spots laay^{4}

designate taaŋ^{1} tiʔ^{4}

desire, want; hungry haat^{6}

dessert, cake ɣaw^{6} nom^{1}

destroy, die, go out, extinguish (a fire) dap^{4}

detour, go around ʔɔɔm^{3}

diagonal biaŋ^{6}, viaŋ^{6}, viaŋ^{6} tooŋ^{6}

diarrhea ɣay^{6} suʔ^{6}

dice, gambling game saŋ^{1} kaa^{1}

die praay^{1}, praay^{1} map^{6}

  cursing expression praay^{1} phɛɛp^{6}, praay^{1} haa^{6}

  squirm, as when dying piat^{6}

die, destroy, go out, extinguish (a fire) dap^{4}

  die; lose; disappear; spoil; pay; pull up (grass) ʔiin^{3}

differ, various, strange taaŋ^{6}

difficult phak^{6}, phak^{6} phɤɤ^{5}

dig khut^{6}

  dig a small hole cɔɔt^{5}

  dig or scratch with the hands; scoop up, search (e.g., in a box) hut^{4}

  dig out (the ear) ɲɔɔn^{4}, ɲɔɔl^{4}

dike, bank of a river ɣan^{4}, ɣal^{4}

diligent, industrious duʔ^{4}, siaŋ^{2}

  diligent, persevere phian^{4}

dip down into cɔk^{4}

dip (food) in sauce cam^{3}

  dip a ball of rice in food and take it up; scratch (of chickens) khuy^{3}

dip up, dip out, draw (water) tak^{4}

  dip up fish with a sieve sɯm^{6}

  dip in water; dye cup^{4}

direction; side; river bank; classifier for one of a pair viaŋ^{3}
direction; side; road, path, way thaaŋ^{4}
dirt, earth, ground ban^{1}, bal^{1}
dried sweat and dirt on the skin ɣay^{6} ɣii^{4}
dirty, soiled pɯan^{3}
disappear rɤɤy^{1}
disappear; die; lose; spoil; pay; pull up (grass) ʔiin^{3}
disappear, vanish vaŋ^{3} vɛɛ^{3}
disappear, vanish by magic power lɯam^{4}
disappear, very (far) lip^{4}
disease (have a); be, become phan^{4}, phal^{4}
have a cold phan^{4} vat^{4}, phal^{4} vat^{4}
dish caan^{1}
dish, bowl, basin saam^{4}
disheveled, mussed (of hair) ɲɔɔŋ^{1}
disheveled, confused, entangled ɲuŋ^{6} ɲaaw^{2}
disheveled, mussed, tangled ɲuŋ^{6} ɲaaw^{2}
dislike, hate; be bored with cee^{1}
dismantle, demolish thaaw^{3}
disorderly ʔon^{1}
disorderly (of children) ʔon^{1} ʔua^{1}
in disorder rum^{2}, ruŋ^{2}, la^{6} nɯɯŋ^{4} la^{6} nɯɯɯt^{5}
displeased with each other, argue tɯk^{4}
disposition, character, personality nit^{4} say^{1}
distressed, worried, troubled ʔaŋ^{6}
distribute, hand out cɛɛk^{6}, yaay^{1}
district, area ɲaan^{5}
disturb kuʔ^{4} kuan^{1}
ditch ta^{6} khɔɔŋ^{4}, mɯaŋ^{1}
dive, swim under water bɔt^{4}
dive in headfirst; press down dik^{4}
divide, share beeŋ^{6}, pan^{1}
divine thip^{6}
divinity, god thee^{4} va^{6} daa^{1}
divorce yaa^{6}
divorce; desert, abandon raaŋ^{6}
divorce; lay aside; leave plii^{6}
do, make hit^{6}
be doing phuam^{4}
be doing, about to kam^{1} laŋ^{4}
doctor, shaman mɔɔ^{2}
dodge, duck lup^{4}

dog   maa^{2}
  exclamation used to chase dogs away   seʔ^{6}
  howl (of a dog)   hɔɔn^{1}
  mad (of dogs)   vɔɔ^{3}
donkey   laa^{4}
don't   kay^{2}, kay^{3}
  don't; stop, refrain from   yaa^{6}
door   pak^{4} tuu^{1}
  close (a door); cover (the face)   ʔɔt^{4}
dorsal fin   khii^{4}, coŋ^{1}
doubt, wonder   soŋ^{1} say^{1}
dove   haw^{2}
down, descend, go down   lɔŋ^{4}
downstream (to go)   lɔɔŋ^{5}
drag, pull   looy^{1}
  descriptive of dragging   ɲɤɤm^{4} ɲɤɤm^{4}, thuu^{4} thaat^{5}
  descriptive of effort of dragging or carrying   thiʔ^{4} thuu^{1} thiʔ^{4} thay^{1}
  drag along   thii^{4} thuu^{4} thii^{4} thaat^{5}
  drag on the ground   laam^{5}
draw, write   khian^{2}
  draw a line, scratch   khiit^{6}
draw (water), dip up, dip out   tak^{4}
dream (to)   van^{4}
dress; prepare; marry   tɛɛŋ^{6}
drip (to), drop   yɔɔt^{6}
drive, chase   raaŋ^{4}
drive (a car)   khap^{4}
drool   ɲuay^{3}
  drool (of saliva); flow   hɤɤy^{1}
drop; to drip   yɔɔt^{6}
drop into water   plum^{6}
drum   trɔɔŋ^{1}, tlɔɔŋ^{1}
  drum variety   thoon^{4}
  sound of gongs and drums   thɯɯt^{6} thɯɯt^{6}
drunk   maw^{4}
  drunkard   hun^{4} kin^{1} law^{3}
  recover from drunkenness, illness   suaŋ^{6}
dry   hɯɯ^{6}, hɯat^{6}
  dry and crisp (of roasted meat)   hɛɛm^{3}
  dry, dried, dried out   khoo^{2}
  dry, dried up   hɛɛŋ^{3}
  dry field   rii^{5}

dry land bɔk^{4}

dry (of weather), dry season lɛɛŋ^{6}

duck pit^{4}

duck, dodge lup^{4}

duckweed nɛɛ^{1}

dumb, unable to speak kɯɯk^{6}

dung beetle kuŋ^{6} khuu^{4}

durian thuʔ^{6} lian^{4}, thu^{6} lian^{4}

seed of jackfruit or durian nuan^{4}

during, in, inside, into, at daŋ^{1}, daaŋ^{1}

dusk, twilight sum^{3}

dust phun^{5}

dust; crushed or smashed to small pieces mul^{4}

dust off, sweep pɛk^{4}

dye ɲum^{6}

to dye, dip in water cup^{4}

dysentery (to have) phan^{4} bit^{4}, phal^{4} bit^{4}

E

each, every dɔɔ^{1}

each other kin^{1}

eagle ʔin^{1} thii^{4}

ear rua^{4}

ear or head of rice ruaŋ^{4}

earring tum^{3} huu^{1}, taaŋ^{3}, taaŋ^{6}, voŋ^{4} vɛɛn^{2}

earth din^{1}

earth, dirt, ground ban^{1}, bal^{1}

easy, simple ŋaay^{5}

eat kin^{1}, deek^{6} (slang)

eat all lɔɔn^{2}

eat or spend every last bit mɔɔt^{6}

eat with a snapping act, as a dog, tiger, fish suap^{5}

eaves yaay^{4}, yɛɛŋ^{4}

edge khɔɔp^{6}, rim^{4}

edge, angle, corner liam^{5}

edge, gunwale of a boat ɣeem^{4}

edge, side; beside thrɛɛm^{1}

go near the edge lɛɛw^{1}

placed near the edge min^{6}

sharp edge, sharp ɣam^{4}

eel   lian^{1}
effective, efficacious   khet^{4}
effeminate man   khan^{4} thɯay^{4}, thɯay^{4}
efficacious, effective   khet^{4}
  magically efficacious   khet^{4} yam^{1}
effort   kooŋ^{1}
  waste of effort   kɯam^{3} kaaŋ^{1}
egg, lay an egg   trɤɤŋ^{3}, tlɤɤŋ^{3}
  eggshell; matchbox; sheath   ta^{6} roop^{5}
eggplant   kee^{3}
eight   peet^{6}
elbow; cubit   suak^{6}, sɔɔk^{6}
elder who arranges at weddings   caw^{3} khoot^{5} voŋ^{4} taa^{1}
electric fan   phat^{6} lum^{4}
elephant   saaŋ^{6}
  elephant rider   khuan^{4}, khwaan^{4}
  elephant's trunk; spout of a teapot   ŋuaŋ^{4}
  sound of elephant chewing up coconut   book^{5}
  sound of elephant trumpeting   phiaʔ^{4} phiaŋ^{6}
  tusk of elephant; ivory   ŋaa^{4}
eleven   sip^{6} ʔɛt^{4}
embarrassed, ashamed   trɤɤy^{1}, tlɤɤy^{1}
embrace   kɔɔt^{6} kum^{1}
  embrace, hug, clasp   kɔɔt^{6}
embroider, plant (a stake)   pak^{4}
employ, use; send (someone)   thraay^{2}
  employee, worker   lɯk^{6} caaŋ^{3}, lɯk^{6} lɛɛŋ^{3}
empty   pruu^{6}, pluu^{6}
enamel, enameled   khɯap^{5}
encounter, meet   phaam^{4}
end, tip   praay^{1}, plaay^{1}
  end, butt; heel   sɔn^{3}
  end, most   sut^{4}
endure, go without   ʔot^{4}, ʔot^{4} ɲɯan^{3}, thon^{4}
  enduring, long-lasting   ɲɯɯn^{4}
enemy; war   khiak^{5}
engaged, get engaged   man^{3}
engine, machine   ɲon^{4}
enjoy one's food, delicious   ŋɔɔn^{2}, nua^{2}, bua^{1}
enough; when   phɔɔ^{4}
entangled, confused, disheveled   ɲuŋ^{6} ɲaaw^{2}
enter   haw^{3}

entertainment, music ŋan^{4}

entreat, wheedle ʔeew^{6}

envelope sɔɔŋ^{4}

envy ʔit^{4} saa^{1}

epidemic haa^{6}

cursing expression praay^{1} haa^{6}

equal, degree, quantity leeŋ^{4}

erase, rub out lɯp^{6}

erect, build, construct kɔɔ^{6}, saaŋ^{3}

erect (of the penis) ŋɔŋ^{1}

establish, set up; all taŋ^{3}

establish, raise up ɲuk^{6}

estimate, guess, assume tuaŋ^{1}

Europe yu^{4} roop^{6}

evaporate hɤɤy^{1}

even, indeed hɔn^{2} (idiomatic)

even, level phiaŋ^{4}

even one (not); one or so; about, approximately sak^{4}

even though; all, both, together with thɯŋ^{4}

even though; arrive, reach thaŋ^{4}

evening, nightfall, night ɣam^{5}

every thuk^{6}

every, each dɔɔ^{1}

every sort sap^{4} phaʔ^{6} phiʔ^{4}

every sort of thing saa^{1} laʔ^{6} phat^{6} saa^{1} laʔ^{6} phaa^{4}

everybody, anybody, who dɤɤ^{1}

everything, something, what tuŋ^{6} thaa^{4}

everywhere thua^{5}

evil, low thɔɔy^{6}

exceed, too kɤɤn^{1}

excellent, very good; certain khak^{6}

excessively, very much vian^{4}, vian^{4} raat^{5}, vɛɛn^{4} raat^{5}

exchange, change pian^{6}

excited; irritated, annoyed rɤɤ^{3} raaŋ^{1}

exclamation thoo^{4}, paa^{4} thoo^{4}, paat^{4} thoo^{4}

exclamation used to chase dogs away seʔ^{6}

excrement ɣay^{6}

existence, race saat^{5}

expect, hope; wait khɔɔŋ^{4}

expensive phɛɛŋ^{4}

expert, artisan; skilled saaŋ^{5}

expose to the sun praak^{6}
extinguish, die, destroy; go out (of a fire) dap^{4}
eye trɔɔŋ^{4}, tlɔɔŋ^{4}, praa^{1}
blink, close (the eye) ɲip^{4}
close one eye, wink liiw^{6}
close the eyes for a moment and then open them ɲip^{4} kɛɛp^{6}
eyebrow khiw^{3}, khiiw^{3}
eyebrow ridge khoom^{4}
eyes staring wide open; open the eyes wide, turn back the eyelid lɯak^{6}
open (the eyes) mlɔɔn^{4}
open the eyes wide, turn back the eyelid; eyes staring wide open lɯak^{6}
poor eyesight kwaaŋ^{3}
shade the eyes pɔɔŋ^{3} praa^{1}

F

face naa^{3}
cover (the face); close (a door) ʔɔt^{4}
face bruised and swollen from a blow; having a long muzzle tuup^{2}
face powder sii^{1} phɔɔŋ^{4}
lie face down ŋam^{3}
lie face up; full moon ŋaay^{2}
lie flat on one's face nuun^{4} meep^{2}
make faces to tease children paak^{6} ɲik^{6} paak^{6} ɲɛɛk^{5}
turn the face away ŋɛɛw^{3}, blɯan^{1}
faggot, bundle lɯm^{4}
faggot, bundle, sheaf roop^{5}
fall, drop tɔk^{4}
fall, fall over lam^{6}
fall flat lam^{6} tɯɯŋ^{4}, lam^{6} phuap^{5}, lam^{6} phuak^{5}
fall in (of a stream bank) yoot^{6}
fall over backwards ŋɤɤk^{5}
fall when overripe (of fruit) yoot^{6}
sound of something falling tum^{1}, pok^{6}, pɔk^{6}
fall (of a leaf) lɔn^{6}
fall off, fall out; slip loose khɔɔn^{5}, khɔɔl^{5}
familiar, well acquainted with kwɛɛn^{6}
familiar, tame khun^{6}
family thrua^{4}
elder who arranges at weddings caw^{3} khoot^{5} voŋ^{4} taa^{1}

family, clan khoot^{5}
family, clan; litter rɔɔk^{5}
famous swaa^{5}
fan, to fan phii^{4}
electric fan phat^{6} lum^{4}
far tray^{1}, tlay^{1}
far apart, widely spaced; coarse, coarsely woven saa^{6}
far, far away dak^{4}
very (far); to disappear lip^{4}
fast, quick, quickly ɲam^{4}
(walk or ride) fast lip^{4} lip^{4}
fasten (a button) khaan^{2}, khaal^{2}
snap fastener tɛp^{6}
fastened, attached tit^{4}
fat tuy^{5}, phuuy^{4}
father; man phɔɔ^{5}
father's younger brother ʔaaw^{5}
father's younger sister ʔɔɔ^{5}
fathom, armspread, measure with armspreads vaa^{4}
favor, merit, good deeds khun^{4}
do a favor for mii^{4} khun^{4} mii^{4} noo^{4}
fear, be afraid laaw^{2}
feast; raise, feed, tend, keep liaŋ^{6}
feed, raise, tend, keep; feast liaŋ^{6}
feed an infant or an invalid puun^{6}
feed animals kua^{1}
fell a tree; wrestle pram^{3}, plam^{3}
fence haŋ^{3}
fence or wall of a monastery taay^{3} vat^{6}
go under (a fence, house, table) lɔɔt^{5}
ferment, pickle mɔɔk^{6}
fern (edible) phrak^{4} kuut^{6}
festival variety (annual) teet^{6}
fever (have a); sick, ill ʔoom^{3}
feel feverish khat^{4}
have a high fever with hands and feet curled up; curled up (of leaves); tangled (of rope) caŋ^{1}
fiber plant pɔɔ^{1}, raay^{3}
fibers of a lotus stem; rubber; gum yaaŋ^{1}
fierce; to scold thuu^{3}
fig (wild) thrua^{6}
fight leew^{4}
fight, make war lop^{6}

fight (of buffalo) seew^{2}

fight (of cocks) tɔɔ^{3}

fight; strike, hit, beat, pound; thresh (rice) mɔk^{6}

figure, shape (of a person) sep^{6}

figure, image hun^{6}

file (the tool) ta^{6} bay^{1}

fill in (a hole) thom^{1}

fine, impose a fine pap^{4}, may^{1}, may^{2}

finger, toe ŋiaŋ^{5}

little finger, little toe ŋiaŋ^{5} kɔɔy^{3}

pick up with the fingers yip^{4}

snap with the fingers; kick (of a horse) bliit^{6}

fingernail, toenail; hoof liip^{5}

finished; already; then lɛɛw^{1}, lɛɛw^{6}

be finished, come to an end; youngest (child); last (oxcart) sɔɔt^{5}

fire vii^{4}

go out (of a fire); extinguish, die, destroy dap^{4}

live coals of a fire haaŋ^{4} vii^{4}

spread (of a fire) laam^{4}

stoke (a fire) khum^{4}

fireplace, stove phiak^{5} vii^{4}, phriak^{5} vii^{4}, phrɯak^{5} vii^{4}

firewood vɯn^{1}, vɯl^{1}

big pile of firewood kɔɔŋ^{1} raa^{6}

light firewood (bamboo) lua^{2}

firm, hard, solid keen^{2}, keel^{2}

first, before kɔɔn^{6}

at first tɛɛ^{6} moʔ^{6}

first (month) ciaŋ^{1}

fish praa^{1}, plaa^{1}

big fish varieties bɯk^{4}, lɤɤm^{4}

bite, nibble (of a fish); sting (of an insect) tɔɔt^{6}

fish basket vak^{4} thaa^{6}

fish bone kaaŋ^{3}

fish hook seet^{6}

fishnet varieties ka^{6} dɤɤt^{6}, tooŋ^{6}, ree^{2}, sa^{6} duŋ^{3}

fish paste (fermented) plaa^{1} dɛɛk^{6}

fish paste wrapped and cooked in fire mɔk^{4} dɛɛk^{6}

fish scales trɛk^{4}, tlɛk^{4}

fish trap; chicken cage sum^{6}

fish trap varieties yay^{4}, sɔɔn^{3}, sɔɔl^{3}

fish varieties ʔiit^{6}, kheŋ^{1}, khɤŋ^{4}, traŋ^{3}, tlaŋ^{3}, thlɛɛ^{5}, pha^{6} lay^{4}, pha^{6} lay^{5}, ɲɔɔn^{4}, lot^{4}, siw^{4}, siiw^{4}, suay^{4}, swaay^{4}, sɯam^{4}, sa^{6} ŋɛɛŋ^{4}

fishy smell ɣaaw^{4}
grope for fish under water ŋum^{4}
sound of fish jumping baap^{5}
to fish, go fishing tɯk^{4}
fitting, suitable khuan^{4}
five haa^{3}
flag thuŋ^{4}
flame preew^{1}, pleew^{1}
flashlight vii^{4} saay^{2}
flat pee^{1}
flat, flattened pɛɛ^{1}, pɛɛ^{3}
flat, flattened; crushed tɤɤt^{6}
flatten, crushed, smashed raa^{5}
flat of woven thatchgrass for roofing plial^{1} ɣaa^{4}
flat (of a tire) vɛɛp^{5}
flavor of orange or lime rinds hɯn^{4}
flavorless, insipid mlaat^{5}
flea mat^{4}
flee; away theew^{4}
flesh, meat mlɔɔ^{5}
flesh on jackfruit seeds mul^{5}
flies (small types) mɛɛŋ^{4} mii^{6}
flirtatious, affected khiaw^{4}
float vuu^{1}
floating on the water surface khɯam^{4} khɯam^{4}
flock (to) poot^{6}
flood (to) thum^{6}
floor, ground phɯɯn^{6}
floorboard joint lines khɛɛ^{5}
flour bɯa^{1}
flour, starch; rice boiled in cakes with a banana pɛɛŋ^{3}
flow trooy^{1}, tlooy^{1}
flow, drool (of saliva) hɤɤy^{1}
flower blɔɔk^{6}, blɔɔk^{6} may^{6}
flower variety koo^{1} mut^{6}
flowering tree varieties cam^{1} pii^{1}, cam^{6} pii^{1}, cam^{1} paa^{1}, cam^{6} paa^{1}
stem of leaf, flower, fruit kaan^{3}
flute khuy^{6}, khuuy^{6}
flute, pipe; spread (a mat) pii^{6}
fly (to) bɯn^{1}, bɯl^{1}, hɔɔp^{6}
fly in circles huʔ^{4} hɔɔp^{6}

fly through the air hɤɤn^{1}, hɔʔ^{4}
fly zigzag bɯn^{1} cɤɤt^{6}
foam, lather, bubbles poop^{6}
fog mɔɔk^{6}
fold thrap^{6}, phap^{6}, phlap^{6}
fold double thop^{6}
fold neatly, arrange tightly liip^{6}
stack or fold up neatly; stick (money) between things stacked up lɛɛp^{6}
follow, accompany; go in search of; with; from; along nam^{4}
follow; search for; along; according to taam^{1}
fond of, like mak^{6}
fontanelle nap^{4} nɤɤ^{4}
food (harmful types) kam^{1}
food; things, possessions; clothing; utensils thrɯaŋ^{5}
enjoy one's food, delicious ŋɔɔn^{2}, nua^{2}, bua^{1}
food eaten with liquor kɛɛm^{3}
food swallowed and returns to the mouth thraak^{5}, thlaak^{5}
go without (food, water); endure ʔot^{4}, ʔot^{4} ɲɯam^{3}, thon^{4}
harmful food kam^{1}
foot, leg ɣeeŋ^{5}
foot, base (of tree) tiin^{1}
foot goes to sleep kɔɔŋ^{5} ɣeeŋ^{5}, mɯn^{4}
have a high fever with hands and feet curled up; tangled (of rope); curled up (of leaves) caŋ^{1}
footprint, track rii^{4}
for, toward suu^{6}
for example thruu^{4} ɣaa^{5}
for, give, cause hɤɤ^{3}
for, to kɛɛ^{6}
force, compel khuu^{1}, cam^{1}
force one's way through phaa^{2}, phaa^{6}, thook^{6}
force through or into mun^{6}, mul^{6}
force, squeeze sap^{4}
forehead phraak^{6}
foreign theet^{5}
maa^{6} theet^{5} foreign horse
forest, thicket paa^{6}, thuan^{6}, thual^{6}
big forest dɔŋ^{1}
deep forest khook^{5}
mythical forest him^{1} ma^{6} phaan^{4}
forget lɔŋ^{2}
fork of a tree ŋaam^{5}

form (rice) into a ball; twist, wring   van^{3}, val^{3}
formerly   rɯa^{6}
formerly, in olden times   tɛɛ^{6} rɤɤ^{4}
fort, police box   pɔm^{3}, pɔɔm^{3}
four   sii^{6}
fragrant   praaŋ^{1}, plaaŋ^{1}
frame (for a picture)   kɔɔp^{6}
free; idle   dɤɤy^{1}
Friday   van^{4} suk^{4}
friend   siaw^{2}, siaw^{6}
friend; group   muu^{6}
frighten, scare; lie, deceive   lɔɔk^{6}
frog   kap^{4}
frog (when talking to children)   ʔuap^{5}
legendary eclipse-causing frog   kap^{4} thaaŋ^{3}
small frog   thrɛɛ^{3}
sound of frog jumping into water   cuap^{5}
trap for frogs; cage   tum^{3}
from   khɔɔy^{6}
from; accompany, follow; go in search of; with; along   nam^{4}
from, since   taŋ^{3} tɛɛ^{6}
from, since, but   tɛɛ^{6}
frontier post; border   daan^{6}
frugal (in eating)   yɔɔm^{1}
fruit   maak^{6}
almost ripe (of fruit)   hɤɤm^{6}
classifier for fruits and certain other round objects, frequent in names of fruit and fruit-bearing trees and plants   maak^{6}
fruit and vegetable dish, first pounded and then spices are added   nian^{6}
fruit varieties   ʔooy^{3}, kan^{1}, ka^{6} thɛn^{4}, khiap^{2}, ŋɛɛw^{4}, tɔɔŋ^{3}, paaŋ^{1} or phaaŋ^{1}, phɔɔk^{5}, mlɔɔt^{6}, ɲom^{4}, lot^{6}, vaa^{2}, viaŋ^{1}
overripe (of fruit)   nuam^{5}
pick fruit with a pole; poke an animal out of its hole with a stick   ɲɔk^{6}
pole for picking fruit; clothesline, pole for drying clothes   yaaw^{6}
soft and mushy (of fruit)   leʔ^{6}
sound of fruit falling   piiŋ^{4}
sound of fruit falling; sound of beating   ʔup^{6}
stem of leaf, flower, fruit   kaan^{3}
thick, abundant (of hair, fruit)   dok^{4}
fry   thɔɔt^{5}
frying pan   mɔɔ^{3} thɛɛŋ^{2}
couplet paired only with mɔɔ^{3} 'pot'   hɛɛk^{6}

full rim^{2}
full after eating ʔiim^{6}
full, satiated ʔiim^{6} nam^{1} sam^{1} raan^{4}
full (of the moon) pheŋ^{4}
full (moon); face up ŋaay^{2}
full to the brim phiap^{5}
not full, partly gone, half empty phrɔŋ^{5}
overly full luat^{5}, lwaat^{5}
fun, amusing muan^{5}
funeral (to have a) soŋ^{6} sa^{6} kaan^{1}
funnel suay^{4}
furlong ɲoot^{5}

G

gable sii^{2} naa^{3}
gadfly lɯap^{6}
gadfly, gnat ɲuan^{6}, ɲual^{6}
galangal haa^{6}
gallbladder blii^{1}
gambling game varieties book^{2}, book^{6}, saŋ^{1} kaa^{1}
game (in sports) meem^{4}
gang up kɯp^{4} (slang)
garden suan^{2}
garlic thiam^{4}
garment (old-fashioned lower one) ka^{6} tɔɔy^{3}
gasoline ʔit^{4} saŋ^{4}, ʔɛt^{4} saŋ^{4}
gather up, put away mian^{6}
gather in (e.g., clothes) rɯɯ^{6}
gather into a heap tɔɔm^{3}
gecko kap^{4} kɛɛ^{5}, kak^{4} kɛɛ^{5}
gem variety phiʔ^{6} thuun^{4}, phi^{6} thuun^{4}, phay^{4} thuun^{4}
general, minister see^{1} naa^{4} bɔɔ^{1} dii^{1}
germinate (seeds), plant ʔɯaŋ^{1}
get, obtain; be able; past tense marker day^{3}
get more than others vɛɛn^{4}
get ahead of another, surpass; more lɯɯn^{5}
get out of the way, avoid trɛɛŋ^{5}, tlɛɛŋ^{5}
get up, stand up, raise, lift luk^{6}
action of many people getting up all at once phɯap^{5}
get up and sit down suddenly phuut^{6} luk^{6} phuut^{6} naŋ^{5}

get up suddenly pɯp^{6} pup^{6}, pup^{6} pap^{6}, pup^{6}
get up, wake up saak^{5}
ghost, spirit pheet^{6}
ghost, spirit; corpse maaŋ^{4}
giant ɲak^{6}
name of giant kum^{1} phan^{4}
type of giant in stories huŋ^{3}
gibbon tha^{6} nii^{4}
gill slit ŋɤɤp^{5}
ginger hiiŋ^{2}
girl, woman mee^{5} bɯk^{4}
give, cause, for hɤɤ^{3}
give, hand over, turn over mɔɔp^{5}
give, offer thuay^{2}, thwaay^{2}
gizzard tɤɤ^{1}
glad, happy sam^{4}
very glad, overjoyed khɤɤn^{3}
glass, drinking glass, bottle kɛɛw^{3}
big glass, cup; old-fashioned Chinese earthen bowl caʔ^{6} ʔɤɤŋ^{1}
glass, cup cɔɔk^{6}
gleaming (red, yellow) cɯɯŋ^{6} khɯɯŋ^{6}, khɯɯŋ^{6}
gleaming (red) huun^{4} huun^{4}
gleaming (red, yellow), bright rɤɤ^{5} rɤɤ^{5}
glory of a king som^{1} phaan^{4}
radiant glory (of a king) raa^{4} sii^{2} som^{1} phaan^{4}
glutinous (rice); tough, sticky niaw^{2}
gnat riin^{6}
gnat, gadfly ɲuan^{6}, ɲual^{6}
gnaw hɛɛn^{3}
go pay^{1}
go around, make a circuit vian^{6}
go down lɔŋ^{4}
go downstream lɔɔŋ^{5}
go out ʔɔɔk^{6}
go see royalty, guard phaw^{3}
go under (a fence, house, table) lɔɔt^{5}
go up, come up, rise, ascend; up hɯn^{3}
go without (food, water) ɲiin^{6}
goat bɛɛ^{3}, phɛʔ^{6}
go-between; spy sɤɤy^{4}

god, divinity   thee^{4} va^{6} daa^{1}

architect of the gods   pha^{6} veet^{5} su^{4} kam^{1}

goiter   ɣɔɔ^{4} ʔɤɤm^{1}

gold   ɣam^{4}

copper and gold in certain expressions; brass, bronze   thɔɔŋ^{4}

gold in a personal name   kham^{4}

gold mine   ɣam^{4} bɔɔ^{6}

silver and gold and jewels   ɲɛn^{4} ɣam^{4} kam^{1} kɛɛw^{3}

gone (partly)   phrɔŋ^{5}, phrɔɔŋ^{5}

gong   khɔɔŋ^{6}

sound of gongs and drums   thɯt^{6} thɯt^{6}

good   cop^{4}, dii^{1}

good, proper   cop^{4} cɯa^{1}

very good, excellent; certain   khak^{6}

goose   haan^{6}

gourd   taw^{3}

bitter gourd   ma^{6} raʔ^{6}

gourd varieties   biap^{6}, mook^{6}, vak^{6}

govern   khɔɔp^{5} khɔɔŋ^{4}

govern, rule   pok^{4} khɔɔŋ^{4}

government, royal   luaŋ^{2}

gradually, slowly   thrɛɛ^{5}

grain, seed, small round object   mlɛt^{6}, mlɛk^{6}

granary   yiaw^{3}, yuŋ^{3}, saaŋ^{1}

couplet paired with saaŋ^{1} 'granary'   lim^{3} (also recorded as lim^{5})

grandchild; nephew, niece   laan^{2}

great-grandchild   leen^{1}, leen^{2}

great-great-grandchild   lɔɔt^{6}

grandfather (paternal)   ʔooŋ^{4}

maternal grandfather; old man   taa^{1}

grandmother (maternal)   ʔaay^{4}

paternal grandmother; old woman   yaa^{5}

grapefruit, pomelo   phuk^{6}

grasp, catch, seize, take hold of   cap^{4}

grass   ɲua^{3}

grass varieties   ɲua^{3} phɛɛt^{6}, ɲua^{3} phrɛɛk^{6}

mat (grass)   biin^{3}

pull up (grass); disappear; die; lose; spoil; pay   ʔiin^{3}

grasshopper   kha^{6} nak^{4}

great (in certain expressions)   ma^{6} haa^{1}

green   khiaw^{1}, heew^{2}

light green   siw^{3}, siiw^{3}

greet; admonish thɔɔŋ^{6}
grey, grey-haired huuk^{6}
groin khɛɛ^{5} kwaa^{1}
grope for fish under water ŋum^{4}
ground, dirt, earth ban^{1}, bal^{1}
ground, floor phɯɯn^{6}
group paa^{6}, phuak^{5}
  group; friend muu^{6}
grow bigger (of a child) phuʔ^{6}
  grow slowly because shaded by a big tree ŋam^{1}
grumble, complain thraam^{4}
guard, watch sɯɯ^{5}
  guard; go see (royalty) phaw^{3}
  guard, take care of rak^{6} saa^{2}
guess, predict thuay^{4}, thwaay^{4}
  guess, assume, estimate tuaŋ^{1}
guest heek^{6}
guilt, punishment, penalty thoot^{5}
gum; rubber; fibers of the lotus stem yaaŋ^{1}
gun thruŋ^{3}
gunwale of a boat, edge ɣeem^{4}
gutter, trough, water pipe haaŋ^{4}

H

haft of a knife kan^{6}
hail mlɛk^{6} tuy^{5}
hair (of the head) phram^{2}
  body hair pun^{1}, pul^{1}
  thick, abundant (of hair, fruit) dok^{4}
  wash (the hair) pɔɔ^{1}
  waves in the hair lɔɔn^{4}
hairknot (make a) treeŋ^{1}, tleeŋ^{1}
hairpin pin^{6}
half khɤŋ^{5}
hall, building rooŋ^{4}
  name of a hall pha^{6} kha^{6} va^{6} dii^{1}
hammer, club ɣɔɔn^{6}, ɣɔɔl^{6}
hand mɯɯ^{4}
  beckon with the hand kwak^{4}
  carry hanging down from the hand riw^{3}, riiw^{3}, hiiw^{5}

cover with the hand   ŋum^{5}
handkerchief   mɛɛŋ^{6} khan^{2}
have a high fever with hands and feet curled up; tangled (of rope); curled up (of leaves)   caŋ^{1}
hold in closed hand   kam^{1}
open (the hand); lie flat on the back   bɛɛ^{1}
hand out, distribute   cɛɛk^{6}, yaay^{1}
hand to someone   yuan^{5}, yual^{5}
handle of a knife or sword   daam^{3}
hang up   veen^{2}
happy   ɲuu^{4} thaaŋ^{6}, sam^{1} raan^{4}, suk^{4}
glad, happy   sam^{4}
happily   sa^{6} nuk^{4} sa^{6} naan^{1}
happy, cheerful   sɯɯn^{5} cɯɯ^{1}, sɯɯn^{5} mɔk^{4} sɯɯn^{6} cɯɯ^{1}
happy, merry   sa^{6} nuk^{4}
live happily   yuu^{6} yen^{1} pen^{1} suk^{4}
hard, solid, firm   keen^{6}, keel^{6}
hard spot in fruit   triaŋ^{1}
hard, stiff   thriaŋ^{2}
hardship, to have trouble; poor   thuk^{6}
harrow (to)   phia^{2}, phɯa^{2}
harvest, reap   sian^{4}
hasty work (to do)   hit^{6} luat^{5} luat^{5}
hat, cap   muak^{2}, muak^{6}
farmer's conical hat   moo^{4}
put on (a hat)   dooy^{3}
put on (a hat, ring); place by inserting or impaling   sup^{4}
hate   saŋ^{4}
hate, dislike; be bored with   cee^{1}
have, there is, there are   mii^{4}
have to, must   tɔŋ^{3}, tɔɔŋ^{3}
hawk   lam^{5}
he, she, it, they   man^{4}
he, you (respectful)   vua^{6}
head   thraw^{3}
back of the head   ŋɔɔn^{5}
hair of the head   phram^{2}
temples of the head   kha^{6} map^{4}
top of the head   thɛɛŋ^{4}
turn the head to look   ŋuak^{5}, ŋwaak^{5}, ŋɛɛk^{5}, ŋwɛɛk^{5}
head louse   raw^{2}
healed (almost, nearly)   ʔeem^{1}
heap, pile; to pile up, heap up   kɔɔŋ^{1}

  big heap or pile   cuun^{6} phuun^{6}
  big (of a heap)   soon^{3} soon^{3}
  heap (of dung)   soo^{6}
  heaped up (in a container)   buun^{1}
  pile in a heap   ʔuak^{5} ɲuak^{5}
hear, listen   ɲia^{2}
  hard of hearing   ʔɯŋ^{3}
heart   cɯɯ^{1}, cit^{4}
heat rash   phot^{6}
heaving motion of the earth   kul^{3} kul^{3}
heavy   nak^{4}
heel; butt, end   sɔn^{3}
help   sooy^{5}
  ask for help; borrow   maan^{6}
  help, rescue, release   phoot^{6}
hemp (Indian), marijuana   saa^{4}
here   nii^{3}
hermit, ascetic   rɯɯ^{4} sii^{2}, lɯɯ^{4} sii^{2}
hide   yɔɔn^{5}, yɔɔl^{5}
  hide oneself   riit^{5}
hide, skin, leather; the movies   naŋ^{2}
high, tall, on, on top of, above   saaŋ^{2}
hire   caaŋ^{3}
history, story   pra^{6} vat^{4}
hit, strike, beat, pound; fight; thresh (rice)   mɔk^{6}
hit; touch; correct; cheap   thɯk^{6}
Hmong   mɛɛw^{3}
hoe, mattock   cok^{4}
hold, carry in the arms   ʔuum^{3}
  hold, carry   thɯɯ^{4}
  hold in closed hand   kam^{1}
  hold in the jaws   khaap^{5}
  hold in the mouth   ʔam^{1}
  hold the breath   kan^{3}
  hold up, support   khɯŋ^{4}
  take hold of   kɔʔ^{4}
  take hold of, catch, seize, grasp   cap^{4}
hole (big)   pɯɯŋ^{6}
  hole in tree or bamboo, hollow   phooŋ^{6}
  hole, pit   lum^{1}
  hole, pit, chasm, crack   sɔɔŋ^{5}
  make a hole with a stick   thuk^{6}

hollow, hole in tree or bamboo phooŋ^{6}
  hollow tube, as of bamboo prɔɔŋ^{6}, plɔɔŋ^{6}
home, village baan^{3}
  couplet paired with baan^{3} 'home' sɔɔŋ^{4}
  house, home raan^{4}, ruuk^{5} raan^{4}
honest, noon, straight thiaŋ^{5}, theeŋ^{5}
  honest; straight yɔɔ^{5}
hoof; fingernail, toenail liip^{5}
hook hɔɔ^{2}
hope vaŋ^{1}
  hope, wait, expect khɔɔŋ^{4}
horn kaw^{1}
  horn of a rhinoceros nɔɔ^{4}
horse maa^{6}
  foreign horse maa^{6} theet^{5}
  kick (of a horse); snap with the fingers bliit^{6}
hot ruun^{6}, ruul^{6}, lɔɔk^{5}
  very hot ʔaw^{3}
hour, time mooŋ^{4}
house, home ruuk^{5} raan^{4}, raan^{4}
  build (a house); plant (plants) prɔɔk^{6}, plɔɔk^{6}
  classifier for houses; back; after laŋ^{2}
  descriptive of a house shaking ɲoop^{5} ɲoop^{5} ɲaap^{5} ɲaap^{5}
  go under (a fence, house, table) lɔɔt^{5}
  side (of the body, of a house); beside rɛk^{4}
  space underneath a house luaŋ^{5}
housefly ɲɛn^{2}, ɲɛl^{2}
howdah bɛŋ^{4}, yɛɛŋ^{6}
how many kii^{3}
howl (of a dog) hɔɔn^{1}
hug, embrace, clasp kɔɔt^{6}
human being, person ma^{6} nut^{6}, hun^{4}
humble, modest ciam^{1}
hump on an ox or buffalo nɔɔk^{6}, lam^{6}
hundred rɔɔy^{6}
  hundred one rɔɔy^{6} ʔɛt^{4}
  hundred thousand sɛɛn^{2}
  three hundred saam^{2} rɔɔy^{6}
hungry, go hungry yuak^{6}
  hungry; desire, want haat^{6}
hunt; smoke meat hoo^{6}
hunter phaan^{4}

hurl down   sɛt^{6}

hurry   thriaw^{2}, thliaw^{2}, leŋ^{5}, hon^{4}

hurry, rush   hɯɯ^{4}

hurt, pain, ache   keet^{6}

husband   hɔɔk^{6}

husk, rind, peel (of a banana)   kaap^{6}

rice husks   ca^{6} prɔɔŋ^{3}, ca^{6} plɔɔŋ^{3}

hut, shack, temporary shelter   tup^{4}

hut in the fields   thiaŋ^{4}

small hut   ka^{6} thɔm^{5}

I

I   kuu^{1}, phaan^{6}, hɔɔy^{6}

ice   nam^{6} khɛŋ^{1}

idle, indolent   maw^{3}

idle; free   dɤɤy^{1}

if   thaa^{3}, hee^{5}, khan^{4}, khan^{4} ɣa^{3}

if ; it is   mɛɛn^{5}

ill, sick; have a fever   ʔoom^{3}

care for, treat the ill   pua^{1}, pin^{6} pua^{1}

illegal   thɯan^{6}

illusion; Mara   maan^{4}

image, figure   hun^{6}

impale   siap^{6}

place by inserting or impaling; put on (a hat, ring)   sup^{4}

impetigo   phay^{4}, hit^{4}

imprison, shut up   thraŋ^{2}

in, inside, into, at, during   daŋ^{1}, daaŋ^{1}

in, at, there   nɛɛn^{1}, nɛɛn^{2}

in, inside   rɤɤ^{1}

incense stick   thuup^{5}, pa^{6} thuup^{5}

incision (make an), mark around   kan^{6}

incorrect, wrong   phit^{4}

incubate, brood   ʔup^{4}

indeed, even   hɔn^{2} (idiomatic)

independent   ʔit^{4} sa^{6} raʔ^{4}

Indian corn, maize   sa^{6} lii^{4}

Indian hemp, marijuana   saa^{4}

Indian, Muslim   khɛɛk^{6}

indigo   khaam^{4}

indirectly (to ask) lak^{6} khit^{6} lak^{6} khay^{4}
indolent, idle maw^{3}
Indra ʔin^{1}
industrious, diligent duʔ^{4}, siaŋ^{2}
infection from a wound, tetanus pham^{2}, pham^{3}
inform, report to khɔɔp^{5}
inhabitants, people saaw^{4}
ink mɯk^{6}
insect mɛɛŋ^{4}
  insect that makes mud nests in walls mɛɛŋ^{4} yay^{1}
  stinger of an insect lay^{4}
  to sting (of an insect); bite, nibble (of a fish) tɔɔt^{6}
insert sɔɔt^{6}
  insert, put inside prɔɔn^{1}, plɔɔn^{1}, prɔɔn^{6}, plɔɔn^{6}
  place by inserting or impaling; put on (a hat, ring) sup^{4}
insipid, flavorless mlaat^{5}
inspect kuat^{6}
installments (to pay in) phɔɔn^{6}
instructions (to give final), order; blow the nose saŋ^{6}
instrument (Lao musical) khɛɛn^{4}
intelligence, wits pan^{1} ɲaa^{4}
  intelligent, clever khuun^{2}
intend, aim; make a mark, mark maay^{2}
interjections ʔɔɔy^{4}, phɔɔ^{3} mee^{5}, buuy^{4}, yoo^{5} (to intensify), hɤɤy^{3}, hɤɤy^{4}, hɤɤy^{5}
interpreter laam^{5}
intestines say^{3}
investigate, trace a secret sɯɯp^{6}
investments (to lose one's) lup^{4} thɯn^{4}
  investment, capital thɯn^{4}
invite ɲua^{6}, sua^{4}, suan^{4}, sɤɤn^{4}
  invite a monk niʔ^{6} mon^{4}
invulnerable khɛɛw^{3} khoŋ^{4}, khoŋ^{4}
iron maa^{4}
  an iron taw^{1} liit^{5}
  to iron clothes liit^{5}
irritated, annoyed; excited rɤɤ^{3} raaŋ^{1}
  irritating or offensive to the ear or eye khiin^{2}
  irritating to the skin ɣaay^{4}
island dɔɔn^{1}
it, he, she, they man^{4}
it is; if mɛɛn^{5}

itch (to)   kii^{1}, ɣum^{4}, ɣum^{4} ɣal^{4}
  itching foot disease from foul water   rɔɔ^{2}
item; joint   ɣɔɔ^{5}
ivory; tusk of elephant   ŋaa^{4}

J

jackal   maa^{2} nay^{4}
jackfruit   praaŋ^{1}, plaaŋ^{1}
  jackfruit when small   phiaŋ^{6}
  seed of jackfruit or durian   nuan^{4}
jail   ta^{6} laaŋ^{4}
jar, jug   hay^{2}
  small jar for lime   khua^{4}, khwaa^{4}
  small jug for water   ʔɛɛŋ^{6}
jaw   haam^{4}
  jaw, chin   kaaŋ^{3} haam^{4}
  hold in the jaws   khaap^{5}
  swollen jaws; mumps   ɣaaŋ^{4} thuum^{4}
jewel   kɛɛw^{3}
  silver and gold and jewels   ɲɛn^{4} ɣam^{4} kam^{1} kɛɛw^{3}
Job's tears   trooy^{1}
join; continue   tɔɔ^{6}
joint; item   ɣɔɔ^{5}
jug, jar   hay^{2}
  pail or jug for washing, not drinking   caʔ^{6} phaŋ^{4}
  small jar for lime   khua^{4}, khwaa^{4}
  small jug for water   ʔɛɛŋ^{6}
jump, leap   doot^{6}
  jump, dance   sɛk^{4}
  jump out of water (of fish)   bɔɔn^{3}
just   ɲut^{6} ti^{4} tham^{4}, ɲot^{6} ti^{4} tham^{4}

K

kapok   ŋiw^{3}, ŋiiw^{3}, nun^{6}
keep, put away   kɯɯ^{3}, yɔɔ^{1}
  keep, tend, raise, feed; feast   liaŋ^{6}
kerosene   nam^{6} man^{4} kat^{4}

kick diit^{6}, teʔ^{4}
  kick (of a horse); snap with the fingers bliit^{6}
kidney tay^{1}
kidneystones diw^{3}, diiw^{3}, niw^{3}, niiw^{3}
kill kaa^{3}
kind nεεw^{4}, yaaŋ^{6}
  kind, like; size sam^{6}
  kind; seed van^{2}
king ka^{6} sεt^{4}, ka^{6} sat^{4}
  king, prince, chief, lord pha^{6} ɲaa^{4}
kingdom laat^{5}
  kingdom, country; city phiaŋ^{4}
kiss cuup^{6}
knee kɔɔ^{6}
kneel down thuk^{6} thraw^{3} kɔɔ^{6}
knife traaw^{1}, miit^{5}
  back of a knife sεn^{2}
  big knife, machete thaa^{6}
  classifier for books, knives, boats, oxcarts, and various sharp objects lεm^{3}
  classifier for tools, knives, and other sharp instruments maak^{5}, maak^{6}
  cleaver-like knife with big curved blade at top maak^{6} thaa^{4} koʔ^{6}
  knife put in waist at back thaa^{6} khat^{4} vuat^{6}
  sheath (of a knife); pod (of beans, etc.) vak^{4}
knit; braid thak^{4}
knob cuum^{1}
knock, strike tɔɔy^{6}, tɔʔ^{4}
  knock aside khiin^{3}
  knock (e.g., on a door) khɔʔ^{6}
  sound of knocking pɔk^{6} pɔk^{6}
knot pum^{1}, plum^{1}, hɔɔt^{6}
  do up the hairknot hɔɔt^{6}
  tie a knot hɔɔt^{6}
knot, bump in a tree puut^{6}
know rɔɔ^{6}, rɔɔ^{6} cak^{4}
  don't know boo^{6} rɔʔ^{6}
knowledge, language thεn^{4}
knuckles maak^{6} kɔɔk^{6}

L

ladder (made from bamboo)   phaʔ^{6} ʔooŋ^{1}
laden heavily (of a boat)   sɛɛm^{1}
ladle, big spoon   ta^{6} mooy^{1}, ta^{6} mooy^{4}
lady   thee^{4} vii^{4}, naaŋ^{4}
lake   nɔɔŋ^{2}
lame, crippled   khee^{4}
lamp   ta^{6} kiaŋ^{1}
land (dry)   bɔk^{4}
landing   thaa^{5}
language; matter, thing   cian^{5}
  language, knowledge   thɛn^{4}
lantern   khoom^{4} fay^{4}
Lao   laaw^{4}
  Lao language   thɛn^{4} laaw^{4}
lap   rum^{3}, ruŋ^{2}, ruŋ^{3}
larva (of a dragonfly)   mɛɛŋ^{4} pɔɔ^{1}
lasso   ɣɔɔŋ^{6}
last (year); pass   traay^{1}, tlaay^{1}
late at night   dɯk^{4}
  late in the morning   thraa^{4}, thlaa^{4}
lath   khɛɛŋ^{6}
lather, bubbles, foam   poop^{6}
laugh   ruaw^{2}
lawsuit (to file)   phɔɔŋ^{3}, fɔɔŋ^{3}
laxative   yaa^{1} thaay^{6}
lay across   kaay^{6}, vaaŋ^{5}
lay aside; leave; divorce   plii^{6}
lay down, set aside   vaaŋ^{1}
layer, stratum (of rocks)   lɯɯp^{6}, lɤɤp^{6}
  layer, level, story   sɛn^{6}
lazy   triik^{6}, tliik^{6}
  move in a lazy manner   kooy^{5} kaay^{5}
lead (the metal)   riak^{6}
  lead ore   ɣay^{6} kɛɛw^{3}
lead, take   yɔɔŋ^{1}
  lead by the hand   ciiŋ^{1}
leaf   bɤɤ^{1}
  big leaf   rɔɔŋ^{2}
  curl up (of a leaf)   koop^{6}

curled up (of leaves); tangled (of rope); have a high fever with hands and feet curled up caŋ^{1}
fall (of a leaf) lɔn^{6}
leaf for cooking yaa^{1} naaŋ^{4}
shrivel from heat (of leaves); sit down ɲoop^{5}
sound of leaves or fruit falling khoop^{5}
stem of leaf, flower, fruit kaan^{3}
strip off leaves; move (e.g., a curtain) along a rod ruut^{5}
leak rɔɔ^{5}
lean back ʔiŋ^{1}, biŋ^{1}
lean over, slant see^{4}
leap, jump doot^{6}
leap into water toon^{1}
learn, practice hat^{4}
leather, skin, hide; the movies naŋ^{2}
leave; lay aside; divorce plii^{6}
leave orders (of a monk) sik^{4}
take one's leave laa^{4}
leech priŋ^{1}, pliŋ^{1}
land leech thaak^{5}
very large leech pɯŋ^{1}
left (hand) vɛɛn^{6}, vɛɛl^{6}
left over lua^{2}
leftover food ŋɯan^{5}
leg kua^{1}, kwaa^{1}
leg; foot ɣeeŋ^{5}
legacy muun^{4}
lemongrass ca^{6} thrɤɤ^{4}, ca^{6} phrɤɤ^{4}
length, piece; lump, classifier thɔɔn^{5}
Lent (Buddhist) phan^{4} saa^{2}
old term for the end of Buddhist Lent paʔ^{6} vɔɔ^{4} la^{6} naa^{4}, vɔɔ^{4} la^{6} naa^{4}
leprosy ka^{6} thuut^{5}, ruan^{5}, ruan^{6}
letter cot^{4} maay^{2}
level, layer, story sɛn^{6}
level, make smooth mɔɔp^{5}
level, even phiaŋ^{4}
lick lia^{4}
lid; wall, partition vaa^{1}
cover, as with a big lid kuam^{1}
cover with a lid ŋam^{4}
lid of empty oil drum; half a bamboo used as a water pipe; empty can used as a container ka^{6} paaŋ^{1}

lie, deceive; scare, frighten   lɔɔk^{6}
lie; tell, narrate   too^{5}
lie down   beet^{6}
lie athwart, block, obstruct   vaaŋ^{2}
lie down, sleep   nuun^{4}
lie face up; full moon   ŋaay^{2}
lie flat on one's face   nuun^{4} mɛɛp^{2}
lie flat on the back; open the hand   bɛɛ^{1}
(lie) on the side   ta^{6} khɛɛŋ^{4}
lie or sit on top of someone   khoom^{4}
life (long)   man^{3} ɲɯɯn^{4}
lift, raise   coom^{1}, pɤɤŋ^{1}
lift, raise; get up, stand up   luk^{6}
lift up   ɲɤŋ^{4}
light   sɛɛŋ^{2}
light, bright; dawn, clear   rɔɔŋ^{5}
light a fire, lamp   taam^{1}, taw^{1}
light a fire, set fire to; burn, cremate   cuk^{4}
light bulb; spindle, spool   luut^{6}
light in weight   vaw^{1}
light (of color); soft; young   ʔuun^{6}
lightning   cɤɤp^{6}
like, alike, similar   thruu^{4}
like that   thruun^{4}, thruu^{4} nan^{6}
like, fond of   mak^{6}
like, kind; size   sam^{6}
like; time, amount   paan^{1}
likely to, worthy of   soŋ^{4} + verb
lime (eaten with betel or used for plaster)   muun^{6}, muul^{6}
lime fruit   naaw^{4}
limit, period   kam^{1} not^{4}, kam^{1} not^{6}
line (a basket) with banana leaves; put something under (e.g., leg of bed or table) to raise it   lɔɔt^{6}
line up in a row   riaŋ^{4}
lion   laat^{5} sa^{6} sii^{2}
lips   muam^{4}, rim^{4} muam^{4}
liquid, soft   lɛɛw^{1}
liquor   law^{3}
drunkard   hun^{4} kin^{1} law^{3}
listen   phaŋ^{4}
listen; hear   ɲia^{2}
litter; family, clan   rɔɔk^{5}

little (a)   ʔiit^{4}, ʔiit^{4} ʔɔɔy^{5}, sip^{4} ʔiit^{4} sip^{4} ʔɔɔy^{5}
   a little, only a little   nɯŋ^{6}
live happily   yuu^{6} yen^{1} pen^{1} suk^{4}
live in a place   ʔaa^{1} say^{2}
liver   tap^{4}
lizard varieties   ɲɛɛ^{3}
   big red-headed lizard   ca^{6} kooy^{1}
   house lizard   yaa^{1} raan^{4}
   skink   caʔ^{6} trɛn^{6}, caʔ^{6} tlɛn^{6}, ca^{6} trɛn^{6}, ca^{6} tlɛn^{6}
   striped lizard   lɛɛn^{4}
log, big piece of wood; lump, piece, classifier   khook^{5}
loincloth   tiaw^{6}
long   ray^{4}
   classifier for long, thin objects   sɛn^{3}, sɛl^{3}
long-lasting, enduring   ɲɯɯn^{4}
   long life   man^{3} ɲɯɯn^{4}
look   nɛɛm^{4}, nɔɔ^{1} khay^{4}, nɔɔm^{1} khay^{4}, liŋ^{1}, sɔɔŋ^{6}
   look at (a mirror)   ɲɛɛŋ^{4}
   look up   sa^{6} ŋaak^{5}
   look, watch, see   nɔɔm^{1}
loom   suaŋ^{4}
   comb-like part of a loom, the beater   via^{1}, via^{4}
   shuttle of a loom   kiiŋ^{6} sɔɔy^{2}
loop (of rope)   huaŋ^{6}
   loop in a snare   buaŋ^{6}
loose fitting   lɔɔŋ^{1}
loose in the ground   prook^{6}, plook^{6}
lord, prince, chief   caw^{3}
   lord, king, prince, chief   pha^{6} ɲaa^{4}
lose; disappear; die; spoil; pay; pull up (grass)   ʔiin^{3}
   hate to lose; love, guard jealously   thɛɛŋ^{4}
   lose one's investments   lup^{4} thɯn^{4}
   lose the skin   lɔɔn^{2}
loud   daŋ^{1}
   loud (noise)   thɛn^{6}, thɛl^{6}
   loud (of talking, crying out)   sɛɛw^{4} sɛɛw^{4}
louse (chicken)   rii^{4}
   body louse   mlɛn^{4}, mlɛl^{4}
   head louse   raw^{2}
love   sɯaŋ^{2}
   love; guard jealously; hate to lose   thɛɛŋ^{4}
lover   yuu^{6}

low, evil   thɔɔy^{6}
low, short   tia^{3}, tam^{6}
lower, put down, take down   prɔŋ^{1}, plɔŋ^{1}
luck   laaŋ^{4}, sook^{5}
  bad luck   thɔʔ^{6} raay^{6}
lump, piece, classifier; log, big piece of wood   khook^{5}
  big lump   ŋoon^{5}
  lump; classifier; piece, length   thɔɔn^{5}
lunch, midday meal   ŋaay^{4}
lungs   phooy^{3}
lye (water)   daŋ^{6}

M

machete, big knife   thaa^{6}
  knife put in waist at back   thaa^{6} khat^{4} vuat^{6}
machine, engine   ɲon^{4}
mad, crazy   kua^{3}, kwaa^{3}
  mad (of a dog)   vɔɔ^{3}
magically efficacious   khet^{4} yam^{1}
magician   mɔɔ^{2} mon^{4}
maize, Indian corn   sa^{6} lii^{4}
make, do   hit^{6}
male, person; carpenter bee   phuu^{6}
  male animal   thak^{4}, thak^{6}
male in-law   khooy^{4}
man   phɔɔ^{5} saay^{2}
  effeminate man   khan^{4} thɯay^{4}, thɯay^{4}
  man; father   phɔɔ^{5}
  old man; maternal grandfather   taa^{1}
  old man, old fellow   phɔɔ^{5} ʔɔɔŋ^{1}
  young man   baaw^{6}
mango   miaŋ^{5}
manner, way   bɛɛp^{6}
  manner, kind, thing   yaaŋ^{6}
mansion, palace   phaa^{1} saat^{2}, phaa^{1} saat^{6}
many, much, very   laay^{1}, laay^{2}
Mara; illusion   maan^{4}
marijuana, Indian hemp   saa^{4}
mark, stripe, design, spots   laay^{4}
  mark, striped   kaan^{6}
mark (make a), intend, aim   maay^{2}

market ta^{6} laat^{6}
marry tɛɛŋ^{6} prɛɛŋ^{1}
  get married, have a wedding feast kin^{1} trɔɔŋ^{1}
  marry; prepare; dress tɛɛŋ^{6}
  related by marriage of children trɔɔŋ^{1}
marsh bɯŋ^{1}
  marsh or pond in a forest with soft clay into which one sinks dɯl^{6}
massage; squeeze biip^{6}
master, boss naay^{4}
mat (grass) biin^{3}
  classifier for mats, cloth articles phɯn^{4}, phɯɯn^{4}
matchbox, eggshell; sheath ta^{6} roop^{5}
matches plɛk^{4} vii^{4}, plak^{4} vii^{4}
mate (of animals) sɤɤŋ^{4}
maternal grandfather; old man taa^{1}
  maternal grandmother ʔaay^{4}
matter phɯɯn^{6}
matter, thing; language cian^{5}
mattock, hoe cok^{4}
mattress sɯa^{6}
meal ɣaap^{5}, thraap^{5}
  evening meal lɛɛŋ^{4}
  midday meal, lunch ŋaay^{4}
means, way thaa^{5}
measure length thɛɛk^{5}
meat, flesh mlɔɔ^{5}
  chopped meat dish saa^{3} mlɔɔ^{5}
  meat; animal nɯa^{3}
medal, coin lian^{1}
meet, encounter phaam^{4}
meet, have a meeting pat^{4} sum^{4}
Mekong River khɔɔŋ^{2}
melon, cucumber priaŋ^{1}
mend, repair, solder cɔɔt^{6}
  repair a boat yaa^{1}
mentally deficient puaŋ^{6}
mention, speak of ɲak^{4}
merit, favor, good deeds khun^{4}
  merit-making ceremony bun^{1} phaʔ^{6} veet^{6}
  merit-making rite yaat^{6} nam^{6}
  merit, merit-making bun^{1}
merry, happy sa^{6} nuk^{4}

Meru su^{4} meen^{4}, su^{6} meen^{4}
middle traaŋ^{1}, tlaaŋ^{1}
middle, in the middle thrɯŋ^{5} tlaaŋ^{1}
midnight theeŋ^{5} ɣɯn^{4}
milk nom^{1}
milk a cow; have an abortion hiit^{5}
millet ɣaw^{6} viaŋ^{3}
million laan^{3}
mine (a) bɔɔ^{6}
gold mine ɣam^{4} bɔɔ^{6}
silver mine ɲɛn^{4} bɔɔ^{6}
minister, general see^{1} naa^{4} bɔɔ^{1} dii^{1}
minute naa^{4} thii^{4}
mirror vɛɛn^{5}
look at (a mirror) ɲɛɛŋ^{4}
miserly; closely spaced, finely woven thii^{5}
misfortune veen^{4}
misfortune, punishment kam^{1}
mix, mixed kɛɛm^{1}, pon^{1}
moan reeŋ^{1}
modest, humble ciam^{1}
moldy (e.g., of food) tɔk^{4} mook^{6}
mollusk, snail ʔook^{6}
moment ago cia^{1}
monastery vat^{6}
monasteries vat^{6} vaa^{4}
wall or fence of a monastery taay^{3} vat^{4}
Monday van^{4} cɛn^{1}
money taaŋ^{1}
ancient money type ɲɛn^{4} haaŋ^{4}
large amount of money in folktales lak^{4}
Lao unit of money triip^{6}, tliip^{6}
tribute money suay^{6}
mongoose cɔn^{1} phɔɔn^{4}, cɔɔn^{1} phɔɔn^{4}
monitor lizard hia^{3}
monk caw^{3} hua^{2}, phaʔ^{6}, ɲaa^{4} khuu^{4}
become a monk to fulfill a promise buat^{6} kee^{3} baʔ^{4}
invite a monk niʔ^{6} mon^{4}
leave orders (of a monk) sik^{4}
man who's been a monk caan^{1}
monk's begging bowl baat^{6}
take orders as a novice or monk buat^{6}

- monkey liiŋ^{4}
- month blian^{1}
  - festival at the end of the ninth lunar month saat^{6}
  - first month blian^{1} ciaŋ^{1}
  - last day of a twenty-nine-day lunar month lap^{6}
  - second lunar month blian^{1} ɲii^{6}
- moon blian^{1}
  - full moon blian^{1} ŋaay^{2}
  - the moon (talking to children) mooŋ^{6} ʔɛɛk^{1}
  - waning moon blian^{1} rɛɛm^{4}
- moor (a boat), park a car; stop cɔɔt^{6}
- more; get ahead of another, surpass lɯɯn^{5}
  - more than, comparative kua^{6}, kwaa^{6}
- morning, early morning lɔɔm^{5}
- mortar rum^{2}, sa^{6} rɔɔy^{4}
  - small mortar for betel khɔɔk^{5} tam^{1} phun^{6}
- mosquito ɲuŋ^{4}
  - mosquito larva ɲuŋ^{6} ɲaaw^{4}
  - mosquito net muŋ^{3}
- most, end sut^{4}
- mother bɤɤy^{5}, mee^{3}, mee^{5}
  - mother's younger sibling naa^{6}
- mother-of-pearl, pearl muk^{6}
- motionless, stiff, paralyzed ka^{6} daaŋ^{3}
- motorcycle mat^{6} tɤɤ^{5} say^{4}
- mountain rɔɔy^{1}
  - a mythical mountain kay^{1} laat^{5}
  - mountain stream rii^{3}
- mouse, rat nuu^{2}
  - mouse varieties luaŋ^{3}, luŋ^{2}
- mouth paak^{6}
  - close (the mouth) hup^{4}
  - having part out (of the mouth) vɛŋ^{6}, vɛɛŋ^{6}
  - hold in the mouth ʔam^{1}
  - open the mouth ʔaa^{3}
  - put out of the mouth ɣaay^{4}
  - squirt (water) from the mouth phiw^{2}, phrɔɔ^{6}
- move, shift ɲap^{4}
  - move (e.g., a curtain) along a rod; strip off (leaves) ruut^{5}
  - move one's dwelling raay^{5}
- move, struggle, writhe khua^{6}
- movies; skin, hide, leather naŋ^{2}

much, many, very   laay^{1}, laay^{2}
mucus of the nose   muuk^{5}
mud   ban^{1} buŋ^{6}, bal^{1} bluŋ^{6}, mun^{5}
  wet and muddy (of a road)   mɯak^{5}
mule   lua^{4}
mumps; swollen jaws   ɣaaŋ^{4} thuum^{4}
mushroom   daaŋ^{3}, het^{4}
  mushroom varieties   daaŋ^{3} ka^{6} tɛl^{6}, daaŋ^{3} la^{6} ŋook^{5}, daaŋ^{3} het^{4} phɔʔ^{4}
mushy and soft (as of fruit)   leʔ^{6}
music, orchestra   phin^{4} phaat^{5}
  music, entertainment   ŋan^{4}
Muslim, Indian   khɛɛk^{6}
mussed, disheveled, tangled   ɲuŋ^{6} ɲaaw^{2}
  mussed, disheveled (of hair)   ɲɔɔŋ^{1}
must, have to   tɔŋ^{3}, tɔɔŋ^{3}
mustard plant   phrak^{4} kɛk^{4}
mute, unable to speak; stupid   yaay^{6}
muzzle (long, of a dog); bruised and swollen from a blow on the face   tuup^{2}
mynah   ʔiaŋ^{3}, ʔiaŋ^{6}

N

nail   ta^{6} puu^{1}
naked   pɯay^{1}, phii^{1} pɯay^{1}
Nakhon Phanom   na^{6} khɔɔn^{4} pha^{6} nom^{4}, la^{6} khɔɔn^{4}
name   sɔɔ^{5}
  named   sɔɔ^{5} ɣa^{3}
  personal name   tham^{4} maʔ^{6} baan^{1}, tham^{4} ma^{6} baan^{1}, sii^{1} vay^{4}
  place name   thaa^{5} khɛɛk^{6}
nap   ŋiip^{5}
narrate, tell; lie   too^{5}
narrow; small; tight-fitting   ɣeep^{5}
naughty, stubborn   ŋaan^{4}
navel   dua^{1}, bɯɯ^{1}
near   trɤɤ^{3}, tlɤɤ^{3}
nearly, almost   kɯap^{6}, thram^{3}
neck   ɣɔɔ^{4}
  up to the neck   ɣɔɔ^{4} cɔɔ^{6} lɔɔ^{4}
necklace   sɔɔy^{3}
  necklace, chain   saay^{1}

needle   kim^{1}
nephew, niece; grandchild   laan^{2}
nest (bird)   rɔɔŋ^{4}, rɔɔk^{5}
net, spiderweb   naaŋ^{5}
  cast-net   lap^{6}
  fishnet variety   naam^{4}
never mind   ciʔ^{6} thooy^{2}
new, again, another   mɔɔ^{6}
New Year's   soŋ^{1} kaan^{1}
  name of soŋ^{1} kaan^{1} day when it falls on Sunday   thuŋ^{4} saʔ^{4} thee^{4} vii^{4}
  name of soŋ^{1} kaan^{1} day when it falls on Monday   khoo^{4} laa^{4} khaʔ^{6} thee^{4} vii^{4}
  name of soŋ^{1} kaan^{1} day when it falls on Tuesday   raak^{5} saʔ^{4}
  name of soŋ^{1} kaan^{1} day when it falls on Wednesday   mon^{4} thaa^{4}
  name of soŋ^{1} kaan^{1} day when it falls on Thursday   kiʔ^{4} liʔ^{6} nii^{4}, ki^{4} li^{6} nii^{4}
  name of soŋ^{1} kaan^{1} day when it falls on Friday   kiʔ^{4} miʔ^{6} thaa^{4}, ki^{4} mi^{6} thaa^{4}
  name of soŋ^{1} kaan^{1} day when it falls on Saturday   ma^{6} hoo^{1} thɔɔn^{4}
news   khaaw^{6}, khaaw^{6} raaw^{4}
next   thɛt^{4} pay^{1}
nibble, bite (of fish); sting (of an insect)   tɔɔt^{6}
nicked, chipped   baan^{6}, baal^{6}
niece, nephew; grandchild   laan^{2}
night   ɣɯn^{4}
  midnight   theeŋ^{5} ɣɯn^{4}
  night, nightfall, evening   ɣam^{5}
  nightfall, afternoon   baay^{6}
nine   kuu^{3}
noise, noisy   nɔɔŋ^{4}
  noise, sound, voice   siaŋ^{2}
noisy   nɛn^{4}, nɔɔŋ^{4} nan^{4}
no matter   kuŋ^{2} taam^{1}
Nong Khai   nɔɔŋ^{1} khaay^{4}
nonglutinous rice   rɛɛ^{3}
nonsense!   kɛɛ^{1} ɣay^{6}
noon, honest; straight   thiaŋ^{5}, theeŋ^{5}
  noon   theeŋ^{5} ɲɛn^{4}
noon meal for monks   pheen^{4}
north, on, above, upper   khɯn^{4}
nose   daŋ^{1}

blow the nose; give final instructions, order saŋ^{6}

term for one who curries favor daŋ^{1} mɯʔ^{4}

not boo^{6}

not yet naay^{5}

novice cua^{1}

now baat^{6} nii^{6}, sɯʔ^{6} sɯɯ^{4} nii^{6}, sɯ^{6} sɯɯn^{4}

now, time, when baat^{6}

numb (slightly) ɲaap^{5}, ɲaap^{5} ɲaap^{5}

number bɤɤ^{1}

a large number koot^{6}

great numbers thaŋ^{6} thee^{4}

nylon nay^{4} lɔn^{5}

O

obeisance (to make) lay^{6}

object, unwilling khat^{4}

obscenely (to speak) phrɤʔ^{6}

obstinate, stubborn bɯɯn^{1}

obstruct baŋ^{1}

obstruct, lie athwart, block vaaŋ^{2}

obtain, get; be able; past tense marker day^{3}

Occidental, white person pha^{6} laŋ^{6}, fa^{4} laŋ^{6}, fa^{6} laŋ^{6}

occupation ʔaa^{1} siip^{5}

ocean sa^{6} mut^{4}, ma^{6} haa^{1} sa^{6} mut^{4}

odd, uneven, not a pair khiik^{5}

odor; steam, vapor sooy^{2}

of, belonging to hɛɛŋ^{6}

of, belonging to; things, possessions hɔɔŋ^{2}

offer, present, give thuay^{2}, thwaay^{2}, tha^{6} vaay^{2}

offer, do reverence buu^{1} saa^{4}

official ʔan^{6} ɲaa^{4}

official building saan^{1}

oh ʔɤɤ^{1}, ʔoo^{1}, ʔoo^{3}, ʔoo^{4}, ʔoo^{5}, ʔɔɔ^{5}, baa^{4}, ʔɤɤy^{3}, ʔooy^{1}, ʔooy^{4}, ʔooy^{5}

oil man^{4}

old kaw^{6}

old man, old fellow phɔɔ^{5} ʔɔɔŋ^{1}

old, old person thua^{4} thaw^{3}, thaw^{3}

old, ripe, dark (color) kee^{6}

olden times dɯk^{4} dam^{1} ban^{1}

older sibling phii^{5}
formerly, in olden times tɛɛ^{6} rɤɤ^{4}
olive (wild) maak^{6} kɔɔk^{6}
omit, skip baa^{1}
on, above, upper, north khɯn^{4}
on, on top of, above, high, tall saaŋ^{2}
one nɯŋ^{5} in counting, ʔɛt^{5} in numbers such as twenty-one, etc.
one or so, not even one, about, approximately sak^{4}
only one diaw^{1}
oneself hiiŋ^{4}
oneself, self ʔeeŋ^{1}
onion phrak^{4} vɔɔ^{6}
only taŋ^{3} thrɔɔ^{6}, thrɔɔ^{6}, thlɔɔ^{6}
only one diaw^{1}
open hay^{2}
open (a door) a little ŋɛɛm^{3}
open (the eyes) mlɔɔn^{4}
open (the hand); lie flat on the back bɛɛ^{1}
open (the mouth) ʔaa^{3}
open up, uncover phiat^{5}
open out, set up kaaŋ^{1}
open out, uncover phiat^{5}
open, undo kɛʔ^{4}, ŋɛʔ^{6}
oppress khen^{1}
oppress, crowd, annoy biat^{6} bian^{1}
or hɛɛ^{4}, hɛʔ^{4}
orange (fruit) kaam^{1}, sum^{3}
orange variety kiaŋ^{3}
section of orange or garlic; petal triip^{6}, tliip^{6}
orange color sɛɛt^{6}
orchestra, music phin^{4} phaat^{5}
order, give final instructions; blow the nose saŋ^{6}
take orders as a novice or monk buat^{6}
ordinal number marker; which, that thii^{6}
ordinary, usual tham^{4} ma^{6} daa^{1}
ornament, adorn ʔee^{5}
orphan kam^{1} phaa^{3}, thraa^{6}, lɯk^{6} thraa^{6}
other ʔɯɯn^{6}
otter naak^{5}
outside lɔɔk^{5}
go out ʔɔɔk^{6}
overcast (of the sky) bot^{4}

overflow   lon^{3}
  overflow, spill, slop over   phɯat^{5}
overjoyed, very glad   khɤɤn^{3}
overripe   dɯm^{5}
  overripe (of fruit)   nuam^{5}
overturn, lie face down   ŋam^{3}
owl   kaw^{1}
own, self   suu^{3}
ox   bɔɔ^{4}
  hump on the back of an ox or buffalo   nɔɔk^{6}, lam^{1}
oxcart   kian^{1}
  classifier for books, knives, boats, oxcarts, various sharp objects   lɛm^{3}
  last (oxcart); youngest (child); come to an end, be finished   sɔɔt^{5}
  sound of oxcarts   khɯk^{6} khɯk^{6}

P

pace, step; to step   yuaŋ^{6}
package, wrap up a package   tuuk^{6}
packsaddle   taaŋ^{6}
padding, stuffing (of a quilt)   nuam^{4}
paddy, unhusked rice   ɣaw^{6} thɔɔk^{6}
pagoda, stupa   thaat^{5}
pail, bucket; tank   thaŋ^{1}
  pail or jug for water   caʔ^{6} phaŋ^{4}
pain, hurt, ache   keet^{6}
  in pain   puay^{6}, puay^{6} soo^{4}
  sharp pain in stomach   cuk^{4}
paint; color   sii^{2}
  paint a picture   teem^{6}
  paint, paint on, smear   thaa^{4}, lɛɛt^{5}
  paint, smear on   thaa^{4}
pair, couple   tooy^{1}
  classifier for one of a pair; side, direction; bank of a river   viaŋ^{3}
palace   vaŋ^{4}
  palace, mansion   phaa^{1} saat^{2}, phaa^{1} saat^{6}
  royal palace   laat^{5} sa^{6} vaŋ^{4}
palm, sole   paa^{6}
pan (frying), couplet only paired with mɔɔ^{3} 'pot'   hɛɛk^{6}
Pandanus tree   caan^{3}, caal^{3}, tɤɤy^{1}
pangolin   nim^{5}, lin^{5}, lil^{5}, lin^{6} lil^{6}

pants, trousers   sooŋ^{3}
papaya   huŋ^{2}
  raw papaya salad   cɛɛw^{6}
paper   ka^{6} daat^{6}, cia^{5}
  crumple up (paper); squeeze clothes when washing   ɲɔɔŋ^{6}
  sound of tearing (e.g., paper)   khuak^{5}, khwaak^{5}, khwɛɛk^{5}
paralyzed   leʔ^{4} caŋ^{1} leʔ^{4} khoo^{1}
  paralyzed and curled up (of arm or leg)   ŋɔʔ^{6}
  paralyzed, stiff, motionless   ka^{6} daaŋ^{3}
park (a car); moor (a boat); stop   cɔɔt^{6}
part, portion (especially fish or meat when cut)   phuut^{5}
  part, section; to castrate   tɔɔn^{1}
  part; while; as for   suan^{6}, sual^{6}
part; phrase, clause   vak^{6}
particles
  final emphatic particle   day^{1}, mɛ^{4}
  final imperative particles   khay^{4}, thɤɤn^{6}, thɤʔ^{4}, thɔʔ^{2}, hay^{4}
  final particles   dee^{1}, dee^{4}, dee^{5}, naa^{4}, naa^{5}, niʔ^{6}, nɔɔ^{4}, nɔʔ^{4}, bɔɔ^{4}, bɔɔ^{5}, mɛɛ^{4}, laa^{1}, laa^{2}, laa^{3}, laʔ^{6}, la^{6} mɛɛ^{4}, hɤɤy^{1}
  final particle meaning 'you see'   law^{6}
  final question particles   lɛʔ^{4}, haa^{3}, haa^{5}
  hesitation particle   ʔaa^{6}, ʔaaʔ^{6}
  vocative particles   ʔɤɤy^{1}, ʔɤɤy^{4}, ʔɤɤy^{5}
partition, wall; lid   vaa^{1}
  partition off a room   kan^{3}, taŋ^{1}
partly gone   phrɔŋ^{5}, phrɔɔŋ^{5}
partridge   thaa^{4}
pass   phaan^{6}
  pass, walk   thiaw^{4}
  pass; last (year)   traay^{1}, tlaay^{1}
past tense marker; get, obtain; be able   day^{3}
patch (a garment)   taap^{6}
paternal grandfather   ʔooŋ^{4}
  paternal grandmother; old woman   yaa^{5}
path, road, way; side; direction   thaaŋ^{4}
pavilion   saa^{1} laa^{4}
paw the ground in anger (of buffaloes)   thɯat^{6}
pay   caay^{6}
  pay in installments   phɔɔn^{6}
peak, pinnacle   cɔɔm^{1}
pearl, mother-of-pearl   muk^{6}
peas   thua^{5} lian^{4}

pedal (a bicycle)   thiip^{6}
peel (of a banana), husk, rind   kaap^{6}
   peel, rind, bark   praak^{6}, plaak^{6}
peel off (of paint)   khwaʔ^{4}
pen (for animals)   ɣɔɔk^{5}
   pen for buffaloes under the house   lɛɛŋ^{5}
pen, pencil   sɔɔ^{2}
   classifier for spoons, pencils, saws   khan^{4}, khal^{4}
   pen (for writing)   paak^{6} kaa^{1}
penalty, punishment, guilt   thoot^{5}
pencil, pen   sɔɔ^{2}
   classifier for spoons, pencils, saws   khan^{4}, khal^{4}
penis   pak^{6} vit^{4}, vit^{4}
people   thay^{4}, thay^{5}, laat^{5} sa^{6} dɔɔn^{1}
   descriptive of many people streaming along; or chicks
      behind a hen   ɲaap^{5} ɲaap^{5}
   other people, they   raw^{2}
   people, inhabitants   saaw^{4}
   sound of people walking barefoot   tɤp^{6} tɤp^{6}
perch   ŋɔɔy^{4}
perfume   nam^{6} ʔop^{4}
period, time   paaŋ^{1}, sen^{5}
   period, limit   kam^{1} not^{4}, kam^{1} not^{6}
   period of time   sua^{5}
permanent wave (to have)   dɛt^{4} phram^{2}
persevere   ʔot^{4} saʔ^{4}
   persevere, diligent   phian^{4}
person; male; carpenter bee   phuu^{6}
   old person   thua^{4} thaw^{3}
   old person; old   thaw^{3}
   person, fellow (males only)   ʔɛɛŋ^{5}
   person, human being   ma^{6} nut^{6}, hun^{4}
   that person   nɔɔy^{6}
   that person, that fellow   threem^{5}
personality, character, disposition   nit^{4} say^{1}
pestle   saak^{6}
petal; section of orange or garlic   triip^{6}, tliip^{6}
phrase, clause; part   vak^{6}
pick up, gather, put away   kip^{4}
   pick fruit with a pole; poke animal out of a hole with a stick   ɲɔk^{6}
   pick, pluck flowers   rɛk^{4}, rak^{4}
   pick (the teeth)   cim^{3}, ciim^{6}

pick up with the fingers yip^{4}

pick with all five fingers or with claws ɲum^{1}

pick with the tips of the five fingers yup^{4}

pickle (to) dɔɔŋ^{1}, bɔɔŋ^{1}

pickle, ferment mɔɔk^{6}

picture ruup^{5}

paint (a picture) teem^{6}

take a picture thaay^{6}

piece, length; a lump, classifier thɔɔn^{5}

couplet paired with mul^{4} ‘small pieces’ phɯt^{6}

having a piece out (of the mouth) vɛŋ^{6}, vɛɛŋ^{6}

piece, lump, classifier; log, big piece of wood khook^{5}

pierce a hole cɔʔ^{4}, bɔɔŋ^{6}

pierced through lɔŋ^{6}

pierce, stab; pound; collide tam^{1}

pig muu^{2}

pile, heap cuun^{6} phuun^{6}

pile a felled tree to block a road thɯp^{6}

pile of dust outside an animal’s hole phrooy^{2}

pile up, heap up; a pile, heap kɔɔŋ^{1}

pillar sooŋ^{5}

pillow heen^{3}, heel^{3}

pimple siw^{1}, siiw^{1}

pincers, pliers, tongs khiim^{4}, khiim^{4} khaw^{3}

pinch yik^{4}

pinch, as a crab; carry under the arm; pick up with chopsticks khɛɛp^{5}, niip^{6}

pineapple maak^{6} nɛt^{6}

pinnacle, peak cɔɔm^{1}

pipe thɔɔ^{5}

pipe, flute; to spread (a mat) pii^{6}

water pipe lin^{4}

water pipe, trough, gutter haaŋ^{4}

pit khum^{1}, khum^{4}

pit, hole lum^{1}

pit, hole, chasm, crack sɔɔŋ^{5}

pity, take pity haay^{6}

place bɔɔn^{6}, book^{5}

favorite place to which people and animals return kɛɛw^{6}

place; continent thiip^{5}

placed near the edge min^{6}

plane (the tool) kop^{4}

plane wood, make sides of a hole smooth sɔʔ^{6}

plant, stick (a stake in the ground)   cam^{3}
  plant a stake; embroider   pak^{4}
  plant a stake; tattoo   sak^{4}
plant, wood, tree   may^{6}
  plant, germinate (seeds)   ʔɯaŋ^{1}
  plant (plants); build (a house)   prɔɔk^{6}, plɔɔk^{6}
  plant varieties   ʔɯaŋ^{3}, ka^{6} phuk^{4}, ka^{6} seet^{6}, ŋaan^{3}, ŋaal^{3}, tɤɤy^{1}, top^{4}, naw^{5}, nɔɔk^{6}, boŋ^{1}, praaŋ^{1}, pɔɔt^{2}, pɔɔt^{6}, lɤɤt^{6}, hɔɔm^{1} hɔɔ^{2}
  water hyacinth   buaŋ^{6}
plaster (mud) on   phɔɔk^{5}
platform in trees   haan^{3}
play (music)   seep^{6}
  play, blow (a wind instrument)   phɔɔ^{6}
play; court, woo   sɤɤn^{6}
playing cards   phay^{3}
pliers, pincers, tongs   khiim^{4}, khiim^{4} khaw^{3}
plodding along   saʔ^{6} saʔ^{6}
plow, a plow   thay^{2}
  plow a second time   plɯɯ^{6}
pluck, pick flowers   rɛk^{4}, rak^{4}
plug (a hole)   ʔɔt^{4}
  plugged up   ʔan^{3}, tɛn^{1}
plumb line   lɯk^{6} diŋ^{6}
pocket, bag   day^{5}
pod (of beans, etc.); sheath (of a knife)   vak^{4}
point   nɛɛ^{4}, ɲii^{6}
poison   phit^{6}
  be poisoned   via^{6}
  to poison   bɯa^{1}, via^{1}
poke in the ribs   kɛɛ^{5}
  poke an animal out of a hole with a stick; pick fruit with a pole   ɲɔk^{6}
  poke an ant's nest to get eggs   suʔ^{6}
  poke a stick in a gunbarrel or hole to clean it   ɲɔɔk^{5}
pole (carrying)   ɣaan^{4}
  carry on one end of a pole over the shoulder   khɔɔn^{4}, khɔɔl^{4}
  carry on two ends of a shoulder pole   raap^{6}
  pick fruit with a pole; poke an animal out of a hole with a stick   ɲɔk^{6}
  pole for drying clothes, clothesline; pole for picking fruit   yaaw^{6}
police box, fort   pɔm^{3}, pɔɔm^{3}
polish   phat^{4}
pomelo, grapefruit   phuk^{6}

pond, pool saʔ^{4}
name of a mythical pool saʔ^{4} ʔaʔ^{6} noo^{4} daat^{6}
pond or marsh in forest with soft clay into which people sink dɯl^{6}
pool in a river vaŋ^{4}
poor khoon^{3}, cɔn^{1}
poor; have hardship, trouble thuk^{6}
popped rice ɣaw^{6} tum^{2} preek^{6}
porcupine men^{3}, man^{3}
portion, part (especially of fish and meat when cut) phuut^{5}
possessions, things thrɯaŋ^{5} throo^{4}
possessions, things; food; clothing; utensils thrɯaŋ^{5}
possessions, things; of, belonging to hɔɔŋ^{2}
post, stake lak^{4}
pot mɔɔ^{3}
couplet only paired with mɔɔ^{3} ‘pot’ hɛɛk^{6}
potato, tuber ʔɛŋ^{3}, man^{4}
potato varieties ʔɛŋ^{3} ta^{6} ʔɤɤn^{1}, luaŋ^{1}, lwaaŋ^{1}, laaŋ^{1}
pounce upon thrup^{6}
pound tɔɔk^{6}
pound, batter thap^{6}
pound; collide; stab; pierce tam^{1}
pound, strike, hit, beat; fight; thresh (rice) mɔk^{6}
pour thee^{4}, riŋ^{6}, raay^{6}, rɔɔt^{6}
pour out thɔɔk^{6}, thɔɔk^{6} lee^{6}
power deet^{6}, lit^{6}
practice, learn hat^{4}
pray, ask vay^{6} vɔɔn^{4}
precepts (royal) laat^{5} sa^{6} tham^{4}
ten royal precepts thot^{6} sa^{6} phit^{6} laat^{5} sa^{6} tham^{4}
predict, guess thuay^{4}, thwaay^{4}
pregnant maan^{4}
prepare thriam^{2}, thram^{2}, thram^{3}
prepare, dress, marry tɛɛŋ^{6}
present, offer thuay^{2}, thwaay^{2}, tha^{6} vaay^{2}
present (to monks) kheen^{4}
press down khom^{6}, ɲɛn^{3}
press down; dive in headfirst dik^{4}
pressed flat bɛɛn^{1}
pressed together, constricted tiip^{6}
presume, assume; guess, estimate tuaŋ^{1}
pretty (not) ʔɯan^{1}
prevent, protect from kan^{1}

price laa^{4} khaa^{4}
prince caw^{3} phaa^{3}
prince, king, chief, lord pha^{6} ɲaa^{4}
prince, lord, chief caw^{3}
procession, have a procession rɛɛ^{6}
project, stick up, stick out thrɔɔ^{5}, thlɔɔ^{5}
promise; a contract sɛn^{2} ɲaa^{4}, sɛn^{3} ɲaa^{4}
prop up, support kham^{6}
proper liap^{5} lɔɔy^{5}
proper, good cop^{4} cɯa^{1}
property som^{1} bat^{4}
prosper huŋ^{6} hɯaŋ^{4}
protect from, prevent kan^{1}
protrude (of teeth) cɤɤŋ^{1}
protrude, of body parts blɛn^{3}, blɛl^{3}
province caŋ^{1} vat^{4}
pry ŋat^{6}, ŋɤɤk^{5}
pry up kɯɯŋ^{6}
pry up, pry open ŋay^{6}
pubic mound kha^{6} moom^{4}, naw^{6}
public saa^{1} thaa^{4} laʔ^{6} naʔ^{6}
pucker up, constrict ɲum^{3}
pull, tug thok^{4}
pull (a rope) taut nɛŋ^{5}
pull down a branch kɔɔŋ^{6}
pull, drag looy^{1}
pull, hold firm by pulling cɔɔŋ^{6}
pull in hand over hand saaw^{2}
pull in one's back when struck ʔeen^{3}
pull; snap or break when pulled rɯt^{6}
pull up (a plant) yook^{6}
pull up, out; take off, remove tuun^{1}
pull (whiskers, feathers) ruk^{4}
pump water suup^{6}
pungent (unpleasant) khiw^{2}, khiiw^{2}, khɛɛt^{6}
punishment, penalty, guilt thoot^{5}
punishment, misfortune kam^{1}
purple ʔit^{4}
pus nɔɔŋ^{2}
push thruut^{5}, soo^{2}
push aside kheew^{2}
push in, stuff ɲeet^{5}

push, shove someone in the back khɯʔ^{6}
push (someone) suu^{2}
push with the feet yɛn^{1}
put cɔɔ^{6}
put around the neck thlɔɔŋ^{6} ɣɔɔ^{4}
put away neatly; save (money) thɔɔn^{3}
put away; pack up, gather kip^{4}, mian^{6}
put inside, insert prɔɔn^{1}, plɔɔn^{1}, prɔɔn^{6}, plɔɔn^{6}
put on (a hat) dooy^{3}
put on (a hat, ring); place by inserting or impaling sup^{4}
put on, wear tɛn^{3}
put out of the mouth ɣaay^{4}
put something under to raise it; line a basket with banana leaves lɔɔt^{6}
put up (an umbrella) kaŋ^{3}
python ŋua^{4} trɔɔ^{1}, ŋua^{4} tlɔɔ^{1}, ŋua^{4} trɛn^{1}, ŋua^{4} tlɛn^{1}

Q

quake, quiver, shake phɯan^{4}
quality (poor) taa^{1} saat^{5}
good quality liap^{5}
quantity, equal, degree leeŋ^{4}
quick, quickly, fast ɲam^{4}
quiet mit^{6}, sa^{6} ŋop^{4}
quiet, silent vaŋ^{3}
very quiet mit^{6} cii^{6} lii^{6}
quilt, coverlet, blanket kha^{6} lɔɔp^{6}
quiver, quake, shake phɯam^{4}
quiver for arrows khɔɔk^{5} lɛɛŋ^{3}

R

rabbit ka^{6} taay^{6}
race, existence saat^{5}
race (to) suaŋ^{5}
radiance, radiant glory laa^{4} sii^{2}, raa^{4} sii^{2}
radio vit^{4} tha^{6} yuʔ^{6}, vit^{4} tha^{6} ɲuʔ^{6}
raft phee^{4}
railing pha^{6} nak^{6}
rain vɯn^{2}

rainbow ŋuak^5 rɔɔŋ^4
raise, feed, tend, keep; feast liaŋ^6
raise, lift coom^1, pɤɤŋ^1
put something under (e.g., leg of bed or table) to raise it; line (basket) with banana leaves lɔɔt^6
raise from a sitting position ŋɤɤŋ^4
raise, lift, get up (from sleep), stand up luk^6
raise, take up (a sheet, tablecloth) phɯɯ^6
raise the head ŋee^4, ŋoo^4
raise up, establish ɲuk^6
rake khaat^5, phia^3
ram with a pole thaŋ^5, thraŋ^5
rambutan ŋɔʔ^6
rank ɲot^6
Vietnamese ranks kaay^1 suu^4, kaay^1 saa^5
ransom, redeem thay^6
rap with the knuckles sap^4
sound of rapping with the knuckles pook^5
rash on the body mɯn^1, mɯɯn^6
heat rash phot^6
rat, mouse nuu^2
rattan vaay^2
raveled out phal^4 pɔɔy^1
raw, unripe rip^4
reach, arrive; even though thaŋ^4
reach for khua^4, khwaa^4
reach to, come very near, almost touch cuʔ^4
read ʔaan^1, ʔaan^2
real, really thɛɛ^3
really tha^6 raay^3
really, truly la^6 vaay^4
really, very ka^6 det^4 ka^6 dɔɔ^3
reap, harvest sian^4
receive, sustain rap^6, rap^6 rɔɔŋ^4, lap^6, lap^6 lɔɔŋ^4
receive, welcome tɔɔn^3
recollect ʔoo^6 thaŋ^4
recording tape thep^6
recover from illness, drunkenness suaŋ^6
red riiŋ^1
redeem, ransom thay^6
redo, repeat lam^1
reed law^4

reel, spool   kɔɔ^{3}
reflection, shadow   ŋaw^{4}
refrain from, stop; don't   yaa^{6}
registry   thaʔ^{6} bian^{1}, tha^{6} bian^{1}
regret the loss   tiak^{6}
regular, usual   pra^{6} cam^{1}
reheat, warm up   hum^{2}, haaŋ^{2}
  reheat dried fish or meat   hiaŋ^{3}
rejoice in another's fortune   thrɯaŋ^{3}
related by marriage of children   trɔɔŋ^{1}
release, rescue, help   phoot^{6}
release, set free   looy^{5}
religion   saat^{6} sa^{6} naa^{2}
remember   ɲɤɤ^{3}
  remember something forgotten   khɯt^{6} suat^{5}
remove, undo   prɛt^{4}, plɛt^{4}
  remove a garment, shoes   thuut^{6}
  remove a thorn   kwii^{6}
  remove, take off; pull up or out   tuun^{1}
  remove, take down; remove (a yoke); undo (a button)   prɛt^{4}, plɛt^{4}
  remove, undo, unbutton, untie   kee^{3}
rent (to)   saw^{6}
repair   sɔɔ^{6}
repair, mend, solder   cɔɔt^{6}
repay a debt   puun^{1}
  ask for repayment   thuaŋ^{4}
repeat; also   yam^{6}
repeat, redo   lam^{1}
reply, answer   ŋaan^{2}, tɔɔp^{6}
report, inform   khɔɔp^{5}
rescue, release, help   phoot^{6}
resin   khii^{2} sii^{4}
  resin, tree variety   yaaŋ^{4}
restless   phuan^{4}
return   prɤɤ^{6}, plɤɤ^{6}, mɯa^{4}
  return, come   maa^{2}, hun^{4}
revere   nap^{6} thɯɯ^{4}
  do reverence, offer   buu^{1} saa^{4}
revile   mɤɤy^{4}, yɤɤ^{5}
revolve, spin, whirl, turn   pin^{6}, mun^{2}, muun^{2}
rhinoceros   rɛɛt^{5}
  horn of rhinoceros   nɔɔ^{4}

ribs, the sides (of the body)   hooŋ^{2}
rice   ɣaw^{6}
  crisp rice   ɣaw^{6} khiap^{2}
  dip ball of rice in food and take it up; scratch (of chickens)   khuy^{3}
  ear or head of rice   ruaŋ^{4}
  form rice into a ball; twist, wring   van^{3}, val^{3}
  nonglutinous rice   rɛɛ^{3}
  popped rice   ɣaw^{6} tum^{2} preek^{6}
  rice boiled in cakes with a banana; starch, flour   pɛɛŋ^{3}
  rice cooked in a bamboo tube   khɔɔk^{5} kwan^{1}
  rice husks   ca^{6} prɔɔŋ^{3}, ca^{6} plɔɔŋ^{3}
  rice seedling   traa^{3}, tlaa^{3}
  rice straw   viaŋ^{1}
  rice that ripens late   ɣaw^{6} ŋaw^{4}
  rice without full kernel   liip^{5}
  thresh (rice); strike, hit, beat, pound; fight   mɔk^{6}
  unhusked rice, paddy   ɣaw^{6} thɔɔk^{6}
  white rice   ɣaw^{6} saan^{2}, ɣaw^{6} saal^{2}
  white rice roasted and pounded   sam^{3} haaŋ^{2}
  wild rice with very short grains   ɣaw^{6} maa^{2} ɲɛɛŋ^{6}
  young rice pounded flat, used in desserts   ɣaw^{6} muu^{3}
ricefield   naa^{4}
  single ricefield   raay^{6} naa^{4}
rich   traw^{1}, ruay^{4}
  rich man   seet^{6} thii^{2}
riddle   ban^{3} haa^{2}
ride   khooy^{5}
right (hand)   khua^{4}, khwaa^{4}
rim, edge   khɔɔp^{6}
rind, peel, bark   praak^{6}, plaak^{6}
  rind, husk, (banana) peel   kaap^{6}
ring   vɛɛn^{2}
  put on (ring, hat); place by inserting or impaling   sup^{4}
  ring around knife handle   heew^{6}
ringworm   laak^{6}
rinse soap off   lay^{4}
ripe, cooked   suk^{6}
  almost ripe (of fruit)   ʔuay^{6}, hɤɤm^{6}
  early ripening (rice, bean)   dɔɔ^{1}
  late ripening (rice, beans)   ŋan^{4}
  put fruit away to ripen   bum^{6}
  ripe, old, dark (of color)   kee^{6}

rise, ascend, go up, come up, up hɯn^{3}
risk, take a chance; make a wish siaŋ^{5}, siaŋ^{6}
river bank; side, direction; classifier for one of a pair viaŋ^{3}
  name of a river ka^{6} diŋ^{1}
road, way, path; side; direction thaaŋ^{4}
  road, way, side raa^{5}
roar phɛɛt^{6} siaŋ^{2}
roast, smoke over a fire yuaŋ^{3}, yaa^{4}, ruut^{6}
rob pun^{3}
rock, swing; stir kway^{1}
  rock a post ɲook^{5}
roll lɛn^{1}
  roll a cigarette ham^{4}
  roll into a ball pum^{5}
  roll, make candles sii^{2}
  roll up, coil up muan^{6}
roof (to) vɔɔŋ^{1}
room hɔɔŋ^{6}
rooster crowing ʔee^{5} kaʔ^{6} reen^{4} ʔee^{5}, ʔee^{5} kaʔ^{6} reel^{4} ʔee^{5}, ʔek^{4} kaʔ^{6} reen^{4} ʔeek^{4}, ʔek^{4} kaʔ^{6} reel^{4} ʔeek^{4}
root raak^{5}, raak^{6}
rope, cord saak^{5}
  coil up (of a rope) kuan^{3}, khwaan^{3}, khuan^{3}, tlooŋ^{1}
  long rope, as a clothesline saak^{5} phiak^{6}
  rope in a buffalo's nose thaw^{4}
rose kuʔ^{4} laap^{6}
rotten naw^{5}
  rotten (of wood) phuʔ^{6}
  rotten wood at base of pole prook^{6}, plook^{6}
  soft and rotten, tender (of meat) pɯay^{6}
round prum^{1}, plum^{1}, mɔn^{4}
row a boat phaay^{4}
row, column thɛɛw^{2}, lian^{4}
royal, the government luaŋ^{2}
  classifier for royal persons ʔoŋ^{1}
  go see (royalty); guard phaw^{3}
  royal palace laat^{5} sa^{6} vaŋ^{4}
  royal precepts laat^{5} sa^{6} tham^{4}
  royalty title phaʔ^{6}, pha^{6}
  say to royalty thuun^{4}
  ten royal precepts thot^{6} sa^{6} phit^{6} laat^{5} sa^{6} tham^{4}

rub   thuu^{2}
  rub out, erase   lɯp^{6}
rubber; gum; fibers of a lotus stem   yaaŋ^{1}
  rubber band   yaaŋ^{1} ka^{6} tiw^{3}
rubbish (small bit of)   pa^{6} ɲool^{6}
rule, govern   pok^{4} khɔɔŋ^{4}
  rule over (a kingdom)   sa^{6} vɤɤy^{1}
ruler (for measuring)   ban^{1} thɛt^{6}
run   luu^{5}
  run over   thap^{6}
  run over (of a car); step on, tread on   yiap^{6}
rush, hurry   hɯɯ^{4}
rust   raak^{5}

S

sad   sook^{6}
  sad and gloomy   kuk^{6}
saddle   ʔaan^{1}
Saek people   thrɛɛk^{6}
Saek villages in Thailand   ʔaa^{1} saa^{1}, ʔa^{6} saa^{1}, ʔaa^{1} saa^{1} maat^{5}, ʔaa^{1} sa^{6} maat^{5}, ʔa^{4} sa^{6} maat^{5}, ʔaat^{6} saa^{1} maat^{5}, ʔeek^{6} ʔaa^{1} saa^{1} [old name], khɔɔŋ^{2}; dɔŋ^{1} sa^{6} mɔɔ^{4} (= doŋ^{1} sa^{6} mɔɔ^{4}, doŋ^{1} su^{6} mɔɔ^{4}, dɔɔn^{1} suʔ^{6} mɔɔ^{4}); baa^{6} vaa^{3} (= baa^{1} vaa^{3}); phay^{6} lɔɔm^{3} (= saw^{1} law^{3})
  abandoned Saek villages in Thailand   thaa^{5} vaay^{4}, naa^{4} laʔ^{6} vaay^{4}
  abandoned Saek villages in Vietnam   bɯk^{4} naa^{4} tɤɤ^{3}, sin^{4} naa^{4} mɤɤy^{4}, trɤɤŋ^{1}, thruu^{3}, sɔɔŋ^{4}
  Saek villages in Laos   thaa^{5} khɛɛ^{4}, thɔɔk^{5}, phoo^{4} kham^{3}
salad (of bamboo shoots)   sip^{6}
saliva   mlaay^{4}, nam^{6} naay^{4}
  drool (of saliva), flow   hɤɤy^{1}
salt   trua^{1}, tlua^{1}
  salty   khɛm^{4}
  to salt (meat, fish)   ʔɯap^{6}
salve for lips of betel chewers   nuat^{5}
sand   yooy^{4}
  sandbar, beach   haat^{6}
sandals   kɤɤp^{6} tɛʔ^{6}
sarong   sa^{6} rooŋ^{3}, sa^{6} looŋ^{2}
satiated, full   ʔiim^{6} nam^{1} sam^{1} raan^{4}

Saturday van^4 saw^1
save (money); put away neatly thɔɔn^3
  be saving, spend (money) cautiously ʔɔɔm^1
save for someone; by the time phɯa^6
  save food for someone coŋ^6
saw, to saw lɯay^6
  classifier for spoons, pencils, saws khan^4, khal^4
say, speak, talk, tell nɔɔy^3
  say; that ɣaa^3, ɣa^3, ɣaa^5
  say to royalty thuun^4
scab on a wound nap^4
scald luak^5
scales, balance siŋ^4
scare, frighten; deceive, lie lɔɔk^6
scattered about ka^6 cat^4 ka^6 caay^1, caan^6 phaan^6
  scattered about, all around ta^6 phɯt^6 ta^6 phɯɯ^4
scholar nak^6 paat^6
  scholar, teacher ʔaa^1 caan^1
scissors kɛɛw^3
scold; fierce thuu^3
scoop up (fish) sɔɔn^3
  scoop of water in the palm to drink vaay^1
  scoop out (water); splash out saat^6
scorch, burn daat^6
scorpion mɛɛŋ^4 ŋaw^4, mɛɛŋ^4 ŋɔɔt^6
scrap (of cloth); bite (of food) mɛɛŋ^6
  scraps of wood tɔɔk^6
scrape khuut^6
  scrape off (fish scales) tɔɔn^6, tɔɔl^6
  scrape out (e.g., rice from a pot); spend all one's money khɔʔ^4
scratch kaw^1
  scratch, as a cat khuut^5
  scratch, as chickens khia^6
  scratch, claw khuaw^4, khwaaw^4, khwaa^4, khwaak^6
  scratch, draw a line khiit^6
  scratch (of chickens); dip ball of rice in food and take it up khuy^3
screwthreads kiaw^1, triaw^1
  screwthreads, strand (of rope) trɛɛw^1, tlɛɛw^1, triaw^1
search khon^3
  search; accompany, follow; with; from; along nam^4
  search; follow; along; according to taam^1
  search, seek yɔɔk^5, lɔʔ^6

season   la^{6} duu^{1}
  season; watch, watchman   ɲaam^{4}
section, part; to castrate   tɔɔn^{1}
  section of garlic   ŋɛŋ^{5}
  section of orange or garlic   ŋiim^{4}
  section or orange or garlic; petal   triip^{6}, tliip^{6}
sedan automobile   lot^{6} keŋ^{1}
sediments, as in water, liquids, soup   saa^{6}
see   rɛn^{2}
  go see royalty; guard   phaw^{3}
  go see someone; seek   sɔɔ^{5}
  see, look, watch   nɔɔm^{1}
  see (someone) off; accompany; send   cɔŋ^{6}
seed, grain, small round object   mlɛt^{6}, mlɛk^{6}
  seed; kind   van^{2}
  seed of jackfruit or durian   nuan^{4}
seek   raa^{2}
  seek; go see someone   sɔɔ^{5}
  seek out   thaaw^{4}
  seek, search   yɔɔk^{5}, lɔʔ^{6}
seize, catch, grasp, take hold of   cap^{4}
self, oneself   ʔeeŋ^{1}
  self, own   suu^{3}
sell   kuay^{1}, kwaay^{1}
send, see someone off; accompany   cɔŋ^{6}
  send (someone); use, employ   thraay^{2}
  send (a present)   kuak^{6}, kwaak^{6}
sermon   theet^{5}
serpent (in stories)   naak^{5}
servant, slave   hɔɔy^{6}
serve   pat^{4} ti^{4} bat^{4}
  serve, wait on   ʔup^{4} pa^{6} thaak^{6}
sesame   vɯŋ^{1}
set (of furniture)   sut^{6}
set up, establish; all   taŋ^{3}
  set down, lay down   vaaŋ^{1}
  set down; shrivel from heat (of leaves)   ɲoop^{5}
  set up; open out   kaaŋ^{1}
seven   cɛt^{4}
sew   ɲip^{6}
  sewing machine   cak^{4}

sexual intercourse sam^{2}, ɲuut^{5}, suut^{5} (latter two modern slang)
move the hips in sexual intercourse nɛt^{4}
shack, hut, temporary shelter tup^{4}
shade yum^{1}
shade the eyes pɔɔŋ^{3} praa^{1}
shadow pɔŋ^{3}
shadow, reflection ŋaw^{4}
shake (a bottle, fruit from a tree) sɛn^{6}, sɛl^{6}
shake something off sit^{6}
shake, quake, quiver phɯan^{4}
descriptive of a house shaking ɲoop^{5} ɲoop^{5} ɲaap^{5} ɲaap^{5}
shaky, in bad condition yoo^{5}
shaman; doctor mɔɔ^{2}
shape, figure sep^{6}
share, divide pan^{1}, beeŋ^{6}
share in something ruam^{5}
sharp haw^{3}
classifier for books, knives, boats, oxcarts, various sharp objects lɛm^{3}
classifier for tools, knives, and other sharp instruments maak^{5}, maak^{6}
sharp (of a knife) trɛɛŋ^{4}
sharp, sharp edge ɣam^{4}
sharpen lap^{6}
sharpen to a point lɛm^{2}
sharpened stake khwaak^{6}
sharp-pointed lɛɛm^{2}
shave thɛɛ^{2}
she, it, he, they man^{4}
sheaf, bundle, faggot roop^{5}
shears to cut areca nuts sa^{6} naak^{5}
sheath (of a knife); pod (of beans, etc.) vak^{4}
sheath; eggshell, matchbox ta^{6} roop^{5}
shed the skin (of snakes) loot^{5}
sheet (of paper) peen^{6}
shelf thraa^{6}
shelter (temporary), shack, hut tup^{4}
shift, move ɲap^{4}
shine (a light) siaŋ^{5}
shiny miaŋ^{4} miaŋ^{4}
smooth and shiny lɯam^{3}
shirt, upper garment phia^{5}
shiver, tremble ruŋ^{1}

shoe, shoes kɤɤp^{6}
  sandals kɤɤp^{6} tɛʔ^{6}
shoot ɲiŋ^{4}, ɲiiŋ^{4}
shop, store laan^{3}
short tin^{3}
short, low tia^{3}, tam^{6}
  too short (of a skirt) khɤɤn^{2}
shoulder khoo^{6} lee^{6}, rɔɔŋ^{4} vaa^{6}, vaa^{6}
  carry on one end of a pole over the shoulder khɔɔn^{4}, khɔɔl^{4}
  carry on the shoulder khuat^{5}
  carry on the two ends of a shoulder pole raap^{6}
  carry slung over the shoulder phaa^{6}
  shoulder bag thɔŋ^{2}
shove someone in the back, push khɯʔ^{6}
shovel, spade yaak^{6}, suan^{3}, swaan^{3}
shower of rain raa^{6}
show off (something) siaŋ^{5}
shrimp kuŋ^{6}
  shrimp paste ka^{6} piʔ^{4}
shrink hot^{4}
shrivel from heat (of leaves); sit down ɲoop^{5}
shut up, imprison thraŋ^{2}
shuttle of loom kiiŋ^{6} sɔɔy^{2}
sibling (older) phii^{5}
  mother's younger sibling naa^{6}
  younger sibling nuaŋ^{6}
sick, ill; have a fever ʔoom^{3}
sickle (short-handled) liam^{4}, vɛɛt^{5}, vɛɛk^{5}
side, part phia^{3}
  side, direction; river bank; classifier for one of a pair viaŋ^{3}
  side; direction; road, way, path thaaŋ^{4}
  side, edge; beside thrɛɛm^{4}
  side (of the body, house); beside rɛk^{4}
  side or corner broken off ka^{6} vaʔ^{4}
  side; way, road raa^{5}
  sides (of the body), ribs hooŋ^{2}
sideburns cɔɔn^{1}
sieve, to sift raŋ^{2}
  sieve thuŋ^{3} raŋ^{2}
sift, sieve raŋ^{2}
silent mit^{6} cit^{6}
  silent, quiet vaŋ^{3}

silver; money ɲɛn^{4}
  silver and gold and jewels ɲɛn^{4} ɣam^{4} kam^{1} kɛɛw^{3}
  silver mine ɲɛn^{4} bɔɔ^{6}
similar, like, alike thruu^{4}
simple, easy ŋaay^{5}
  simply sɤɤy^{1}
sin baap^{6}
since hay^{3}
since, from taŋ^{3} tɛɛ^{6}
  since, from; but tɛɛ^{6}
sing lɔɔŋ^{3}, hap^{4}
  singer, singing mɔɔ^{2} lam^{4}
sink cam^{1}, cɔm^{1}
sip (a hot liquid) yuut^{5}
sister (older) cii^{5}
  father's younger sister ʔɔɔ^{5}
sit naŋ^{5}
  sit down; shrivel from heat (of leaves) ɲoop^{5}
  sit leaning against a triangular pillow thɤɤŋ^{3}
  sit or lie on top of someone khoom^{4}
Sita, wife of Rama sii^{4} daa^{1}
six rɔk^{4}
  sixty rɔk^{4} sip^{6}
  sixty five rɔk^{4} sip^{6} haa^{3}
size kha^{6} naat^{6}
  size; kind, like sam^{6}
skein; spindle nay^{4}
  skein-like device ʔak^{4}
skilled, clever keŋ^{6}, keeŋ^{6}
  skilled; artisan, expert saaŋ^{5}
skin, hide, leather; the movies naŋ^{2}
  dried sweat and dirt on the skin ɣay^{6} ɣii^{4}
  skin diseases moo^{3}, laaŋ^{4} bɛɛn^{1}
skin (the penis) laan^{4}
skink caʔ^{6} trɛn^{6}, caʔ^{6} tlɛn^{6}, ca^{6} trɛn^{6}, ca^{6} tlɛn^{6}
skinned luun^{2}, luun^{3}
  skinned, having the skin abraded plɤɤk^{5}
  skinned; to stop, stop work lɤɤk^{5}
  take skin and flesh off bones lɤɤk^{5} saak^{5}
skip, omit baa^{1}
skirt ka^{6} pooŋ^{1}, sin^{3}

skull ta^{6} poʔ^{4} bak^{2} thraw^{3}
sky, weather bɤn^{1}
sky, atmosphere ʔaa^{1} kaat^{6}
slack, not taut yaan^{4}, yaal^{4}
slant, lean over see^{4}
slap; clap tap^{4}
slash, cut van^{1}, val^{1}
slave, servant hɔɔy^{6}
sleep, lie down nuun^{4}
get up (from sleep); stand up; raise, lift luk^{6}
(sleep) curled up khot^{4}
sleepy raw^{3} nuun^{4}
talk in one's sleep thrɤɤ^{2}, thlɤɤ^{2}
slice rɔɔn^{6}, han^{6}
slice thin seet^{5}
slingshot ŋaam^{5} maak^{5} ka^{6} thun^{1}
slip loose, fall off, fall out khɔɔn^{5}, khɔɔl^{5}
slip and fall thrɤɤt^{5}, thlɤɤt^{5}
slip loose, slip from the hand luut^{6}
slip off, slip down (of lower garment) prooŋ^{5}
slippery mlɯɯn^{5}, mlɯɯl^{5}
slow trɯm^{5}
slowly, gradually thrɛɛ^{5}
small nɔɔy^{5}, nɔɔy^{6}, lɛk^{6}
small; narrow; tight-fitting ɣeep^{5}
very small nay^{5} nay^{5}, nɔɔy^{5} nɔɔy^{5}
smart (of a wound) seep^{6}
smashed, flatten, crushed raa^{5}
smear, spread baay^{6}
smear on, paint thaa^{4}, lɛɛt^{5}
smell dam^{1}
smell bad ŋaw^{2}
smell very bad ŋaw^{2} phriŋ^{4} phriŋ^{4}, ŋaw^{2} phliŋ^{4} phliŋ^{4}
smoke ɣɔn^{4}
smoke; steam hom^{4}
smoke tobacco duup^{6}
very smoky, hot and airless ʔuut^{6}
smoke over a fire; roast yuaŋ^{3}
smoke (meat); hunt, go hunting hoo^{6}
smoke (tobacco) duup^{6}

smooth triaŋ^{3}, tliaŋ^{3}
smooth and shiny lɯam^{3}
smooth; clean prian^{3}, plian^{3}, mɔt^{4}
make smooth and level; level mɔɔp^{5}
not smooth phɯɯt^{6}
use a knife to cut away and smooth a knot in wood lɔʔ^{6}, sɔʔ^{6}
snail, mollusk ʔook^{6}
snake ŋua^{4}
discarded snake skin; corpse thraap^{5}
snap fastener tɛp^{6}
snap with fingers; kick (of a horse) bliit^{6}
snare reew^{6}
snatch thɯɯn^{3}
sneeze muy^{6}, muuy^{6}
snore trɛn^{1}, tlɛl^{1}
so, and then, but phat^{2}
so, and so, then, and then, therefore lee^{4}, leʔ^{4}, le^{4}, lɤɤy^{4}
so, then kuŋ^{2}, kuŋ^{3}, ciʔ^{2}, ci^{2}
So people soo^{3}, sa^{6} roo^{3}
soak (e.g., rice) maa^{6}, see^{5}
soap sa^{6} buu^{1}
socks thuŋ^{1} thaw^{3}
soft, decayed ɲuay^{3}, yuay^{3}
soft and mushy (as fruit) leʔ^{6}
soft, liquid lɛɛw^{1}
soft; young; light (of color) ʔuun^{6}
soiled, dirty pɯan^{3}
solder, repair, mend cɔɔt^{6}
soldier tha^{6} haan^{2}
sole, palm paa^{6}
solid, hard, firm keen^{6}, keel^{6}
some dɛɛ^{6}, laŋ^{4}, laaŋ^{4}
something, what, everything tuŋ^{6} thaa^{4}
soot mɛɛw^{4} mɔɔ^{3}
soul, spirit miŋ^{5}
sound, noise, voice siaŋ^{2}
sour sam^{3}
south, below, under tɤɤ^{3}
sow, throw, cast vaan^{6}, vaal^{6}
space under a house luaŋ^{5}
couplet paired with luaŋ^{5} ‘space under a house’ sɔɔŋ^{4}
spaced (widely), far apart; coarse, coarsely woven saa^{6}

spade, shovel   yaak^{6}, suan^{3}, swaan^{3}

  use a spade to make sides of hole smooth; plane wood   sɔʔ^{6}

span (finger); move as a measuring worm   khɯɯp^{5}

sparkle   ɲaap^{5} ɲaap^{5}

speak   traaw^{3}, tlaaw^{3}

  speak, talk, say, tell   nɔɔy^{3}

  speak, tell   kaaw^{6}

  (speak) obscenely   phrɤʔ^{6}

  speak of, mention   ɲak^{4}

  unable to speak   nɔɔy^{3} naaŋ^{6}

  unable to speak, dumb   kɯɯk^{6}

  unable to speak; mute; stupid   yaay^{6}

spear   sum^{2} muu^{2}, sam^{3} muu^{2}

spend (money) cautiously, be saving   ʔɔɔm^{1}

spend money wastefully, to waste   sɔɔn^{3}

  spend all one's money; scrape out (e.g., rice out of a pot)   khɔʔ^{4}

  spend a lot of money on something   phoʔ^{6} (slang)

  spend every bit of one's money; eat every last bit of something   mɔɔt^{6}

spicy hot   thaat^{5}, phet^{4}

spider   thruŋ^{6} thraaw^{2}, mɛɛŋ^{4} mum^{4}

  spiderweb   vaaŋ^{3}

  spiderweb; net   naaŋ^{5}

spill   phraaw^{5}, phlaaw^{5}

  spill, overflow, slop over   phɯat^{5}

spin (cotton)   thray^{4}, pan^{1}, pan^{6}, pal^{1}

  spin (a top)   han^{1}

  spin, whirl, turn, revolve   pin^{6}, mun^{2}, muun^{2}

spindle, spool; light bulb   luut^{6}

  spindle; skein   nay^{4}

  spinning wheel   lua^{2}, lwaa^{2}

spirit, soul   miŋ^{5}

  spirit, ghost   pheet^{6}

  spirit, ghost; corpse   maaŋ^{4}

  spirit shrine   deen^{4}

  spirit varieties   ʔoŋ^{1} muu^{5}, maaŋ^{4} phrɔɔŋ^{4}

  spirit; whorl in the hair   hɔn^{2}

spit   pruut^{6}, pluut^{6}

  spittoon   ka^{6} thoon^{1}, khɔɔk^{5} ŋiaŋ^{5}, ŋiaŋ^{5}

spit for roasting   rap^{4} yaa^{4}

splash (of water); swirl up (dust)   phoŋ^{3}

  splash out, scoop out (water)   saat^{6}

spleen   paaŋ^{3}, maam^{3}, maam^{6}

splinter kheen^{6}, kheel^{6}
split phaa^{6}
split (bamboo) strips sak^{4}
spoiled (of food) siw^{2}, siiw^{2}
spoiled, damaged hɯɯ^{2}
spool, reel kɔɔ^{3}
spool, spindle; light bulb luut^{6}
spoon buaŋ^{6}
big spoon, ladle ta^{6} mooy^{1}, ta^{6} mooy^{6}
classifier for spoons, pencils, saws khan^{4}, khal^{4}
spots, stripe, design, mark laay^{4}
spotted, many colored daaŋ^{6}
spout of teapot; elephant's trunk ŋuaŋ^{4}
spread, smear baay^{6}
spread (a mat); flute, pipe pii^{6}
spread in the sun to dry phɤɤy^{1}
spread apart thaaŋ^{6}
spread (of fire) laam^{4}
spring (of water) nam^{6} cɛn^{3}
sprinkle rooy^{4}, hot^{4}
sprout ŋɔɔk^{5}
sprout, bud (as in coconut) caaw^{1}
squirt (water) from the mouth phrɔɔ^{6}, phiw^{2}
spy; go-between sɤɤy^{4}
squat yɔɔŋ^{3} yɔɔ^{3}, yɔɔŋ^{3} yɔɔ^{6}
squat down naŋ^{5} yɔɔŋ^{3} yɔɔ^{3}, naŋ^{5} yɔɔŋ^{3} yɔɔ^{6}
squeeze; massage biip^{6}
squeeze clothes when washing; crumple up (paper) ɲɔɔŋ^{6}
squeeze, force sap^{4}
squeeze juice out khan^{6}, khal^{6}
squirm, as when dying piat^{6}
squirrel rɔɔk^{5}
flying squirrel paaŋ^{6}
squirt (water) from the mouth phrɔɔ^{6}, phiw^{2}
stab thrɔɔk^{5}
stab deeply cam^{1}
stab, pierce; pound; collide tam^{1}
stack (of paper) tap^{4}
stack of small dry sticks thɤɤp^{5}
stack up, fold neatly; stick (money) between things lɛɛp^{6}
stairs ŋan^{5} ray^{1}
stairs, ladder ray^{1}

stake, post lak^{4}
stammer ʔan^{3}
stand yɔŋ^{4}
  stand leaning against something mɛʔ^{6}
  stand on a branch and bounce up and down ɲoom^{2}, ɲoom^{3}
  stand up; get up (from sleep); raise, lift luk^{6}
  stand with legs apart caaŋ^{6}
stand (a footed) khan^{2}
star traaw^{1}
  morning star traaw^{1} phek^{6}
starch, flour; rice boiled in cakes with a banana pɛɛŋ^{3}
stare fixedly kɯŋ^{3} praa^{1}
  stare with amazement praa^{1} khaaŋ^{6}
  staring with wide open eyes; open eyes wide or turn back an eyelid lɯak^{6}
startled ruk^{4}, sa^{6} dɤɤt^{6}
steadily, continually lɯay^{3}, lɯay^{5}
steal lak^{6}
steam (to) nɯŋ^{3}
  steam; smoke (to) hom^{4}
  steam, vapor; odor sooy^{2}
  vessel for steaming glutinous rice ruat^{6}
steamboat kam^{6} pan^{6}
steep sɛn^{4}, san^{4}
stem of leaf, flower, fruit kaan^{3}
step, pace yuaŋ^{6}
  step on, tread on; run over (of a car) yiap^{6}
sterile ka^{6} dɛɛŋ^{3}, man^{1}
stew, cook for a long time ʔɔɔm^{6}
stick (a stake in the ground), plant cam^{3}
  stick (money) between things; stack up or fold neatly lɛɛp^{6}
stick in the throat kheen^{6}
stick of firewood prɔɔ^{6}, plɔɔ^{6}
  stack of small dry sticks thɤɤp^{5}
stick out (the tongue) blɔɔ^{3}
  stick up, stick out, project thrɔɔ^{5}, thlɔɔ^{5}
sticklac thraŋ^{5}
sticky, thick (of liquids) trɛɛw^{6}
  sticky, tough; glutinous (rice) niaw^{2}
stiff, hard thriaŋ^{2}
stiff, motionless, paralyzed ka^{6} daaŋ^{3}
still, yet khaa^{4}, lii^{6}, haʔ^{6} lii^{6}, ha^{6} lii^{6}, hay^{2}

sting (of an insect); bite, nibble (of fish)   tɔɔt^{6}
stinger of an insect   lay^{4}
stir; swing, rock   kway^{1}
stir-fry, sauté   phat^{4}
stoke (a fire)   khum^{4}
stomach, belly   thuŋ^{6}
have a sharp pain in the stomach   cuk^{4}
sound of stomach rumbling with hunger   kook^{5} kaak^{5}
sound of stomach rumbling with hunger; tiger roaring   kook^{5}
stomp   thɯɯp^{5}
stone   riin^{2}, riil^{2}
stone or other objects used as a weight   toon^{3}
stool   taŋ^{6}
stop   coʔ^{4}, caŋ^{3}, yut^{4}
stop; moor (a boat); park (a car)   cɔɔt^{6}
stop, refrain from; don't   yaa^{6}
stop, stop work; skinned   lɤɤk^{5}
stop the flow of blood   khat^{4} luat^{5}
stop in, visit   vɛɛ^{5}
stopper of clay for sky rocket   thɯat^{6}
store, shop   laan^{3}
storehouse; treasury   khaŋ^{4}
story   niʔ^{4} thaan^{4}, niʔ^{6} thaan^{4}, lɯaŋ^{6}
story, history   pra^{6} vat^{4}
story, level; layer   sɛn^{6}
story, level   phɯɯn^{6}
stove, fireplace   phiak^{5} vii^{4}, phriak^{5} vii^{4}, phrɯak^{5} vii^{4}
straight; honest   yɔɔ^{5}
not straight, crooked   khot^{6}, vii^{5}
straight; noon; honest   thiaŋ^{5}, theeŋ^{5}
straighten or bend as desired   blɛt^{4}
strain, as in defecating or childbirth   beŋ^{6}, bɛŋ^{6}
strand (of rope); screwthreads   kiaw^{1}, triaw^{1}, trɛɛw^{1}, tlɛɛw^{1}
strange   ŋɯt^{6} ŋɔɔ^{5}
strange, differ, various   taaŋ^{6}
strange, amazing   ʔat^{4} sa^{6} cɛn^{1}
stratum, layer of rocks on a mountain   lɯɯp^{6}, lɤɤp^{6}
stream along   ɲaap^{5} ɲaap^{5}
strength, strong   reeŋ^{4}
stretch taut   neŋ^{5}
stretch taut, pull taut   khɯŋ^{1}

strike, knock   tɔʔ^{4}, tɔɔy^{6}
  strike, beat, batter   thap^{6} thoo^{4}
  strike, hit, beat, pound; fight; thresh (rice)   mɔk^{6}
  strike something to free it of mud, etc.   khuʔ^{4}
  strike with a pole   paay^{6}
string (to)   rɔɔy^{6}
  sound of string breaking when pulled   top^{6}
strip off (leaves); move (e.g., a curtain) along a rod   ruut^{5}
stripe, design, mark, spots   laay^{4}
  striped   laay^{4} lɔɔŋ^{6}
  striped; to mark   kaan^{6}
stroke, wipe   luup^{5}
strong, strength   reeŋ^{4}
  strong-smelling (of tobacco)   puk^{4}
  strong, vigorous   maŋ^{4}
struggle, writhe, move   khua^{6}
  struggle over, vie for   siiŋ^{2}
stubble, stump   kɔn^{6}, kɔl^{6}
stubborn   dɯɯ^{3}
  do stubbornly, do alone   ʔɯa^{1}
  stubborn, naughty   ŋaan^{4}
  stubborn, obstinate   bɯɯn^{1}
stuck   khaa^{4}, khaaŋ^{6}
  stuck in the flesh (of a knife)   cup^{6}
student   nak^{6} rian^{1} (also recorded as rian^{4})
study   rian^{4}
stuff, push in   ɲeet^{5}
  stuffed; crowded   neen^{3}
  stuffing, padding   nuam^{4}
stump, stubble   kɔn^{6}, kɔl^{6}
stupa, pagoda   thaat^{5}
stupid, dull-witted   pɯk^{4}
  stupid; mute, unable to speak   yaay^{6}
subjugate, bring under control   naap^{5}
submit, yield, consent, allow   ɲɔɔm^{4}
substance that is chewed   miaŋ^{6}
substitute   taaŋ^{1}
  substitute for   thɛɛn^{4}
suck   duut^{6}
sudden, suddenly (of grabbing, seizing, embracing)   kap^{6}
sugarcane   ʔɔɔy^{3}

sugar palm taan^{1}
sugar palm tree khoo^{6} taan^{1}
suitable, fitting khuan^{4}
suitcase, box, trunk hiip^{6}
suitcase, bag ka^{6} paw^{1}
summon, call; be called (so-and-so) reek^{5}
sun taŋ^{1} ɲɛn^{4}, taaŋ^{1} ɲɛn^{4}
spread in the sun to dry phɤɤy^{1}
sun, day, daytime ɲɛn^{4}
sunshine riit^{6}
Sunday van^{4} ʔaa^{1} thit^{6}, van^{4} ʔa^{6} thit^{6}, van^{4} thit^{6}
support, prop up kham^{6}
support (as a pillow) under the head muun^{2}
support, hold up khɯŋ^{4}
sure, certain nɛɛ^{5}
surpass, get ahead of another; more lɯɯn^{5}
surprised, amazed ŋɯt^{6}
sustain; receive rap^{6} rɔɔŋ^{4}, lap^{6} lɔɔŋ^{4}
swallow (to) trɯɯn^{1}, tlɯɯn^{1}
swallow (the bird) ʔeen^{6}, ʔɛɛn^{6}
swarm tɔɔm^{1}
swarm on fruit and pastry (of ants, flies) cɯʔ^{4}, ɲɯʔ^{4} ɲɯʔ^{4}
sway, as a house in the wind phɯan^{4} ɲut^{6}
sweat nam^{6} tum^{6}
dried dirt and sweat on the skin ɣay^{6} ɣii^{4}
sweep kuat^{6}, kwaat^{6}
sweep, dust off pɛk^{4}
sweet vaan^{1}, vaan^{2}, vaal^{2}
swift (of a current) riw^{4}, riiw^{4}
swim yuu^{4}
swim or dive under water bɔt^{4}
swing (to) hoon^{1}
swing, rock; stir kway^{1}
swing for children; cradle vɔŋ^{5}
swirl up (of dust); splash (of water) phoŋ^{3}
switch (a) rɔɔy^{1}
sound of a switch striking a child thop^{4}
swollen, bruised vɔk^{6}
swollen, as from a bruise noo^{4}
swollen jaws; mumps ɣaaŋ^{4} thuum^{4}
swollen (of the eye) khɯaŋ^{4}

swoop down   sɛɛw^{6}
swoop back and forth   vɤɤn^{6}
sword   daap^{6}, raaw^{2}

T

table   toʔ^{4}, toʔ^{6}
go under (a fence, house, table)   lɔɔt^{5}
tadpole   ruuk^{6}
Tai, Thai   thay^{4}
tail   ruaŋ^{2}
take   ʔaw^{1}
take a picture   thaay^{6}
take care of, guard   rak^{6} saa^{2}
take down, remove; remove (a yoke); undo (a button)   prɛt^{4}, plɛt^{4}
take hold of   baay^{1}
take up in both arms   ʔoom^{1}
take, lead   yɔɔŋ^{1}
take off, remove; pull up or out   tuun^{1}
talk, say, speak, tell   nɔɔy^{3}
talk in one's sleep   thrɤɤ^{2}, tlɤɤ^{2}
tall, high; on, on top of, above   saaŋ^{2}
couplet paired with saaŋ^{2} 'tall, high (of people, elephants)'   vɔɔŋ^{4}
very tall (of people)   yooŋ^{1}
tallow   khay^{1}
tamarind   trɛɛw^{2}, tlɛɛw^{2}, thrɛɛw^{2}, thlɛɛw^{2}
tame, familiar   khun^{6}
tangled, mussed, disheveled   ɲuŋ^{6} ɲaaw^{2}
tangled (of rope); curled up (of leaves); to have a high fever with hands and feet curled up   caŋ^{1}
tank; bucket, pail   thaŋ^{1}
target   paw^{3}
taste (to)   deem^{3}
tattoo (to); plant (a stake)   sak^{4}
tattoo, tattoo designs   sak^{4} laay^{4}
taut   khɛŋ^{5}, tɯŋ^{1}
not taut, slack   yaan^{4}, yaal^{4}
pull (a rope) taut   nɛŋ^{5}
tax   phaa^{4} sii^{2}
tax; value   khaa^{5}
taxi   thɛk^{4} sii^{5}

tea saa^{4}
spout of teapot, elephant's trunk ŋuaŋ^{4}
teakettle, teapot kaa^{1}
teach sɔɔn^{2}, sɔɔl^{2}
teacher khuu^{4}
teacher, scholar ʔaa^{1} caan^{1}
tear (to) siik^{6}
sound of tearing (e.g., paper) khuak^{5}, khwaak^{5}, khwɛɛk^{5}
tease kɛɛw^{1}
teeter-totter may^{6} yooŋ^{1} yeek^{6}
teeth, tooth nɛɛŋ^{1}
bare the teeth siik^{6} nɛɛŋ^{1}
tell thɔɔy^{4}
tell, narrate; lie too^{5}
tell, speak kaaw^{6}
tell, talk, say, speak nɔɔy^{3}
temples of the head kha^{6} map^{4}
ten sip^{6}
ten thousand mɯɯn^{6}
tend, keep, raise, feed; feast liaŋ^{6}
tender; crisp, brittle cɔɔn^{1}
tender (of meat), soft and rotten pɯay^{6}
tendon ʔin^{1}
termite mɔɔt^{5}
territory; boundary kheet^{6}, dɛɛn^{1}
testicle ram^{2}
tetanus, infection from any wound pham^{2}, pham^{3}
textbook bɛɛp^{6} rian^{4}
Thai, Tai thay^{4}
thank you khɔɔp^{5} cɯɯ^{1}, day^{3} yɤɤ^{4}
that nan^{6}, man^{6}, kan^{6}, tan^{6}, yan^{6}, rɛn^{6}
that, there ʔan^{6}, man^{6}
that way raan^{5} raa^{5} ʔan^{6}
that, which; ordinal number marker thii^{6}
that; say ɣaa^{3}, ɣa^{3}, ɣaa^{5}
thatchgrass ɣaa^{4}
then, and then, so, and so, therefore lee^{4}, leʔ^{4}, le^{4}, lɤɤy^{4}
and then lɛɛw^{6} kuŋ^{2}
and then, so; but phat^{2}
then, and so, expresses finality loot^{5}
then; finished; already lɛɛw^{1}, lɛɛw^{6}
then, so kuŋ^{2}, kuŋ^{3}, ciʔ^{2}, ci^{2}

there han^{3}

there, at, in nεεn^{1}, nεεn^{2}

there, that ʔan^{6}, nan^{6}, man^{6}

there, yonder ʔun^{3}, phun^{3}

therefore, then, and then, so, and so lee^{4}, leʔ^{4}, le^{4}, lɤɤy^{4}

there is, there are; to have mii^{4}

thermos bottle ka^{6} tik^{4}

these, this nii^{6}

they, it, he, she man^{4}

they, other people raw^{2}

thick naa^{2}

thick, abundant (of hair, fruit) dok^{4}

thick, sticky (of liquids) trεεw^{6}

thicket, forest paa^{6}

thief kha^{6} mooy^{4}

thin, not fat phrɔɔm^{2}

classifier for long, thin objects sεn^{3}, sεl^{3}

thin, not thick vaaŋ^{1}

very thin soo^{4}

thing, kind, manner yaaŋ^{6}

thing, matter; language cian^{5}

things, possessions thrɯaŋ^{5} throo^{4}

things, possessions; food; clothing; utensils thrɯaŋ^{5}

things, possessions; of, belonging to hɔɔŋ^{2}

things (classifier for) ʔan^{1}, ʔal^{1}

think khɯt^{6}, ŋɤʔ^{4}

thirteen sip^{6} saam^{2}

this, these nii^{6}, niʔ^{6}

this one ʔa^{6} rii^{6}

thorn ʔɔn^{1}

thousand phan^{4}

thread daay^{3}, mii^{2}

threaten khuu^{6}

hold up threateningly ŋɯat^{5}

three saam^{2}

thirteen sip^{6} saam^{2}

three hundred saam^{2} rɔɔy^{6}

thresh (rice); strike, hit, beat, pound; fight mɔk^{6}

threshing ground laan^{4}

throw kεεŋ^{6}, kwεεŋ^{6}

throw (e.g., a stone) cɤɤt^{6}

throw away loʔ^{6}

throw, throw away tuŋ^{6}
throw, toss ɲoon^{4}
throw, cast, sow vaan^{6}, vaal^{6}
thrust in all the way khuŋ^{4}
thumb; big toe ŋiaŋ^{5} poo^{3}
thunder phraa^{3}
Thursday van^{4} phaʔ^{6} hat^{4}
tick rip^{4}
tie kɔn^{3}
tie in bundles phay^{4}
tie or bind tightly rɛt^{6}, rɛt^{6} rɯŋ^{4}
tie up (an animal) laam^{5}
tiger kuuk^{6}
sound of tiger roaring; sound of stomach rumbling kook^{5}
tight, close cɛɛp^{6}
tight-fitting; narrow; small ɣeep^{5}
tile ka^{6} bɯaŋ^{3}
tilted, not straight ʔiaŋ^{1}
tilt the head back nɤɤy^{4} naa^{3}
time vee^{4} laa^{4}, sɯɯ^{4}, sɯ^{6} sɯɯ^{4}, sɤɤ^{4}, baat^{6}
formerly, in olden times tɛɛ^{6} rɤɤ^{4}
long time ɲɯa^{4}
olden times dɯk^{4} dam^{1} ban^{1}
period of time sua^{5}
time, amount; like paan^{1}
time, hour mooŋ^{4}
time passed yuu^{6} maa^{2}
time, period paaŋ^{1}, sen^{5}
time, when hooy^{4}
waste time khɤɤk^{5}
time (a) thɯa^{5}
time (to be in), catch up with thɛn^{4}
by the time; save for someone phɯa^{6}
tin sɯɯn^{4}, saŋ^{1} ka^{6} sii^{1}
tin, can ka^{6} pɔŋ^{1}
tip, end praay^{1}, plaay^{1}
tip, highest point ɲuut^{5}
tired ʔit^{4}
very tired hiw^{2}, hiiw^{2}
tired, weak, crippled pia^{3}
tired of something khɛʔ^{6}, pɤɤt^{6}, naay^{6}

title of hero in stories   thaaw^{6}
to   ka^{6}
to, for   kεε^{6}
toad   ɣal^{4} ɣaak^{5}
tobacco   hɯɯt^{6}
toe, finger   ŋiaŋ^{5}
big toe, thumb   ŋiaŋ^{5} poo^{3}
little toe, little finger   ŋiaŋ^{5} kɔɔy^{3}
toenail, fingernail; hoof   liip^{5}
together   room^{4}
together, altogether   phrɔɔm^{6}
together, with   duay^{3}, yɔɔy^{5}
together with, all, both; even though   thɯŋ^{4}
toilet   thaan^{1}
tomato   khɯa^{1} khɯa^{4}
tomorrow   thɔɔk^{5}, mɯɯ^{6} thɔɔk^{5} nii^{6}
tongs, pincers, pliers   khiim^{4}, khiim^{4} khaw^{3}
tongue   liin^{6}
stick out (the tongue)   blɔɔ^{3}
too, too much   phoot^{5}
too; exceed   kɤɤn^{1}
tools (classifier for implements and other sharp tools)   maak^{5}, maak^{6}
tooth, teeth   nεεŋ^{1}
bare the teeth   siik^{6} nεεŋ^{1}
top for spinning   tuan^{3}, tual^{3}
torch   ka^{6} bɔɔŋ^{1}
torn, broken, break   kaat^{6}
torn; chipped   hian^{2}
having a piece torn off   vin^{6}, viil^{6}, viik^{5}
tortoise (water)   plaa^{1} pha^{6} ʔɔɔŋ^{1}, via^{3}
toss, throw   ɲoon^{4}
touch   cɔɔt^{6}, tooŋ^{1}
touch; hit; correct; cheap   thɯk^{6}
touch lightly   tɔɔy^{3}, tlɔɔy^{3}, suun^{4}
touch with the tongue to taste   cεʔ^{4}
tough, sticky; glutinous (rice)   niaw^{2}
tough, coarse (of meat, food)   ɲiap^{6}
toward, for   suu^{6}
tower   hɔɔ^{2}
traces of an animal passing   phɔɔt^{6}
track, footprint   rii^{4}
trade   khaa^{6}

traditions hiit^5 thɯk^6 khɔɔŋ^4
  traditions, ceremony riit^5
  traditions, customs praʔ^6 phee^4 nii^4, hiit^5
transform oneself kap^4 pheet^5
transplant rice tram^1
transport, carry khun^2
travel around thiaw^6
tray thraa^2, thlaa^2
tread on, step on; run over (of a car) yiap^6
treasury; storehouse khaŋ^4
treat (the ill), care for pua^1, pin^6 pua^1
tree, plant, wood may^6
  cut a blaze in a tree to mark it baak^6
  cut a piece off the side of a tree or log thaak^6
  fell a tree; wrestle pram^3, plam^3
  tree (in expressions) ton^3
  tree, plant; base, first part khoo^6
  tree varieties ka^6 baw^1, ka^6 bok^4, cuaŋ^1, tiiw^3, thɯaŋ^4, thɔɔn^6, laan^6, laal^6
trellis yoon^6, yool^6
tremble, shiver ruŋ^1
tribute money suay^6
trim rɔɔn^4
trim a fallen tree; cut into pieces rɛɛm^3
tripod khiaŋ^4
troops kam^1 laŋ^4 vaŋ^4 saa^4
troubled, worried ʔuk^4
  troubled, worried, stressed ʔaŋ^6
trough, gutter, water pipe haaŋ^4
  trough for pigs rua^2
trousers, pants sooŋ^3
trudge along without paying attention ŋup^4 ŋup^4
true ciŋ^1
truly, really la^6 vaay^4
trumpet (of an elephant) phiaʔ^4 phiaŋ^6
trunk, box, suitcase hiip^6
trunk of an elephant; spout of a teapot ŋuaŋ^4
trunk of a tree lam^4
try khɤɤŋ^6, lɔɔŋ^4
  try, make an effort phiʔ^4, phaay^6
tuber, potato ʔɛŋ^3, man^4
  tuber variety kɔɔy^1

tuck into nεp^{4}, nεεp^{5}

tuck up cɔɔn^{3}

Tuesday van^{4} ʔaŋ^{1} khaan^{4}

tug, pull thok^{4}

turbid khun^{2}

turmeric ŋiin^{6}, ŋiil^{6}

turn something over vɔɔn^{3}

turn upside down or inside out priin^{3}, pliin^{3}

turn, spin, whirl, revolve pin^{6}, mun^{2}, muun^{2}

turn (a car) around ʔuay^{6}, ʔwaay^{6}

turn freely on a wheel mlɔɔn^{5}

turn the face away ŋεεw^{3}, blɯan^{1}

turn the head to look ŋuak^{5}, ŋwaak^{5}, ŋεεk^{5}, ŋwεεk^{5}

turtle rɔɔ^{4}

tusk of elephant; ivory ŋaa^{4}

tusk of a boar nεεŋ^{1} ŋεε^{4}

tweezers maak^{5} niip^{6}

twenty saaw^{4}

twenty-one saaw^{4} ʔεt^{4}

twig, branch kaaŋ^{6}

twig; one chopstick kiŋ^{6}

twilight, dusk sum^{3}

twins phaŋ^{1} phεεt^{6}

twist bit^{4}

have dysentery phan^{4} bit^{4}, phal^{4} bit^{4}

twist strands of rope sap^{4}

twist, wring; form rice into a ball van^{3}, val^{3}

twisted, crooked biaw^{3}

twisted (mouth) bii^{6}

two ɲii^{6}, sɔɔŋ^{2}

second lunar month blian^{1} ɲii^{6}

U

Ubon ʔuʔ^{4} bon^{1}

Udorn ʔuʔ^{4} dɔɔn^{1}

ugly siim^{4}

umbrella khan^{4}

cloth umbrella khan^{4} kot^{4}

paper umbrella khan^{4} ɲuu^{4}

unbutton, undo, untie, remove kee^{3}

uncle, older brother of either parent   luŋ^{4}
uncover, open up   phiat^{5}
underneath the house (a space)   luaŋ^{5}
undo, open   kɛʔ^{4}, ŋɛʔ^{6}
  undo (a button); remove (a yoke); remove, take down   prɛt^{4}, plɛt^{4}
  undo, unbutton, untie, remove   kee^{3}
uneven, odd, not a pair   khiik^{5}
unhusked rice, paddy   ɣaw^{6} thɔɔk^{6}
unripe, raw   rip^{4}
unroll, come unrolled   laay^{1}
  unroll (cloth)   phɯŋ^{6}, phɯɯŋ^{6}
  unroll, unwrap   tii^{6}
untie, unbutton, undo, remove   kee^{3}
until   kii^{4}, maʔ^{6} kii^{4}, ma^{6} kii^{4}
  until, so much that   con^{1}
unwilling, object to   khat^{4}
unwrap, unroll   tii^{6}
up; rise, ascend, go up, come up   hɯn^{3}
  upper, on, above; north   khɯn^{4}
urinate   ɲuu^{5}
use   pa^{6} ɲoot^{6}
  use, employ; send (someone)   thraay^{2}, say^{3}
used to, have ever   khɤɤy^{4}
usual, ordinary   tham^{4} ma^{6} daa^{1}
usual, regular   pra^{6} cam^{1}
utensils; things, possessions; food; clothing   thrɯaŋ^{5}

V

vagina, female organ   moʔ^{5}, siat^{5}
value, tax   khaa^{5}
vanish, disappear   vaŋ^{3} vɛɛ^{3}
  vanish, disappear by magic power   lɯam^{4}
vapor, steam; odor   sooy^{2}
various   naa^{4} naa^{4}
  various, differ, strange   taaŋ^{6}
vase   cɛɛ^{1} kan^{1}
vegetable   phrak^{4}
  vegetable varieties   tiiw^{3}, vɛɛn^{6}, sa^{6} ŋɛɛŋ^{4}
  water hyacinth   buaŋ^{6}

vehicle, car, bicycle   lot^{6}
  sedan automobile   lot^{6} keŋ^{1}
very, many, much   laay^{1}, laay^{2}
very much, excessively   vian^{4}, vian^{4} raat^{5}, vɛɛn^{4} raat^{5}
very, really   ka^{6} det^{4} ka^{6} dɔɔ^{3}
vie for, struggle over   siiŋ^{2}
Vientiane   viaŋ^{4} cɛn^{1}
Vietnamese   keew^{1}
  Vietnamese honorific   ʔoŋ^{1}
  Vietnamese ranks   kaay^{1} suu^{4}, kaay^{1} saa^{5}
vigorous   hɯŋ^{1} haaw^{3}
  vigorous, strong   maŋ^{4}
village, home   baan^{3}
vine   thaa^{4}, saak^{5}
vision (poor)   praa^{1} thua^{2}
visit, stop in   tham^{2}, vɛɛ^{5}
vocative particles   ʔɤɤy^{1}, ʔɤɤy^{4}, ʔɤɤy^{5}
voice, sound, noise   siaŋ^{2}
vomit   ruak^{5}
vulture   rɛɛŋ^{6}

W

waist   ʔɛɛw^{1}, vuat^{6}
  carry tucked in the waist   phɔk^{6}
  knife put in waist at back   thaa^{6} khat^{4} vuat^{6}
wait   khɔɔy^{4}, thaa^{3}
  wait, hope, expect   khɔɔŋ^{4}
wait on, serve   ʔup^{4} pa^{6} thaak^{6}
wake up, get up   saak^{5}
walk   thɛɛw^{4}, ɲaaŋ^{5}
  walk, pass   thiaw^{4}
  walking stick   cooŋ^{3} thrɯŋ^{6}, thrɯŋ^{6}
wall, partition; lid   vaa^{1}
  wall of woven bamboo   vaa^{1} ka^{6} tɛʔ^{4}
  wall or fence of a monastery   taay^{3} vat^{6}
waning (moon)   rɛɛm^{4}
  waning moon   blian^{2} rɛɛm^{4}
want, would like to   man^{2}, man^{3}
  want, desire; hungry   haat^{6}
war; enemy   khiak^{5}

warm raw^{3}
warm up, reheat hum^{2}, haaŋ^{2}
warp length (one) say^{3}
wart truut^{6}
wash sooy^{6}
wash (clothes) yak^{6}
wash (the hair) pɔɔ^{1}
wasp tɔɔ^{6}, thiin^{4}, thiil^{4}
waste (to) pɯaŋ^{1}
waste of effort kɯam^{3} kaaŋ^{1}
waste, spend money wastefully sɔɔn^{3}
waste time khɤɤk^{5}
watch, clock naa^{4} li^{4} kaa^{1}
watch, guard sɯɯ^{5}
watch (to) cɔɔp^{6}
watch, look, see nɔɔm^{1}
watch, watchman; season ɲaam^{4}
water nam^{6}
go without (food, water); endure ʔot^{4}, ʔot^{4} ɲɯam^{3}, thon^{4}
high water nam^{6} maak^{5}
sound of water falling or being poured cook^{5}, cɔɔk^{5}
to water plants rɛk^{6}
water in which glutinous rice is cooked mɔɔk^{6}
water pipe, trough, gutter haaŋ^{4}
water hyacinth buaŋ^{6}
water tortoise plaa^{1} pha^{6} ʔɔɔŋ^{1}, via^{3}
watermelon priaŋ^{1} moo^{4}
waves in water phɔɔŋ^{4}
waves in the hair lɔɔn^{4}
way, manner bɛɛp^{6}
that way raan^{5} raa^{5} ʔan^{6}
way, means thaa^{5}
way, road, side raa^{5}
get out of the way, avoid trɛɛŋ^{5}, tlɛɛŋ^{5}
way, path, road; side; direction thaaŋ^{4}
we pruu^{1} (two or more), roo^{4} (you and I, not others)
weak, tired, crippled pia^{3}
wealth laap^{5}
wear, put on tɛn^{3}
wear diagonally vak^{4}
weather, sky bɯn^{1}

weave tam^{3}, tam^{3} huuk^{6}
weave a basket saan^{2}
wedge liim^{3}
Wednesday van^{4} phut^{6}
weep, cry tay^{3}
weigh tit^{4}, saŋ^{5}
weigh down with something heavy nɛŋ^{2}
weigh a matter, consider ŋii^{5}
weight equal to a gram kam^{1}
welcome, receive tɔɔn^{3}
well (of water) nam^{6} saaŋ^{3}
wet ram^{4}
wet and muddy (of a road) mɯak^{5}
what thuʔ^{6} thaa^{4}
what, anything; why thaa^{4}, thrɤɤ^{4}
what, something, everything tuŋ^{6} thaa^{4}
what, which, any nɤɤ^{4}
wheedle, entreat ʔeew^{6}
wheel khiŋ^{3}, koŋ^{1}
wheel; cart lɔɔ^{3}
when buay^{3}
when, time, now baat^{6}
when; enough phɔɔ^{4}
when, time hooy^{4}
where nɤɤ^{1}, nɤɤ^{2}
where, why nɤɤ^{1}, nɤɤ^{2}
which, that; ordinal number marker thii^{6}
which, what, any nɤɤ^{4}
while; part; as for suan^{6}, sual^{6}
whirl, spin, turn, revolve pin^{6}, mun^{2}, muun^{2}
whirlpool nam^{6} bun^{3}, nam^{6} pun^{3}
whisper ɲiim^{5}
whisper; be careful ɲiim^{5} ɲia^{2}
whistle thiw^{2}, phriw^{2}, hiw^{2}, hiiw^{2}
white haaw^{2}
white, albino phɯak^{6}
white person, Occidental pha^{6} laŋ^{6}, fa^{4} laŋ^{6}, fa^{6} laŋ^{6}
whittle law^{1}
whittled stick diw^{3}, diiw^{3}
who, everybody, anybody dɤɤ^{1}
whorl in the hair; spirit hɔn^{2}

why, where nɤɤ^{1}, nɤɤ^{2}
why; what, anything thaa^{4}, thrɤɤ^{4}
wide khwaaŋ^{2}
wide, broad rooŋ^{6}
widowed maay^{6}
wife phaa^{4}
father's younger brother's wife luaw^{4}
will si^{2}
will, about to daa^{1}, raaŋ^{2}, raaŋ^{3}
will, would; about to daa^{1}
will, almost to, almost sam^{5} maʔ^{6}
win, victorious, defeat phɛɛ^{5}
wind lum^{4}
name of a wind ka^{6} diŋ^{1}
wind, bind a cord around ɲak^{6}
wind around trɛɛw^{3}, tlɛɛw^{3}
wind a cord around khian^{4}
wind a rope into a coil khwaan^{3}
window pak^{4} tuu^{1} bɔɔŋ^{6}
wing viat^{5}
wink, close one eye liiw^{6}
winnow vii^{6}
winnowing basket thuŋ^{3} vii^{6}
wipe sɛt^{6}
wipe after defecating mooŋ^{1}
wipe, stroke luup^{5}
wire luat^{5}
wish (make a); take a chance, risk siaŋ^{5}, siaŋ^{6}
with, together duay^{3}, yɔɔy^{5}
with, and kap^{4}
with, by dooy^{1}
with; from; along; accompany, follow; go in search of nam^{4}
without, have none ray^{5}
go without (food, water); endure ʔot^{4}, ʔot^{4} ɲɯam^{3}, thon^{4}
wits, intelligence pan^{1} ɲaa^{4}
woman, girl mee^{5} bɯk^{4}
old woman mlaaw^{6}
old woman; paternal grandmother yaa^{5}
young woman saaw^{2}
wonder, doubt soŋ^{1} say^{1}
woo, court; play sɤɤn^{6}

wood, tree, plant   may^{6}
  big piece of wood; lump, piece; classifier; log   khook^{5}
work   ŋaan^{4}, viak^{5}
  work, act, action   kaan^{1}
worker, employee   lɯk^{6} caaŋ^{3}, lɯk^{6} lɛɛŋ^{3}
world   look^{5}, peen^{6} ban^{1}, peen^{6} bal^{1}
worm   truan^{1}, trual^{1}
  worm   nɔɔn^{1}, nɔɔn^{2}, nɔɔl^{2}
worried   huaŋ^{3}, hwaaŋ^{3}
  worried, troubled   ʔuk^{4}
  worried, troubled, distressed   ʔaŋ^{6}
worship   buu^{1} saa^{4}
worth it   trum^{3}, tlum^{3}
worthy of, able to be   taa^{1}
  worthy of, likely to   soŋ^{4} + verb
would like to, want   man^{2}, man^{3}
would, will; about to   daa^{1}
wound (to)   baat^{6}
  infection from any wound; tetanus   pham^{2}, pham^{3}
woven (closely), coarse; far apart, widely spaced   saa^{6}
  finely woven, closely spaced; miserly   thii^{5}
wrap up, cover   hum^{3}
  wrap up a package, a package   tuuk^{6}
wrestle; fell a tree   pram^{3}, plam^{3}
wring, twist; form rice into a ball   van^{3}, val^{3}
wrinkled   hɛɛw^{3}
write, draw   khian^{2}
  writing, book   naŋ^{4} sɯɯ^{2}
writhe, struggle, move   khua^{6}
wrong, incorrect   phit^{4}

Y

yam   bɔɔn^{1}
yawn   raaw^{2}, haaw^{2}, haap^{6} haaw^{2}
year   khuap^{6}, tuay^{3} used only in songs, pii^{1}
  first year in the Saek 12-year cycle   tii^{6}
  second year in the Saek 12-year cycle   thriw^{3}
  third year in the Saek 12-year cycle   rɯn^{4}
  fourth year in the Saek 12-year cycle   mɛɛw^{3}
  fifth year in the Saek 12-year cycle   sin^{4}
  sixth year in the Saek 12-year cycle   tii^{5}

seventh year in the Saek 12-year cycle ŋɔɔ^{5}
eighth year in the Saek 12-year cycle muy^{4}
ninth year in the Saek 12-year cycle thrɯn^{1}
tenth year in the Saek 12-year cycle raw^{3}
eleventh year in the Saek 12-year cycle tut^{4}
twelfth year in the Saek 12-year cycle hɤɤy^{5}

Year of the Rat, first year in the 12-year cycle suat^{5}
Year of the Ox, second year in the 12-year cycle sa^{6} luu^{1}
Year of the Tiger, third year in the 12-year cycle khaan^{1}
Year of the Rabbit, fourth year in the 12-year cycle thɔʔ^{4}
Year of the Dragon, fifth year in the 12-year cycle ma^{6} looŋ^{4}
Year of the Snake, sixth year in the 12-year cycle ma^{6} seŋ^{1}
Year of the Horse, seventh year in the 12-year cycle ma^{6} mia^{4}
Year of the Goat, eighth year in the 12-year cycle ma^{6} mɛɛ^{4}
Year of the Monkey, ninth year in the 12-year cycle vɔɔk^{5}
Year of the Cock, tenth year in the 12-year cycle la^{6} kaa^{1}
Year of the Dog, eleventh year in the 12-year cycle cɔɔ^{1}
Year of the Pig, twelfth year in the 12-year cycle kun^{1}

four years from this year pii^{1} ʔɛn^{3}
last (year); to pass traay^{1}, tlaay^{1}
next year pii^{1} naa^{3}
three years from this year pii^{1} ʔun^{3}
two years from this year, year after next pii^{1} rɯɯ^{1}
year before last pii^{1} luaŋ^{5}

yellow vaaŋ^{4}
yes, ok ʔɤɤ^{3}, ʔɤɤ^{4}, ʔɤɤ^{5}
yesterday luan^{4}
yet, not yet phaa^{5}, haa^{2} lii^{5}
yet, still khaa^{4}, lii^{6}, haʔ^{6} lii^{6}, ha^{6} lii^{6}, hay^{2}
yield, submit, consent, allow ɲɔɔm^{4}
yoke ʔɛɛk^{6}
part of yoke under the neck ʔɔŋ^{3}
remove (a yoke); remove, take down; undo (a button) prɛt^{4}, plɛt^{4}
yonder, there ʔun^{3}, phun^{3}
you ʔay^{5}, caw^{3} (very polite), mɯŋ^{4}
you, he vua^{6} (respectful)
you (plural) suu^{2}
young num^{6}
father's younger brother ʔaaw^{5}

father's younger sister ʔɔɔ^{5}
young man baaw^{6}
young woman saaw^{2}
younger sibling nuaŋ^{6}
youngest (child); last (oxcart); come to an end, be finished sɔɔt^{5}
young; soft; light (of color) ʔuun^{6}

References

Aymonier, Étienne. 1895. *Voyage dans le Laos*. Paris: Annals du Musée Guimet, Bibliothèque d'Études, vols. 5, 6. A reference to 'savages' called Sak, v. 5, pp. 112–13.

Benedict, Paul K. 1979. Linguistic Prediction: the Case of Saek. A paper delivered at the Eleventh International Conference on Sino-Tibetan Languages and Literatures, Tucson, AZ. Published in Edmondson and Solnit, pp. 161–87.

Blanchard, Wendell. 1957. *Thailand, its people, its society, its culture*. New Haven: HRAF Country Survey Series.

Boltz, William G. 1991. The Old Chinese Terrestial Rames in Saek. In *Studies in the Historical Phonology of Asian Languages*, edited by William G. Boltz and Michael C. Shapiro, 53–67. *Current Issues in Linguistic Theory Vol.77*. Amsterdam/Philadelphia: John Benjamins Publishing Co.

Bonifacy, Auguste Louis. 1919. *Cours d'ethnographie indochinoise*. Hanoi-Haiphong: Imprimimerie d'Extrême-Orient. Saek listed on p. 81.

Chamberlain, James R. 1998. The Origin of the Sek: Implications for Tai and Vietnamese History. *Journal of the Siam Society* 86.1&2: 27-48.

Chao, Yuen Ren. 1930. A System of Tone Letters. *Le Maître phonétique* 45:24–27.

Credner, Wilhelm. 1935. *Siam, das Land der Tai*. Stuttgart: J. Engelhorns nachf.

Edmondson, Jerold A., and David B. Solnit. 1997. *Comparative Tai: The Tai Branch*. Arlington, TX: Summer Institute of Linguistics and The University of Texas at Arlington.

Fraisse, André. 1950. Les tribus Sek et Kha de la province de Cammon (Laos). *Bulletin de la Société des Études Indochinoises* 25.3:333–48. Saek vocabulary on pp. 338–40.

Gedney, William J. 1965. Saek, a Displaced Northern Tai Language. A paper delivered at the Annual Linguistic Society Meeting.

______. 1970. The Saek Language of Nakhon Phanom Province. *Journal of the Siam Society* 57.1:67–87. Reprinted in Gedney 1989, pp. 373–99.

______. 1982. The Twelve Year Names in Saek. A paper delivered at the Fifteenth International Conference on Sino-Tibetan Languages and Literatures, Peking. Reprinted in Hudak 1993, pp. 975–89.

______. 1989. *Selected Papers on Comparative Tai Studies*, edited by Robert J. Bickner, John Hartmann, Thomas John Hudak, and Patcharin Peyasantiwong, 373–99. Michigan Papers on South and Southeast Asia

No. 29. Ann Arbor: Center for South and Southeast Asia, The University of Michigan.

Haudricourt, André. 1958. Les Sek de la province du Cammon (Laos), migration thai ou déportation chinoise? *Journal Asiatique* 246:107–08.

______. 1960. Note sur les dialects de la region de Moncay. *Bulletin de l'École Française d'Extrême-Orient* 50:161–77.

______. 1963a. Remarques sur les initiales complexes de la langue Sek. *Bulletin de la Société Linguistique de Paris* 58:156–63.

______. 1963b. La langue Sek. *Proceedings of the International Congress of Orientalists* 25 (Moscow) 4:414–15. Abstract.

______. 1976. La tonologie du Sek. *Bulletin de la Société Linguistique de Paris* 71.1:299–304.

Hudak, Thomas John, ed. 1993. *William J. Gedney's The Saek Language: Glossary, Texts, and Translations.* Michigan Papers on South and Southeast Asia No. 41. Ann Arbor: Center for South and Southeast Asian Studies, The University of Michigan.

Khanittanan, Wilaiwan. 1975. Saek Revisited. In *A Tai Festschrift for William J. Gedney on the Occasion of his Fifth Cycle of Life Birthday Anniversary, April 14, 1975*, edited by Thomas W. Gething, 128–39. Southeast Asian Working Papers No. 8. Honolulu: University of Hawaii Southeast Asian Studies Program.

______. 1976. Phaasaa Saek [The Saek Language]. Bangkok: Thammasat University Press. In Thai.

______. 2008. Saek Revisted. In *The Tai-Kadai Languages*, edited by Anthony V.N. Diller, Jerold A. Edmondson, and Yongxian Luo, 389–92. Routledge Language Family Series. London and New York: Routledge.

LeBar, Frank M., Gerald C. Hickey, and John K. Musgrave. 1964. *Ethnic Groups of Mainland Southeast Asia*. New Haven: HRAF Press.

Macey, Paul. 1905. Étude ethnographique sur diverses tribus, aborigènes ou autochtones habitant les provinces des Hua-phano, Ha-tang-hoc et du Cammon, au Laos. *Actes, IVe Congrès International des Orientalistes, Alger 1905.* 1re Partie, 5e Sect.:3–63. Description of Sek on pp. 36–43; vocabulary on pp. 52–57.

Maspero, Henri. 1912. Étude sur la phonétique historique de l'annamite. Les initiales. *Bulletin de l'École Française d'Extrême-Orient* 12.1:1–127. Saek tones on pp. 3–5.

Morev, L.N. 1988. Yozik sek [The Saek Language]. Moscow: Nauka. In Russian.

Rivière, Armand. 1902. Vocabulaire hang-tchek, khas Xos, Harème. In *Mission Pavie, Géographie et Voyages IV*, 285–90. Paris: E. Leroux.

Seidenfaden, Erik. 1930. Ethnology. In *Siam, Nature and Industry*, Ministry of Commerce and Communication, 82–106. Bangkok: The Bangkok Times Press Ltd.

Smalley, William A. 1994. *Linguistic Diversity and National Unity: Language Ecology in Thailand.* Chicago and London: The University of Chicago Press.

Thongkum, Theraphan L. 1976. The Saek Language of Ban Ba Wa: Some Phonetic Notes. In *Genetic Relationship, Diffusion, and Typological Similarities of East and Southeast Asian Languages*, edited by Mantaro J. Hashimoto, 398–409. Tokyo: Japan Society for the Promotion of Science.

Appendix I
The Saek Names for the Twelve Cyclical Years

While doing fieldwork on thc Sack language, Gedney regularly encountered the following forms for the names of the twelve years, borrowed from Lao or Northeastern Thai as evidenced by the [s] for [ch] in the first and second form and [l] for [r] in the fifth and tenth form. Gedney notes that these forms were provided by young and educated Saek speakers who were also fluent in Lao and Siamese. For comparative purposes, the Siamese forms are also listed in parentheses.

pii^{1} suat^{5}	Year of the Rat, first year in the twelve-year cycle (Siamese pii^{1} chuat^{3})
pii^{1} sa^{6} luu^{1}	Year of the Ox , second year in the twelve-year cycle (Siamese pii^{1} cha^{2} luu^{5})
pii^{1} khaan^{1}	Year of the Tiger, third year in the twelve-year cycle (Siamese pii^{1} khaan^{5})
pii^{1} thɔʔ^{4}	Year of the Rabbit, fourth year in the twelve-year cycle (Siamese pii^{1} thɔʔ^{2})
pii^{1} ma^{6} looŋ^{4}	Year of the Dragon, fifth year in the twelve-year cycle (Siamese pii^{1} ma^{4} rooŋ^{1})
pii^{1} ma^{6} seŋ^{1}	Year of the Snake, sixth year in the twelve-year cycle (Siamese ma^{4} seŋ^{5})
pii^{1} ma^{6} mia^{4}	Year of the Horse, seventh year in the twelve-year cycle (Siamese pii^{1} ma^{4} mia^{1})
pii^{1} ma^{6} mɛɛ^{4}	Year of the Goat, eighth year in the twelve-year cycle (Siamese pii^{1} ma^{4} mɛɛ^{1})
pii^{1} vɔɔk^{5}	Year of the Monkey, ninth year in the twelve-year cycle (Siamese pii^{1} wɔɔk^{3})
pii^{1} la^{6} kaa^{1}	Year of the Cock, tenth year in the twelve-year cycle (Siamese pii^{1} ra^{4} kaa^{1})
pii^{1} cɔɔ^{1}	Year of the Dog, eleventh year in the twelve-year cycle (Siamese pii^{1} cɔɔ^{1})
pii^{1} kun^{1}	Year of the Pig, twelfth year in the twelve-year cycle (Siamese pii^{1} kun^{1})

In 1966, Gedney encountered an elderly Saek speaker said to be in his nineties. This informant provided the following list of names. In subsequent trips, the original informant having died, Gedney could not find anyone else who knew these terms. Afterwards, Gedney notes that younger Saek speakers interested in their heritage sought him out for these terms.

pii^{1} tii^{6}	first year in the Saek twelve-year cycle
pii^{1} thriw^{3}	second year in the Saek twelve-year cycle
pii^{1} rɯn^{4}	third year in the Saek twelve-year cycle
pii^{1} mɛɛw^{3}	fourth year in the Saek twelve-year cycle
pii^{1} sin^{4}	fifth year in the Saek twelve-year cycle
pii^{1} tii^{5}	sixth year in the Saek twelve-year cycle
pii^{1} ŋɔɔ^{5}	seventh year in the Saek twelve-year cycle
pii^{1} muy^{4}	eighth year in the Saek twelve-year cycle
pii^{1} thrɯn^{1}	ninth year in the Saek twelve-year cycle
pii^{1} raw^{3}	tenth year in the Saek twelve-year cycle
pii^{1} tut^{4}	eleventh year in the Saek twelve-year cycle
pii^{1} hɤɤy^{5}	twelfth year in the Saek twelve-year cycle

Appendix II
The Names of Songkan

Songkan (soŋ^{1} kaan^{1}, Siamese soŋ^{1} kraan^{1}) is the astrological New Year occurring on the twelfth or thirteenth day of April with the passage of the sun into the zodiac sign of Aries. The name given to the day on which soŋ^{1} kaan^{1} falls in any particular year depends upon the name of one of the seven daughters of Lord Kabil Maha Phrom, a Brahma divinity in the heavenly realm. Each of the names can be followed by thee^{4} vii^{4} 'lady, queen' because the seven daughters are grouped together and referred to as the Songkan Ladies, e.g., mon^{4} thaa^{4} thee^{4} vii^{4} 'Lady Monthaa'. Following the list of names is the Saek version of this tale along with an English translation.

thuŋ^{4} saʔ^{4}	name of soŋ^{1} kaan^{1} day when it falls on Sunday
khoo^{4} laa^{4} khaʔ^{6}	name of soŋ^{1} kaan^{1} day when it falls on Monday
raak^{5} saʔ^{4}	name of soŋ^{1} kaan^{1} day when it falls on Tuesday
mon^{4} thaa^{4}	name of soŋ^{1} kaan^{1} day when it falls on Wednesday
kiʔ^{4} liʔ^{6} nii^{4} (= ki^{4} li^{6} nii^{4})	name of soŋ^{1} kaan^{1} day when it falls on Thursday
kiʔ^{4} miʔ^{6} thaa^{4} (=ki^{4} mi^{6} thaa^{4})	name of soŋ^{1} kaan^{1} day when it falls on Friday
ma^{6} hoo^{1} thɔɔn^{4}	name of soŋ^{1} kaan^{1} day when it falls on Saturday

On 7 August 1966, Gedney recorded the following Saek text which relates the origin of the Songkan festival. It was dictated by Prasop Suwannamaacoo, a young generation (YG) speaker of Saek.

The Story of Songkan
Saek Text

1.	mii^{4}	seet^{6}thii^{2}	hun^{4}	nɯŋ^{5}.	boo^{6}	mii^{4}	lɯk^{6}.	raan^{4}
	there is	rich man	person	one	not	have	child	house

yuu^{6}	trɤɤ^{3}	kin^{1}	kap^{4}	hun^{4}	kin^{1}	law^{3}.	hun^{4}	kin^{1}	law^{3}	mii^{4}
be at	near	each other	with	person	eat	liquor	person	eat	liquor	have

lɯk^{6} yuu^{6} sɔɔŋ^{2} hun^{4}. hay^{+} hay^{1} lɯk^{6} kan^{6}.
child be at two person beautiful beautiful child that

2. mɯɯ^{6} nɯŋ^{5} hun^{4} kin^{1} law^{3}, haw^{3} pay^{1} yɤɤ^{5} seet^{6}thii^{2}.
day one person eat liquor enter go revile rich man

seet^{6}thii^{2} lɤɤy^{4} thaam^{2} ɣaa^{5}, "phan^{4}thaa^{4} caw^{3} laŋ^{2} hun^{4} yɤɤ^{5}
rich man and so ask that why you then come revile

hɔɔy^{6} thruu^{4} nii^{6}?"
I like this

3. hun^{4} kin^{1} law^{3} lɤɤy^{4} tɔɔp^{6} ɣaa^{5}, "caw^{3} phan^{4} hun^{4}
person eat liquor and so answer that you be person

mii^{4} ɲɛn^{4} mii^{4} ɣam^{4} laay^{2}, tɛɛ^{6} boo^{6} mii^{4} lɯk^{6}. baat^{6} praay^{1}
have silver have gold much but not have child time die

lɛɛw^{6} thrɯaŋ^{5}throo^{4} ɲɛn^{4} ɣam^{4} kuŋ^{2} rɤɤy^{1}. hɔɔy^{6} ciʔ^{2}
completive possessions silver gold then disappear I so

thuk^{6} khoon^{3} kuŋ^{2}taam^{1} tɛɛ^{6}ɣaa^{3} mii^{4} lɯk^{6}. phan^{4} hun^{4} cop^{4}
poor poor no matter but have child be person good

kwaa^{6} caw^{3}."
comparative you

4. seet^{6}thii^{2} nan^{6} lɤɤy^{4} trɤɤy^{1}, laŋ^{2} pay^{1} lay^{6}
rich man that and so ashamed then go pay obeisance

taaŋ^{1}ɲɛn^{4}, blian^{1} siaŋ^{6} thrɔɔ^{2} lɯk^{6}. siaŋ^{6} naay^{6} kuŋ^{2} boo^{6} mii^{4}
sun moon wish beg child wish tired of then not have

lɯk^{6} con^{1} rɤɤ^{3}raaŋ^{1}. ʔiin^{3} vee^{4}laa^{4} pay^{1} saam^{2} pii^{1}.
child until irritated disappear time go three year

5. yuu^{6}maa^{2}, thaŋ^{4} mɯɯ^{6} nɯŋ^{5}, phan^{4} mɯɯ^{6} hɯn^{3},
time passed reach day one be day go up

sip^{6}haa^{3} ɣam^{5}, blian^{1} haa^{3}. seet^{6}thii^{2} lɤɤy^{4} pay^{1} sɔɔ^{5} khoo^{6}hay^{4}.
fifteen night month five rich man and so go seek banyan tree

lɛɛw^{6} ʔaw^{1} ɣaw^{6}saan^{2}, sooy^{6} nam^{6} cɛt^{4} thɯa^{5}. lɛɛw^{6} ruŋ^{2} hɯn^{3}
then take white rice wash water seven a time then cook go up

buu^{1}saa^{4}. lɛɛw^{6} seep^{6} ŋan^{4} phin^{4}phaat^{5} siaŋ^{6} thrɔɔ^{2} lɯk^{6}.
worship then play music music string orchestra wish beg child

6. thee^{4}va^{6}daa^{1} yuu^{6} nɛɛn^{2} khoo^{6}hay^{4}. vua^{6} lɤɤy^{4} haay^{6}.
divinity be at in banyan tree he and so take pity

vua^{6} laŋ^{2} pay^{1} sɔɔ^{5} pha^{6}ɲaa^{4} ʔin^{1}, thrɔɔ^{2} hɤɤ^{3} vua^{6} phoot^{6}.
he then go name lord Indra beg allow he help

pha^{6}ɲaa^{4} ʔin^{1} laŋ^{2} hɤɤ^{3} tham^{4}maʔ^{6}baan^{1} thee^{4}va^{6}but^{4} lɔŋ^{4}
lord Indra then cause personal name divine child go down

kɤɤt^{6} nam^{4} phaa^{4} seet^{6}thii^{2}.
born with wife rich man

7. baat^{6} day^{3} lɯk^{6} ʔɔɔk^{6} lɛɛw^{6} hɤɤ^{3} sɔɔ^{5}ɣa^{3}
time get child come out completive give named

tham^{4}maʔ^{6}baan^{1} ku^{6}maan^{4}. phɔɔ^{5} laŋ^{2} prɔɔk^{6} phaa^{1}saat^{2} cɛt^{4}
personal name male child father then build palace seven

sɛn^{6} hɤɤ^{3} yuu^{6} nɛɛn^{2} trɤɤ^{3} khoo^{6}hay^{4} yan^{6}. phɔɔ^{4} bɯk^{4} hɯn^{3}
level cause be at there near banyan tree that when big go up

tham^{4}maʔ^{6}baan^{1} day^{3} rian^{4} cian^{5} nɔk^{6}. lɛɛw^{6}kuŋ^{2} rian^{4}
personal name past time study language bird and then study

thɛn^{4}rɔɔ^{6} con^{1} ʔa^{6}ɲuʔ^{6} day^{3} cɛt^{4} pii^{1}.
knowledge until age get seven year

8. taŋ^{3}tɛɛ^{6} ʔun^{3} ci^{2} hun^{4} thaŋ^{4} laay^{2} raw^{2} nap^{6}thɯɯ^{4}
since yonder then people all many they revere

thaaw^{6} ma^{6}haa^{1}phom^{4} kap^{4} ka^{6}bin^{1}la^{6}phom^{4}. phom^{4} thaŋ^{4} sɔɔŋ^{2}
lord great Brahma with name of Brahma Brahma all two

ʔoŋ1 nii6 rɔɔ6 ɣaa5 tham4ma6baan1 niʔ6 phan4 hun4 mii4
classifier this know that personal name this be person have

thɛn4rɔɔ6 laay2. lɤɤy4 hɔʔ4 lɔŋ4 tɛɛ6 saaŋ2 bɯn1 ɣa3 daa1
knowledge much and so fly go down from above sky say will

lɔŋ4 thuay4 ban3haa2 nam4 tham4ma6baan1 saam2 ɣɔɔ5. sɛn3ɲaa4
go down guess riddle with personal name three item agree

kin1 ɣaa5 thaa3 tham4ma6baan1 thuay4 thɯk6 phom4 si2
each other that if personal name guess correct Brahma will

tɛk4 ɣɔɔ4 thua4phɔɔ5suu3 buu1saa4. khan4ɣaa5 tham4ma6baan1 thuay4
cut neck his own worship if personal name guess

boo6 thɯk6, lɛɛw6 hɤɤ3 tɛk4 ɣɔɔ4 tham4ma6baan1.
not correct then cause cut neck personal name

9. tɔk4lɔŋ4 kin1 lɛɛw6, phaʔ6phom4 lɤɤy4 thaam2
agree each other completive Brahma and so ask

ban3haa2 ɣaa5, "ɣɔɔ5 nɯŋ5, tɔɔn1 lɔɔm5 laa4sii2 yuu6 book5
riddle that item one part morning radiance be at place

nɤɤ4. sɔɔŋ2, tɔɔn1 thiaŋ5 laa4sii2 yuu6 book5 nɤɤ4. saam2, tɔɔn1
which two part noon radiance be at place which three part

ɣam5 laa4sii2 yuu6 book5 nɤɤ4?"
evening radiance be at place which

10. tham4ma6baan1 thrɔɔ2 phat4 pay1 cɛt4 mɯɯ6.
personal name beg ask delay go seven day

day3 rɔk4 mɯɯ6 lɛɛw6, tham4ma6baan1 ha6lii6 khɯt6 boo6
get six day completive personal name still think not

day3 ɣa3 laa4sii2 yuu6 book5 nɤɤ4. laŋ2 khɯt6 ɣaa5,
be able that radiance be at place which then think that

"mɯɯ6thɔɔk5nii6 kuu1 daa1 praay1 day1 nih6." lɤɤy4 theew4
tomorrow I will die particle particle and so flee

lɔŋ4 khɔɔy6 phaa1saat2. pay1 nuun1 riit5 yuu6 tiin1 khoo6taan1.
go down from palace go sleep hide be at foot sugar palm tree

11. con1 ɣam5, mii4 nɔk6 ʔin1thii4 sɔɔŋ2 hɔɔk6 phaa4 maa2
until night there is bird eagle two husband wife come

tɛɛ6 raa2 kin1. lɤɤy4 hun4 nuun4 yuu6 nɛɛn2 khoo6taan1 nan6.
from seek eat and so come sleep be at in sugar palm tree that

nɔk6 ʔin1thii4 thua4 phaa4 lɤɤy4 thaam2 hɔɔk6 ɣaa5,
bird eagle classifier wife and so ask husband that

"mɯɯ6thɔɔk5nii6 hiiŋ4 daa1 pay1 raa2 kin1 thaaŋ4 nɤɤ4?"
tomorrow ourselves will go seek eat way which

12. hɔɔk6 tɔɔp6 ɣaa5, "phak6phɤɤ5 thaa4. mɯɯ6thɔɔk5nii6
husband answer that difficult what tomorrow

tham4ma6baan1 ku6maan4 daa1 praay1. phaʔ6phom4 daa1 kaa3
personal name male child will die Brahma will kill

thruu4ɣaa5 kee3 ban3haa2 boo6 day3."
as solve riddle not be able

13. phaa4 lɤɤy4 thɔɔy4 hɤɤ3 hɔɔk6, "kee3 hɤɤ3 ɲia2."
wife and so tell for husband solve cause hear

14. hɔɔk6 lɤɤy4 loo5 ɣaa5, "hooy4 lɔɔm5 laa4sii2 yuu6
husband and so tell that time morning radiance be at

naa3, hun4 laŋ2 sooy6 naa3. hooy4 thiaŋ5 ŋan6 laa4sii2 yuu6
face person then wash face time noon that radiance be at

tam1ʔaaŋ1, hun4 laŋ2 ʔaw1 nam6ʔop4 ʔaw1 ŋeen6 thaa4 tam1ʔaaŋ1.
chest person then take perfume take turmeric paint chest

hooy4 ɣam5 laa4sii2 yuu6 ɣeeŋ5, hun4 laŋ2 sooy6 ɣeeŋ5."
time evening radiance be at feet people then wash feet

tham4ma6baan1 nuun4 yuu6 tɤɤ3 khoo6taan1 nan6 lɤɤy4 ɲia2.
personal name sleep be at under sugar palm tree that and so hear

phɔɔ^{4} ɲia^{2} lɛɛw^{6} thruu^{4} nan^{6} kuŋ^{3} lɤɤy^{4} prɤɤ^{6} maa^{2} ma^{4}
when hear completive like that then and so return come at

phaa^{1}saat^{2} tan^{6}.
mansion that

15. phɔɔ^{4} rɔɔŋ^{5} hɯn^{3}, mɯɯ^{6} mɔɔ^{6}, ka^{6}bin^{1}laʔ^{6}phom^{4} kuŋ^{2}
when dawn go up day another name of Brahma then

hun^{4} thaam^{2} ban^{3}haa^{2}. tham^{4}ma^{6}baan^{1} ku^{6}maan^{4} kuŋ^{2} loo^{5} thruu^{4}
come ask riddle personal name male child then tell like

day^{3}ɲia^{2} nam^{4} thua^{4} nɔk^{6} ʔin^{1}thii^{4} nɔɔy^{3} kin^{1} nan^{6}
hear with classifier bird eagle speak each other there

lɛɛw^{6}.
completive

16. thaaw^{6} ka^{6}bin^{1}la^{6}phom^{4} laŋ^{2} reek^{5} lɯk^{6} saaw^{2} thaŋ^{4}
lord name of Brahma then call child young woman all

cɛt^{4} hun^{4} nan^{6} hun^{4} loo^{5} ɣaa^{5}, "thraw^{3} hɔɔŋ^{2} phɔɔ^{5} nii^{6}
seven person that come tell that head belong to father this

daa^{1} thɯk^{6} raw^{2} tɛk^{4}, buu^{1}saa^{4} tham^{4}ma^{6}baan^{1} day^{1}. thraw^{3}
will touch they cut worship personal name particle head

hɔɔŋ^{2} phɔɔ^{5} nii^{6}, khan^{4}ɣa^{3} taŋ^{3} kɯɯ^{3} nɛɛn^{2} peen^{6}ban^{1},
belong to father this if set up keep in earth

vii^{4} kuŋ^{2} daa^{1} ham^{2} look^{5}. khan^{4}ɣa^{3} tuŋ^{6} hɯn^{3} saaŋ^{2} bɯn^{1},
fire then will burn world if throw go up above sky

vɯn^{2} kuŋ^{2} daa^{1} lɛɛŋ^{6}, boo^{6} tɔk^{4}. khan^{4}ɣa^{3} tuŋ^{6} lɔŋ^{4} nɛɛn^{2}
rain then will dry not fall if throw go down in

ma^{6}haa^{1}sa^{6}mut^{4}, nam^{6} kuŋ^{2} daa^{1} hɛɛŋ^{3}. hɤɤ^{3} caw^{3} thaŋ^{4} cɛt^{4}
ocean water then will dry up cause you all seven

hun^{4} nii^{6} ʔaw^{1} khan^{2} hun^{4} rap^{6} ʔaw^{1}."
person this take stand come catch take

17. traaw^{3} thruu^{4} nan^{6} lɛɛw^{6}kuŋ^{2} tɛk^{4} maak^{6} thraw^{3}
speak like that and then cut classifier head

thua^{4}phɔɔ^{5}suu^{3} hɤɤ^{3} ka^{6} lɯk^{6} saaw^{2} khoo^{6}. naaŋ^{4} kuŋ^{2}
of himself give to child young woman first lady then

lɤɤy^{4} ʔaw^{1} khan^{2} hun^{4} rap^{6} ʔaw^{1}. lɛɛw^{6} rɛɛ^{6}
and so take stand come catch take then carry in procession

rɔɔp^{5} rɔɔy^{1} su^{6}meen^{4} rɔk^{4}sip^{6} naa^{4}thii^{4}. lɛɛw^{6}laŋ^{2} sɤɤn^{4}
around mountain Mt. Meru sixty minute so then invite

pay^{1} kɯɯ^{3} rɤɤ^{1} tham^{3} khan^{4}tha^{6}thu^{6}lii^{1} rɔɔy^{1} kay^{1}laat^{5}.
go keep in cave name of cave mountain Mt. Kaylaat

mii^{4} thrɯaŋ^{5} thip^{6} buu^{1}saa^{4}. pha^{6}veet^{5}su^{4}kam^{1} laŋ^{2}
there is things divine worship name of gods' architect then

nii^{4}mit^{6} rooŋ^{4}. ʔaw^{1} kɛɛw^{3} cɛt^{4} van^{2} ʔee^{5}. rooŋ^{4} ʔan^{6}
create hall take jewel seven kind adorn hall classifier

nan^{6} hɤɤ^{3} sɔɔ^{5}ɣa^{3} pha^{6}kha^{6}va^{6}dii^{1}. hɤɤ^{3} phan^{4} book^{5} pat^{4}sum^{4}
that give named name of hall make be place meet

thee^{4}va^{6}daa^{1}. thee^{4}va^{6}daa^{1} laŋ^{2} ʔaw^{1} blɔɔk^{6}may^{6} hun^{4} sooy^{6} nɛɛn^{2}
divinity divinity then take flower come wash in

saʔ^{4} ʔaʔ^{6}noo^{4}daat^{6} cɛt^{4} thɯa^{5}.
pool name of pool seven a time

18. phɔɔ^{4} thaŋ^{4} kam^{1}not^{6} saam^{2}rɔɔy^{6} rɔk^{4}sip^{6}haa^{3} mɯɯ^{6}, vua^{6}
when reach limit three hundred sixty-five day they

laŋ^{2} taaŋ^{1}tiʔ^{4} ɣaa^{5} pii^{1} nɯŋ^{5}. phan^{4} soŋ^{1}kaan^{1} rɛk^{6} nam^{6}.
then designate that year one be Songkan sprinkle water

lɯk^{6} saaw^{2} thaŋ^{4} cɛt^{4} hun^{4} kuŋ^{2} pian^{6} kin^{1}
child young woman all seven person then take turns each other

rɛɛ^{6} thraw^{3} phɔɔ^{5} rɔɔp^{5} rɔɔy^{1} dɔɔ^{1} pii^{1}. lɯk^{6}
carry in procession head father around mountain every year child

saaw^{2} cɛt^{4} hun^{4} hɔɔŋ^{2} thaaw^{6} ma^{6}haa^{1}phom^{4} man^{6}
young woman seven person belong to lord great Brahma that

taaŋ^{1}tiʔ^{4} ɣaa^{5} phan^{4} naaŋ^{4} soŋ^{1}kaan^{1}. mii^{4} sɔɔ^{5} taam^{1} mɯɯ^{6}.
designate that be lady Songkan there is name follow day

vua^{6} ɣaa^{5} soŋ^{1}kaan^{1} pii^{1} nɤɤ^{4} yɔɔ^{5} kap^{4} mɯɯ^{6} nɤɤ^{4} kuŋ^{2}
they say Songkan year which straight with day which then

hɤɤ^{3} ʔaw^{1} sɔɔ^{5} nan^{6}. thruu^{4}ɣaa^{5} thaa^{3} mɯɯ^{6} soŋ^{1}kaan^{1} yɔɔ^{5}
give take name that for example if day Songkan straight

kap^{4} van^{4}ʔa^{6}thit^{6} kuŋ^{2} sɔɔ^{5} ɣaa^{5} thuŋ^{4}saʔ^{4}thee^{4}vii^{4}. khan^{4} yɔɔ^{5}
with Sunday then name that name of Sunday if straight

kap^{4} van^{4}cɛn^{1} kuŋ^{2} ɣa^{3} khoo^{4}laa^{4}khaʔ^{6}thee^{4}vii^{4}. khan^{4} yɔɔ^{5}
with Monday then that name of Monday if straight

van^{4}ʔaŋ^{1}khaan^{4} kuŋ^{2} sɔɔ^{5} ɣaa^{3} raak^{5}saʔ^{4}. khan^{4} yɔɔ^{5}
Tuesday then name that name of Tuesday if straight

van^{4}phut^{6} kuŋ^{2} sɔɔ^{5} ɣaa^{3} mon^{4}thaa^{4}. khan^{4} yɔɔ^{5}
Wednesday then name that name of Wednesday if straight

van^{4}pha^{6}hat^{4} kuŋ^{2} sɔɔ^{5} ɣaa^{3} ki^{4}li^{6}nii^{4}. khan^{4} yɔɔ^{5}
Thursday then straight that name of Thursday if straight

van^{4}suk^{4} kuŋ^{2} sɔɔ^{5} ɣaa^{3} ki^{4}mi^{6}thaa^{4}. khan^{4} yɔɔ^{5} van^{4}saw^{1}
Friday then name that name of Friday if straight Saturday

kuŋ^{2} sɔɔ^{5} ɣaa^{3} ma^{6}hoo^{1}thɔɔn^{4}.
then name that name of Saturday

19. pii^{1} nii^{6} thruu^{4} kin^{1}. van^{4} thii^{6} sip^{6}saam^{2} blian^{1}
year this like each other day ordinal thirteen month

haa^{3} yɔɔ^{5} kap^{4} van^{4}phut^{6}. sɔɔ^{5} naaŋ^{4} soŋ^{1}kaan^{1} ɣaa^{5}
five straight with Wednesday name lady Songkan that

mon^{4}thaa^{4}thee^{4}vii^{4}. ʔaw^{1} blɔɔk^{6} cam^{1}paa^{1} nɛp^{4} rua^{4}. ʔaw^{1}
name of Wednesday take flower flower type tuck ear take

phay^{4}thuun^4 phan^4 thrɯaŋ^5 ʔee^5. kin^1 nom^4 nɤɤy^4. mɯɯ^4 khwaa^4
gem type be thing adorn eat milk cheese hand right

thɯɯ^4 kim^1. mɯɯ^4 vɛɛn^6 thɯɯ^4 may^{6}cooŋ^{3}thrɯŋ^6. nuun^4
hold needle hand left hold walking stick lie down

mlɔɔn^4 praa^1 hun^4 saaŋ^2 laŋ^2 bɛɛ^3.
open eyes eye come on back of back goat

The Story of Songkan
English Translation

1. Once there was a rich man who had no children. His house was near a drunkard's, and the drunkard had two children. Very, very beautiful were those children.

2. One day the drunkard went and berated the rich man. So the rich man asked, "Why do you come and berate me like this?"

3. The drunkard answered, "You're a person with a lot of silver and gold, but you have no children. When you die, your possessions and your silver and your gold will disappear. Even though I'm poor, I've got children. I'm a better man than you."

4. And so the rich man was ashamed. He went before the moon and made a wish for a child. He wished until he was exhausted, but he still had no children. And so he continued on until he was irritated. He had wasted three years.

5. Time passed, and then the fifteenth day of the waxing phase of the fifth lunar month arrived. So the rich man went and looked for a banyan tree. Then he took white rice and washed it in water seven times, cooked it, and raised it up in obeisance. Then he played music and made a wish, begging for a child.

6. And so the divinity living in the banyan tree took pity on him. He went to see the Lord Indra and beseeched him to help. And so Lord Indra had Thammabaan, the divine child, come down and be born to the rich man's wife.

7. When the boy had been born, they gave him the name Thammabaan. Then the father built a seven-story palace for him to live in near that banyan tree. When he grew up, Thammabaan studied the language of the birds and other knowledge until he was seven years old.

8. Since the olden days, all the people have revered Lord Mahaphom and Kabinlaphom. These two Brahma divinities knew that Thammabaan was a person with great knowledge. So they flew down from the sky, saying they would come down and ask three riddles to Thammabaan. They made an agreement with one another that if Thammabaan guessed correctly, the Brahma would cut off his own head and offer it in worship. If Thammabaan did not guess correctly, then they would cut off Thammabaan's head.

9. When they had agreed, the Brahma divinities asked the riddles, "First, in the morning, where is the radiance? Second, at noon, where is the radiance? Third, in the evening, where is the radiance?"

10. Thammabaan asked for a delay of seven days. When six days had passed, he still could not think where the radiance was. Then, he thought, "Tomorrow, I shall die for sure." So he fled from the palace and lay down, hiding himself at the foot of a sugar palm tree.

11. At nightfall, two eagles, a husband and a wife, returned from searching for food. They came to sleep in that sugar palm tree. The wife asked her husband, "Tomorrow, where will we go to look for food?"

12. The husband answered, "What's the difficulty? Tomorrow, Thammabaan will die. The Brahmas will kill him because he can't solve the riddles."

13. So the wife told her husband, "Solve them and let me hear it."

14. So her husband told her, "In the morning, the radiance is on the face, so people wash their faces. At noon, the radiance is on the chest, so people take perfume and turmeric and put them on their chests. In the evening, the radiance is on the feet, so people wash their feet." Thammabaan was lying under the sugar palm tree and heard the eagles. When he heard the solutions, he returned to the palace.

15. When it was daylight the next day, Kabinlaphom came and asked the riddles. And so Thammabaan answered as he had heard it from the two eagles talking to each other.

16. Then Lord Kabinlaphom called all seven of his daughters to come and told them, "Your father's head is going to be cut off and offered up to Thammabaan. Your father's head here, if it touches the earth, then fire will burn up the world. If it's thrown up into the sky, then there'll be a drought and no rain will fall. If it's thrown down into the sea, then the water will dry up. The seven of you should bring a basin and catch it."

17. Having spoken thus, he cut off his own head and gave it to his eldest daughter. And she brought a basin and caught it. Then they carried it in a procession around Mt. Meru for sixty minutes. Then they took it and placed it in Khanthathulii cave on Mount Kaylaat. There were divine things to offer in worship and so Phraveetsukam created a hall and adorned it with seven kinds of jewels. To that hall they bestowed the name Phakhavadii and made it a meeting place for the divinities. And then the divinities brought flowers and rinsed them in the Anoodaat pool seven times.

18. When a period of 365 days was completed, they designated it as a year. This is Songkan for sprinkling water. And all the seven daughters take turns carrying their father's head in procession around the mountain every year. The seven daughters of Lord Mahaphom are designated as the Ladies of Songkan.

They have names according to the days. For example, if Songkan day coincides with Sunday, then it is named Thungsatheevii. If it coincides with Monday, then it is Khoolaakhatheevii. If it coincides with Tuesday, then it is named Raaksa. If it coincides with Wednesday, then it is named Monthaa. If it coincides with Thursday, then it is named Kilinii. If it coincides with Friday, then it is named Kimithaa. If it coincides with Saturday, then it is named Mahoothorn.

19. This year is the same. The thirteenth day of the fifth lunar month coincides with Wednesday. The name of the Lady of Songkran is Monthaatheevii. She has a campaa flower tucked behind her ear, and she uses the phaythuun gem as an ornament. She partakes of milk and cheese. Her right hand holds a needle and her left holds a walking stick. She lies with her eyes open and comes on the back of a goat.

The above Saek text and English translation were originally published in slightly different form in Thomas John Hudak, ed. 1993. *William J. Gedney's The Saek Language: Glossary, Texts, and Translations*. Michigan Papers on South and Southeast Asia No. 41. Ann Arbor: Center for South and Southeast Asian Studies, The University of Michigan. Reprinted courtesy of the publisher.

Appendix III
Saek Villages

Thailand. In Thailand, four Saek villages are generally cited, all located in Nakhon Phanom province in Northeastern Thailand. Morev's 1988 study of Saek (p. 9) lists the same four villages.

1. baan^{3} ʔaat^{6} saa^{1} maat^{5}, five kilometers north of Nakhon Phanom on the Mekong River on the road to Uthen. Also known locally as baan^{3} khɔɔŋ^{2}.
Old name ʔeek^{6} ʔaa^{1} saa^{1}. Variant pronunciations of the current name include the following: ʔa^{4} sa^{6} maat^{5}, ʔa^{6} saa^{1}, ʔaa^{1} saa^{1}, ʔaa^{1} sa^{6} maat^{5}, ʔaa^{1} saa^{1} maat^{5}, ʔaat^{6} sa^{6} maat^{5}.
2. baan^{3} phay^{6} lɔɔm^{3}, one mile inland from baan^{3} ʔaat^{6} saa^{1} maat^{5}. Also known as baan^{3} saw^{1} law^{3}.
3. baan^{3} dɔŋ^{1} sa^{6} mɔɔ^{4}, in sii^{1} soŋ^{1} khraam^{4} district. Variant pronunciations include baan^{3} dɔɔn^{1} suʔ^{6} mɔɔ^{4}, baan^{3} doŋ^{1} su^{6} mɔɔ^{4}, baan^{3} doŋ^{1} sa^{6} mɔɔ^{4}.
4. baan^{3} baa^{6} vaa^{3}, in kiŋ^{6} naa^{4} vaa^{3} district. Also recorded as baan^{3} baa^{1} vaa^{3}.

Abandoned villages in Nakhon Phanom province include the following:

1. baan^{3} thaa^{5} vaay^{4}, between Nakhon Phanom and baan^{3} ʔaat^{6} saa^{1} maat^{5}.
2. baan^{3} naa^{4} laʔ^{6} vaay^{4}, on the road to Sakon Nakhon.

Laos. In texts collected by Gedney, the following Saek villages are said to be found in Laos:

1. baan^{3} thaa^{5} khɛɛ^{4}
2. baan^{3} thɔɔk^{5}
3. baan^{3} phoo^{4} kham^{3}

In a notebook entry in Siamese, Gedney lists baan^{3} phaa^{5} thuŋ^{1} with a true Saek population and baan^{3} phoon^{3} ŋaam^{1} with a half Saek and half Lao population. Morev (p. 9) notes there are about ten Saek villages in Khammouane province in the districts of Nhommarat, Mahaxay, Kham Khet, and Tha Khek.

Vietnam. The villages of baan^{3} trɤɤŋ^{3} and baan^{3} tɛɛn^{1} are said to have Saek inhabitants. Because of the uncertain status of the Saek population in these two villages, they have not been included in the lexicon. Abandoned Saek villages include baan^{3} bɯk^{4} naa^{4} tɤɤ^{3}, baan^{3} sin^{4} naa^{4} mɤɤy^{4}, baan^{3} trɤɤŋ^{1}, baan^{3} thruu^{3}, and the phiaŋ^{4} sɔɔŋ^{4}.

Saek villages cited in Chamberlain 1998. Without providing any phonological descriptions, Chamberlain lists two Saek dialects in Laos: 1) the dialect found in Khamkeut District in Borikhamxay Province; and 2) the dialect found in Khammouane Province as well as in Thailand. Romanizations are taken from Chamberlain.

Borikhamxay Province, Khamkeut District, Laos:

1. Ban Na Kadok in Nam Veo Subdistrict (originally from Phu Quan village in Nghê An Province in Vietnam).
2. Ban Som Sanouk, Ban Nam Phao, and Ban Houay Toun in Lak Xao Subdistrict.
3. Ban Na Tham Kwang (or Ban Nam Hoy) in Khammouane Subdistrict.

Khammouane Province, Nakai District, Laos:

1. Ban Toeng (baan^{3} trɤɤŋ^{1})
2. Ban Na Meo
3. Ban Na Moey (baan^{3} sin^{1} naa^{4} mɤɤy^{4})
4. Ban Beuk (baan^{3} bɯk^{4} naa^{4} tɤɤ^{3})

Chamberlain (note 6, p. 45) notes that the above villages are in Laos, not in Vietnam as cited in Gedney's research (see above under **Vietnam**).

Khammouane Province, Gnommarath District, Laos:

1. Ban Pha Thoung, said to have originally come from Ban Toeng
2. Ban Khène, said to have originally come from Ban Toeng

Other Saek villages can be found in Thakhek District and Hinboun District.

Chamberlain, James R. 1998. The Origin of the Sek: Implications for Tai and Vietnamese History. *Journal of the Siam Society* 86.1&2:27-48.
Morev, L.N. 1988. *Yozik sek* [The Saek Language]. Moscow: Nauka.

OCEANIC LINGUISTICS SPECIAL PUBLICATIONS

Oceanic Linguistics Special Publications are occasional publications issued under the sponsorship of the Department of Linguistics of the University of Hawai`i. The series consists of independently subsidized studies bearing on the languages of the Oceanic area. The "Oceanic area" is defined for this purpose as the combined Austronesian, Papuan, and Australian language areas. The Special Publications are published and distributed for the Department by the University of Hawai`i Press.

Manuscripts may be submitted to:

Oceanic Linguistics Special Publications
Department of Linguistics
1890 East-West Road
Moore Hall 569
University of Hawai`i
Honolulu, Hawai`i 96822